Souvenir par a'...

Black into White

Black into White

Race and Nationality in

Brazilian Thought

With a Preface to the 1993 Edition and Bibliography

Thomas E. Skidmore

Duke University Press   Durham and London 1993

© 1993 Duke University Press, first paperback printing
All rights reserved
Originally published by Oxford University Press in 1974
Printed in the United States of American on acid-free paper ∞
Library of Congress Cataloging-in-Publication Data appear on
the last printed page of this book.

For my parents
who took a lively interest

Contents

Preface to the 1993 Edition

Every author who introduces the reprint of a monograph without revisions faces the inevitable question: what changes *would* you have made, if the publisher had not offered the irresistible option of republication in the original form? Let me suggest a few answers.

The hardest task for most intellectual historians is to tie together the ideas in question, the articulators of those ideas, and the world in which they lived and thought—including not only their socio-economic context, but also the cultural institutions through which they reached their audience and the nature of that audience.

Most difficult among these connections, and the one I feel I was least successful in making, is the one between ideas, ideologies and intellectual consensuses, on the one hand, and the socio-economic reality that produced them on the other hand. I claim only to have opened some avenues of inquiry, which clearly need further exploration.

We still do not understand well, for example, the socio-economic bases of the liberal, republican ideology (which included racist assumptions) that triumphed in the 1880s. How was that ideology—heterodox, complex, and inconsistent as it was—related to the growing gap between the declining agrarian economies of the once-dominant Northeast and the increasingly dynamic agro-export economy of the Center-South? Viotti da Costa (1985) and Nachman (1977) have offered stimulating analyses. How did the emergence of what became the Third World's first major industrial powerhouse in São Paulo relate to the controversies over national identity, popular participation, and the question of Brazil's racial future? And how are we to explain the conception of, and social space allocated or denied to, the mixed blood—especially the mulatto—in the evolution of Brazilian society (Schwartz 1992b; Skidmore 1992, 1993; Vainfas 1986)?

Many subtleties in the intellectual context also were incompletely explored in my book. How, for example, did the tradition of Brazilian Romanticism continue to influence the intellectuals and politicians who agonized over race and national identity after 1870? What are the links between Modernism—the most original Brazilian literary expression of the twentieth century—and the continuing (if often unstated) preoccupation with Brazil's racial character? How did the Brazilian elite's perception of the contrast between European (especially French) and U.S. culture affect its understanding of its national and cultural destiny (Massi 1989)? How did the United States, with its unambiguously racist society, mold the Brazilian elite's image of its own society and racial formation? How did the relative disorganization of formal academic life (no universities before 1930) affect the pattern of Brazilian thought about as complex a matter as the country's ethnic evolution and contemporary social reality?

Finally, my book focused on the thought and aspirations of only a small fraction of the Brazilian population. I used the term "elite" to refer to the thin stratum of the literate who controlled the instruments of "high" culture. They could be numbered at most in the tens of thousands in the late Empire and in the hundreds of thousands by 1940.

But what of the rest of the millions of Brazilians? We are only beginning to gain insight into the world according to the "nonelites" through case studies such as the innovative monographs of

Chaloub (1986, 1990) and Diacon (1991). Research on popular
attitudes toward such subjects as race and national identity will
offer an essential and enlightening counterpoint to my focus on
elite thought and behavior.

1974 –
1988
— ?

In the fourteen years since this book was first published, relatively little new research has been done on the themes defined
here, especially the link in thought between race and nationality.
This can perhaps best be explained by the fact that Brazilian scholars, especially from the established academic institutions, continue
for the most part to avoid the subject of race, in virtually all its
aspects, at least for the twentieth century. Indeed, Brazilians often
regard non-Brazilians who pursue the subject as having misunder-
stood it. They are sometimes inclined to dismiss U.S. scholars, in
particular, as being unable to avoid projecting onto Brazil assumptions about U.S. society. Undoubtedly this criticism is often valid.
Race relations is certainly a sufficiently emotion-laden subject,
especially for anyone from the United States, to raise the danger of
an ethnocentric approach to the only other continent-sized country
in the New World to have experienced African slavery on a massive
scale, as Hellwig (1992) has so well documented.

Even so, one cannot fail to be impressed by the manner in which
the vast majority of the Brazilian intellectual elite continue to
regard the question of race and race relations as a virtual nonsubject
(Skidmore 1985, 1991). This is all the more striking given the
massive amount of new information that has become available on
the realities of race relations in contemporary Brazil.

When I wrote my book in the early 1970s, there had been
virtually no empirical analysis of social stratification in Brazil. This
was especially true for the variable of race, since race had been
omitted from the 1970 census—itself an interesting indicator of
that military government's attitude toward race. Beginning in the
late 1970s, however, Brazilian census authorities launched a series
of highly detailed household surveys that did include race. A few
researchers began to analyze these data, including a team from the
census bureau (Oliveira et. al. 1985). The officially sponsored set of

descriptive statistics, whose release was held up for two years by a census bureau director who apparently feared it would damage Brazil's favorable image in race relations (*Veja* 1985), revealed gross differences in income by race, with blacks earning only 35 percent of the income of whites, and *pardos* (mixed bloods) earning only 45 percent. Later research based on subsequent household surveys, the 1980 census, and the 1940, 1950, and 1960 censuses (which did include race) established beyond doubt that race was a significant *independent* variable affecting key life chances, such as education, infant mortality, life expectancy, morbidity, and income. Yet in the early 1990s a widespread debate over the role of race in Brazilian society had yet to begin in Brazil (Skidmore 1991). Aside from a small number of Afro-Brazilian activists and scholars, a few progressive elements in the Catholic Church (CNBB 1988) and on the political left, primarily the Partido Democrático Trabalhista (PDT) and the Partido dos Trabalhadores (PT), and a thin band of academics and intellectuals, those dominating public life in Brazil continue to ignore the subject.

The few Brazilian social scientists who have chosen to pursue in-depth research on the role of race have been primarily anthropologists, sociologists, and demographers. Pathbreaking work on the quantitative dimensions of racial inequality has been done by Hasenbalg (1979), Hasenbalg and Silva (1988, 1990), Silva (1981, 1985), and Wood and Carvalho (1988), and similar quantitative studies are found in the collection edited by Lovell (1991). Education is one of the few areas where other systematic research has been done, as in the issue of *Cadernos de Pesquisa* edited by Rosemberg and Pinto (1987). Occasional attitudinal studies, including the one by Souza (1983) on black views about upward mobility and a collaborative examination of blacks in Protestant denominations (Novaes and Floriano 1985), have supplemented the quantitative approach.

The bulk of anthropological research has continued to fall within the traditional "culturalist" approach, focusing on African cultural survivals in religion, dance, music, food, language, and folklore.

While this has yielded a rich portrait of a vital aspect of Brazilian life, it has contributed relatively little to our understanding of the broader questions of race relations in contemporary Brazil. There remains a great opportunity for anthropologists to use their methodology in analyzing the larger cultural and social context within which the quantitative studies are conducted and, no less important, the way these findings are perceived and interpreted in Brazilian society.

Several anthropologists who contributed greatly to my understanding of the role of race and slavery in the creation of twentieth-century Brazil have continued to produce important work: Thales de Azevedo (1975), Fernandes (1989), and Ianni (1978, 1987). Prominent among the historians who fit this category are Viotti da Costa (1982, 1985) and Afro-Brazilian writers and activists such as Moura (1983, 1988, 1990) and Nascimento (1978, 1982).

There is a rich literature on the agonies of being an Afro-Brazilian, most of which appears outside the established network of publishing and public debate. One exception is the collective volume edited by Costa (1982), but the common pattern tends to be very limited editions of poetry or fiction by black authors (*Cadernos Negros* 1991; Camargo 1986; Colina 1982).

Let me now turn to a more general review of the literature that has subsequently appeared on the themes treated in this book. I concentrate on book-length studies, with only occasional reference to the extensive periodical literature. Interested researchers will want to consult the bibliographies cited in the updated bibliography on p. 291. Also included here are works on political issues such as immigration, monarchism, and political and criminal activity of urban nonwhites, as well as works which focus directly on thought about race and nationality.

Of the themes treated in this book, the one that has continued to attract most attention is the history of slavery (and the struggle for its abolition in the nineteenth century). Both Brazilian and foreign researchers on the history of race relations and racial ideologies have focused almost exclusively on the period up to slavery's final abolition in 1888. This continuing restriction of focus was high-lighted by the observance of the centennial of abolition in 1988 (Maggie 1989), when many scholarly conferences virtually ignored the fate of Afro-Brazilians over the century *since* legal servitude ended. The richness of the recent work on slavery and abolition has been explored in the excellent bibliographical survey by Stuart Schwartz (1992a), and readers are referred there for a detailed discussion of recent scholarly trends. Those who are interested in the use of primary sources should consult the guide published by the Arquivo Nacional (1988).

The most comprehensive bibliographical guide for those inter-ested in recent publications on both slavery and race relations is the catalog edited by Luiz Claudio Barcelos et. al. (1991) and published by the Centro de Estudos Afro-Asiáticos in Rio de Janeiro. It includes approximately 2,500 entries, primarily in anthropology, history, political science, and sociology, and is especially valuable for the large number of Brazilian master's and doctoral theses cited. The latter (often lost to scholars because of the lack of any central reporting mechanism among Brazilian universities) are the product of a surge of academic research in Brazil in the last several decades. All entries, though not annotated, are grouped into five categories: (1) bibliography, printed sources, and general studies on slavery and race relations; (2) slavery and abolition; (3) race relations and inequality; (4) political participation, culture, and identity; and (5) religion.

For race relations since 1888, the most important book-length study is by Andrews on São Paulo (1991), which gives readers the first well-documented historical picture and includes several work-place case studies in Brazil's most dynamic industrial region. A more restricted monograph is the study of Campinas by Maciel (1987). The political (and sometimes criminal) activity of urban nonwhites in the decade after the fall of the empire in 1889 has also received some attention. The role of the Guarda-Negra, the black volunteer shock troops who harassed the Republican party organiz-ers, is studied briefly in Ricci (1990) and the suppression of the infamous *capoeiras* is treated by Holloway (1989). The dramatic case of André Rebouças, the mulatto abolitionist leader who joined the deposed Emperor Dom Pedro II in exile in Portugal in 1889, and then wandered in disillusionment in Africa, is sympathetically portrayed in Spitzer (1989).

One of my central arguments in this book is the close link between thought about race and thought about national identity. The latter includes not only intellectual history, but also the history of nationalist movements. In recent years there has been significantly more work on nationalism and concepts of national identity than on post-1888 race relations or racial ideologies. The most comprehensive new study for the 1889–1930 era is by Oliveira (1990). The succeeding era is analyzed from a São Paulo-centered perspective in Mota (1978). Mota's work includes one of the most critical revisionist interpretations of Gilberto Freyre, typical of the widely shared (but less often publicly stated) views of Brazilian intellectuals in the 1970s. The 1920–45 era is also treated in Miceli (1979).

Two ideologically significant, if historically minor, political movements with strong implications for debates over national identity were the Jacobins and the Monarchists, which both proved troublesome for the Republican governments of the 1890s. The Monarchists have received their first serious monographic study in Janotti (1986), the Jacobins in Suely de Queiroz (1986).

The study of elite culture in the First Republic (1889–1930) continues to attract attention. An invaluable reference work on intellectual and cultural history has been provided by Martins, whose encyclopedic seven-volume survey (1976–79) includes five volumes on the years between 1855 and 1960. A general historiographical survey of recent work on the First Republic has a useful section on intellectual history (Gomes and Ferreira 1989). Two studies of literary culture, both emphasizing the social context, are especially relevant to the themes of race and national identity. Ventura's exploration of "literary polemics" (1991) in the 1870–1914 period opens with a discussion of the key themes of race, geography, and climate in Brazilian thought and centers on the many battles waged by Sílvio Romero in defending his ideas about Brazil's cultural identity. Sevcenko (1983) has followed a similar approach, focusing on the social implications of the literary struggles of Euclides da Cunha and Lima Barreto. Finally, Needell (1987) has provided an in-depth portrait of elite culture and society in early twentieth-century Rio de Janeiro, giving rich detail about the institutions crucial to both the production and consumption of that culture.

One of the most important features of Brazilian intellectual life in these years was the continuing predominance of a juridical culture (captured in the untranslatable term *bacharelismo*), which infused the worlds of both culture and politics. Venancio Filho (1977) has provided an excellent perspective on the history of legal education in Brazil, while Adorno (1988) has given a penetrating sociological analysis of the rise of the *bacharel* in Brazilian politics between 1827 and 1883.

The presence of race as a theme in literature has attracted the attention of several non-Brazilian authors. Haberly (1983) argues that agony over race, especially the place of the Afro-Brazilian, was a component in national consciousness and is central to an under-standing of such influential writers as Gonçalves Dias, José de Alencar, Castro Alves, Machado de Assis, Cruz e Sousa, and Mário de Andrade. Surveys on race in literature are offered in Marotti (1987) and Brookshaw (1983). Brazilian scholars exploring this theme include Vainfas (1986) on how the Portuguese and Brazilian "literati" of the colonial era dealt with the slavery and all its racial implications, Gomes (1988) on the theme of the Afro-Brazilian in Brazilian Romanticism, Queiroz Júnior (1975) on the depiction of the mulatto in Brazilian literature, and Moura (1976) on racial prejudice in a preeminent form of popular culture, *literatura de cordel*.

Immigration policy was another important theme in my analysis. Research on immigration continues to produce a growing litera-ture. A useful listing of recent contributions is given in Hall et. al. (1989). Celia de Azevedo (1987) has analyzed the elite's obsession with the need to replace Afro-Brazilian labor with European workers. The link between the drive to recruit immigrants and the need for additional labor in the São Paulo coffee sector is analyzed in Holloway (1980). Luebke (1987) has explored the controversies surrounding German ethnics during World War I. Meade and Pirio (1988) document how the Brazilian and U.S. governments collaborated in preventing U.S. blacks from emigrating to Brazil. Finally, the Instituto Panamericano de Geografia e Historia (1987) has published a useful reference work on immigration policies and legislation in Argentina, Brazil, and Uruguay.

One of the key features of the pre-1930 intellectual era in Brazil was the lack of organized social sciences. Their origins have now been traced in an important collaborative study edited by Miceli (1989). The history of anthropology, one of the most relevant disciplines, has been documented in Corrêa (1987). The subfield of eugenics, which enjoyed a Brazilian vogue in the 1920s and 1930s, is well analyzed in Stepan (1991). The structure of the publishing industry—including books, periodicals, and newspapers—was highly important in determining which ideas and authors reached the reading public. Hallewell (1982) has produced a pioneering study of book publishing; Dimas (1983) has analyzed one of the most influential cultural journals of the belle epoque.

Of the individual writers who continue to merit attention from scholars, none is more prominent than Machado de Assis, who said almost nothing directly about either race or national identity. Yet his novels continue to furnish a rich source of interpretation on the Brazilian elite's conception of its society's historical destiny in the late nineteenth and early twentieth centuries. No critic has been more penetrating on the relationship between Machado's unique creative universe and the harsh realities of Brazil's agro-exporting society than Roberto Schwarz (1977, 1990). Gledson (1984, 1986) and Faoro (1974) have offered their own analyses of Machado's approach to the contradictions of Brazilian elite consciousness in this era. The most important work on Euclides da Cunha, in addition to Sevcenko (1983), is by Galvão, who has provided a critical edition of *Os Sertões* (1985), along with a major study of the contemporary press treatment of the Canudos rebellion (1974) and essays on Euclides and Canudos (1976).

One of the few monarchist political thinkers to receive attention is Eduardo Prado, who merited extended discussion in Rodrigues's study of conservative historiography (1988a) and in Levi's portrait of the Prado family (1987). Oliveira Vianna, one of the most influential of all twentieth-century writers on ethnic factors in Brazilian history, is a frequent subject for Brazilian analysis, as in Paulo Queiroz (1975), Vieira (1976), and Medeiros (1978). Rodrigues (1988b) subjected Vianna to a highly hostile critique, while Carvalho has offered a more sympathetic portrait (1991). Two of the early-twentieth-century thinkers who dissented from the prevailing racist theories, Alberto Torres and Manoel Bomfim, have been discussed by Marson (1979) and Alves Filho (1979). The role of Monteiro Lobato, a key intellectual figure who has yet to gain the analysis he deserves, has been studied by Landers (1988) in connection with the Modernist movement.

No figure is more central to the present century's Brazilian thought about race and nationality than Gilberto Freyre. Yet we still lack any satisfactory in-depth study of his work, placing it in the context of Brazilian intellectual and social history. Interesting suggestions in that direction have been made by Da Matta (1987) and Bastos (1986), while the Fundação Joaquim Nabuco, which Freyre was instrumental in founding, has furnished the raw material on which future research can draw, in Fonseca (1983) and Miranda (1988).

Race and nationality are no less central to present-day Brazilians' thought about their nation's destiny than they were in the years between 1870 and 1940, on which this book focused (Winant 1992). Indeed, much of the language used in that era remains current, with the exception of the virus of "scientific racism," which Brazilians, along with the rest of its onetime advocates in the Western world, have repudiated.

As Brazil enters the twenty-first century, it will continue, like all the republics of the New World, to face agonizing questions about its identity. Surely one of the most constructive ways in which non-Brazilians can help in clarifying that challenge is to join in laying bare the assumptions of past thought. If I have contributed to that enterprise then I shall consider my scholarly efforts to have been amply rewarded.

References cited in this Preface may be found in the Bibliography to the 1993 Edition at the back of the book.

Preface

When I began work on this book I thought I was going to write a collection of intellectual portraits, studying representative figures of the years between 1870 and 1930. To my dismay, I soon found myself launched into an examination of all the major intellectual currents of the era. Only slowly did I realize that I was heading toward a detailed analysis of racial thought in Brazil. While offering my interpretation I have tried to give enough background information about Brazilian history—political, economic, and social—to make the context intelligible.

Readers should not expect to find here anything resembling a history of Brazilian thought between 1870 and 1930. That would require a far more detailed and comprehensive analysis of thinkers and institutions than I have included. Many writers and schools of thought are omitted or mentioned only briefly, on the grounds that they said little about race, or at least that their views did not differ significantly from other figures examined here. By the same token, many writers appearing in these pages are analyzed only insofar as they grappled with the central problem of race. Other aspects of their thought are perforce neglected. (A more detailed discussion on this point will be found in the Note on Sources and Methodology in the Appendix). The danger of such an approach is that their ideas will be distorted by being viewed through a narrow prism which does not allow us to see the total context of their intellectual position. On the other hand, such a focus may permit us to see more clearly the continuity of elite thought on one question they considered fundamental to their nation's future.

*   *   *

Before the achievement of total abolition in Brazil in 1888, most of the Brazilian elite had given little hard thought to the problem of race per se, nor the connection between Brazil's racial characteristics and her future development. Although apprehensions regarding these issues clearly underlay much of their discussion of abolition and other reforms after 1850, Brazilians did not often talk directly about race as a social phenomenon, preferring to concentrate on institutional and legal reforms. These very apprehensions, of course, strengthened their temptation to focus attention on legal reforms; and the lateness with which these reforms came about—total abolition only in 1888, for example, and the end of the monarchy the following year—reinforced their willingness to assume that institutional changes alone would put Brazil on the path of rapid historical progress.

But the Brazilian who favored change faced a far greater task than had his English or French counterpart. Not only did he have to undertake the many tasks of modernization already being tackled in Europe and North America, he also had to begin by eliminating anachronisms such as human slavery and creating basic modern institutions such as a comprehensive school system. Brazilian liberals were fighting the battles of both the eighteenth and the nineteenth centuries at once. The lack of political support for the reformers' prime targets—slavery, the crown, the established Church—misled liberals into thinking that their victory over these enemies would bring the fundamental transformation which liberalism assumed to be the prerequisite for national progress.

The issues of race (and the related ones of climatic determinism) *were*, however, being discussed in Europe, and Europeans did not shrink from expressing themselves in unflattering terms about Latin America, and especially Brazil, because of its large African influence. Brazilians read these writers, usually uncritically, and grew apprehensive. Derivative in their culture, self-consciously imitative in their thought, mid-nineteenth-century Brazilians, like other Latin Americans, were ill-equipped to argue about the latest social doctrines from Europe.[1]

This is not to say that determinisms of race and climate were universally believed in Brazil. It would be more accurate to say that many tacitly accepted them and others implicitly assumed their *possible* validity. A few Brazilian thinkers did, however, grapple with the basic issue of race before 1888. Their thinking presaged the painful dilemmas that formed a major part of Brazilian intellectual life in the decades following the total abolition of slavery in 1888.

One point must be made clear at the start. When I speak of what "Brazilians" thought and wanted, I am describing the Brazilian elite. Any member of this elite necessarily existed in two worlds. On one hand, he was part of a tiny educated minority within his own country. His ideas and training were European, shaped by the Jesuitical and humanistic cultural traditions of Portugal, but increasingly modified during the nineteenth century by French culture, which brought the message of the Enlightenment with its secular and materialistic assumptions. Then came the growth of liberalism, nourished especially from England and the United States, which meant that even the models for political and social organization came from abroad. On the other hand, the elite actually lived in Brazil, not Paris or London. Eça de Queirós or Anatole France might visit Brazil, but they were certainly not of Brazil.

As if the challenge of transforming their backward society were not enough, Brazilians also had to grapple with the possibility that their ideology was irrelevant. Could it be true that modern progress was meant only for white men in temperate zones? This question and the attempts made to answer it form the basis of this book. In 1880 the ambitious young politician Joaquim Nabuco published an abolitionist manifesto in which he said "if abolition should mean suicide, then humanity would be rendered a service by those incapable of independent survival."[2] When abolition eventually became a reality, the issues underlying this statement were laid bare.

Acknowledgments

I have accrued many debts since this study began in the mid-1960's. Among the friends who have given me great help in finding sources are Vamireh Chacon, Antônio Cândido, José Honório Rodrigues, and Brady Tyson. Alexandre Eulálio and Francisco de Assis Barbosa spent many hours patiently introducing me to the history of Brazilian thought, and giving critical reactions to earlier versions of these ideas. Help came from other colleagues who exist now only in the realm of memory: George C. A. Boehrer, Luiz Washington Vita, Cavalcanti Proença, Lourenço Filho, and Araujo Ribeiro.

A very different version of this book was seen in manuscript by a number of friends. Extremely useful comments were sent by Nancy Stepan, Donald Cooper, Robert Toplin, Joseph Love, John Wirth, Fábio Lucas, and Harold Davis. Three Brazilian friends who have helped at every stage of the research and sent invaluable comments on drafts were Francisco Iglésias, Alberto Venâncio Filho, and João Cruz Costa. Since none of these friends saw the final (much revised) manuscript, they can hardly be implicated in any of my interpretative or factual vagaries. This disclaimer is worth stressing because I am acutely conscious of the irony involved in a study of Brazilian race-thinking coming from a country whose racial attitudes constitute one of the twentieth century's most destructive historical legacies.

Consultations in the Oliveira Lima Library at the Catholic Uni-

versity of America (Washington, D.C.) were greatly facilitated by
the Director, Professor Manoel Cardozo, and his staff. The Oliveira
Lima Collection is an excellent working library for the history of
Brazilian thought between 1870 and 1930. In Brazil much material
was located in the Casa de Rui Barbosa, whose Director (now President of the Fundação Rui Barbosa), Américo Jacobina Lacombe,
offered valuable suggestions for research. The clipping collection
and library of the Archive of O Estado de São Paulo proved an important source, thanks to the helpfulness of the staff under Sr.
Bordallo. Extended consultation of the newspaper collection in the
Biblioteca Nacional was greatly aided by Zilda Galhardo de
Araujo, who worked under difficult circumstances. Consultation of
a virtually complete collection of newspaper and magazine articles
by and about Alberto Tôrres was made possible by the kindness of
his daughter, Professor Dona Helíosa Alberto Tôrres. Special
thanks is due the staffs of the following libraries who located
little-used printed sources: the University of Wisconsin Memorial
Library (and its Inter-Library Loan Department), the Division of
Spanish, Portuguese and Latin America (formerly the Hispanic
Foundation) of the Library of Congress, the Centro Brasileiro de
Pesquisas Educacionais in Rio de Janeiro, and the Harvard College
Library.

My research began while on a three-year postdoctoral fellowship
in the History Department of Harvard University. Harvard had invited me to shift from my previous specialization in modern German History (I had already completed a doctoral dissertation on
the German Reichschancellor Caprivi) to modern Latin America.
Given complete freedom with Harvard funding, I was able to discover modern Brazil and the challenges of interpretation it offers
the historian. Subsequently I received financial support for research
leave and research expenses from the Committee on Latin American Studies at Harvard University, the Ibero-American Studies
program at the University of Wisconsin, and the Joint Committee
on Latin American Studies of the Social Science Research Council
and the American Council of Learned Societies. All these funds

came from the Ford Foundation, whose large-scale support meant so much to Latin American studies in the 1960's.

I also received support from the University of Wisconsin Graduate School, whose research financing has been made possible by the foresight and ingenuity of Wisconsin scientists, administrators, and benefactors over the decades. Revision of the manuscript continued while I held a fellowship at the Woodrow Wilson International Center for Scholars, housed at the Smithsonian Institution in Washington, D.C. I am most grateful to the former Director of the Center, Benjamin H. Read, and the staff for the excellent working conditions, and especially to the library staff who filled a large number of orders for books from the Library of Congress.

A succession of patient research assistants helped gather materials for this project: Joel Lazinger, Keith Hewitt, Ellen Brow, Thomas Holloway, Joan Westgate, and Rodney Hurd. James Lauer and Mary Karasch, my former students at Wisconsin, made many useful bibliographical suggestions. Typing help has come from the History Department, the Ibero-American Studies Office and the Industrial Relations Research Institute at Wisconsin, as well as the Woodrow Wilson International Center for Scholars in Washington.

My wife's career is as a ghost writer. In this book she has used her peculiar expertise extensively on my behalf. Before she attacked it, my manuscript was a long meandering treatise on liberalism and nationality. Her efforts over the last year and a half have enabled it to become a book about race. For the writing she bears fully half the responsibility. If history were her professional field she would accept coauthorship.

Thomas E. Skidmore

Madison, Wisconsin
February 1974

Black into White

1 ■ The Intellectual Context of Abolition in Brazil

THE BRAZIL OF 1865

In 1865 Brazil stood out in the Americas as a political anomaly—an Empire with a hereditary monarchy. While the Spanish Americans had fought to expel the Spanish crown in toto, the Brazilians marched to independence under the royal banner of one Braganza fighting the rest of Portuguese royalty. Brazil also stood out as an economic and social anomaly—an essentially rural economy that continued to tolerate slavery, despite the end of the slave trade in 1850. Both the traditional sugar plantations of the North and the newly booming coffee plantations of the South were fueled by slave labor.

In 1865 Brazil was Catholic, although, compared to New Spain, the Brazilian Church lacked both the wealth and the personnel to operate as a powerful and independent institution.[1] The Catholic Church had been reorganized as the established church under the Brazilian Constitution of 1824. Cemeteries were owned and administered by the Church; public primary and secondary education was made a Church responsibility; neither civil marriage nor divorce was permitted; non-Catholics could not be elected to the national assembly; and non-Catholics (although permitted to gather for worship) could not give their meeting place the external appearance of a church. The same Constitution, however, brought a large part of Church finances under Imperial control. Along with this weak power base, the nineteenth-century Brazilian Church had inherited a less militant tradition than that of the crusading Spanish Church. The Brazilian clergy's reputation for personal corruption reflected a similar spirit. As a result, although individual clergy were active in politics, especially in the early Empire, the Brazilian Church itself was not a center of vigorous thought on social and political questions.

The basis for both the philosophy and the political theory which prevailed in the Empire up to 1865 was a curious amalgam of ideas imported from France.[2] It was called Eclecticism, and as its name implies it was little more than a synthesis of the philosophical and religious ideas prevalent in France.[3] Its very vagueness made it the perfect companion to the weak religious tradition, and it carried the day among the leading thinkers of mid-nineteenth-century Brazil—hardly a center of philosophical thought.[4] As Antônio Paim has explained:

> Since it was synonymous with a simple juxtaposition of ideas and lacked any guiding principles, it [Eclecticism] lost any negative connotation in Brazil and was almost always combined with the label "enlightened," a qualifier doubtless meant to ennoble it. More important, the victory of political conciliation during the Second Empire can be attributed to the mentality identified with [it].[5]

In politics the climate was dominated by "party conciliation." Two political parties had emerged by 1860—the Liberal and the Conservative.[6] They competed in the national legislature according to the model of the English House of Commons—even their debating style was often derivative. The Liberals had originated as a party dedicated to defending Brazilian interests against the Portuguese. The Conservatives had begun as the defenders of absolutism, which some Conservatives took to mean defending Portuguese interests even when the latter opposed independence. By the 1840's, however, their original character was blurred. Regionalism and republicanism had divided the politicians along new lines, and by the early 1860's the two parties looked very similar (although the Liberals were soon to change). An equilibrium had been reached between, on one side, the powerful planter oligarchies of the most important provinces (Bahia, Pernambuco, Minas Gerais, São Paulo, Rio de Janeiro) and, on the other side, the Emperor. Even the politicians were often straightforwardly frank about their lack of ideological differences.

This political system appeared stable until the strains produced by a war with Paraguay (1865–70) led Pedro II to assert his authority against the parliamentary majority, thereby provoking a torrent of criticism of the entire monarchical structure. In one sense the liberal critics of the crown were justified. However enlightened Pedro II might have been, he stood at the apex of a hierarchical society based on human enslavement. It was under the authority of the Emperor and his ministers that the police and the Army hunted down runaway slaves and returned them to their masters, sometimes for torture and mutilation. An authoritarian structure, however ameliorated in practice, extended down into the family system, where the male head of the household enjoyed a power over the women and children which could border on sadism.[7]

It was also true that the Empire was more centralized than could remain acceptable to the leaders of dynamically growing regions such as the province of São Paulo. They wanted more autonomy to exploit their own resources and demonstrate their ingenuity in areas such as education and economic development. The issue of overcentralization also offered a convenient vehicle for political "outs" who had been unable to break into power because they could not or did not wish to collaborate with the political oligarchies of their provinces. The role of court favor was enormous in the composition of the Senate, for example, since the Emperor had the power to designate the final winner among a short list of three senatorial nominees. Furthermore, the Emperor exercised an effective veto over appointees to administrative posts down to the provincial level, further accentuating the need of local politicians to earn personal support at court. Thus, it could be alleged with some reason that the unitary monarchy

was strangling local initiative and distorting the formation of local opinion.

Notwithstanding these complaints, however, established political authority and the cogency of its theoretical justification in
1870 were as weak as established religion. In both cases the object of criticism was more vulnerable than the critics could have
believed. Far from being the tyrant depicted by the Republican
pamphleteers, Pedro II was more liberal and open-minded on social issues than most of the older political elite, although he resisted liberal efforts to reduce the "moderating power."[8] His real
role had been rationalized by the pragmatic constitutional lawyers and the Eclectic Philosophers.[9] This did not save him from
becoming the convenient whipping boy of liberal critics, however, because he was easier to attack—more personal and visible
—than the tradition of amorphous political thought that had
blurred party lines and left the younger generation without a
clear justification for the anomaly of a slaveholding, Catholic-
oriented agrarian monarchy.

The accompanying intellectual and literary tradition that dominated mid-century literature amply deserved its title of "Romantic."[10] It originated with a small number of writers who had
emerged in Brazil at the end of the eighteenth century. Their
thought and work was greatly influenced by Europe, as could be
seen in their pursuit of the cult of nature so characteristic of
European Romanticism. When Brazil broke away from Portugal
in 1822, these writers believed that they were articulating an
independent national consciousness—glorifying *Brazilian* natural
splendors. Couched in exuberant hyperbole, their romantic invo-
cations of Brazilianness served as a literary mantle for the anti-
Portuguese campaigns of the politicians.

In the years immediately following Brazil's independence in
1822 Indianism became a social and intellectual fad among the
elite. Portuguese names were discarded in favor of Indian ones.
Aspirants to high society even tried to prove they had noble Indian blood. Although there were virtually no dictionaries of

Tupí, the most widely spoken Indian language, and although the minor Indian languages of the Amazon basin and the interior highlands (Mato Grosso) went totally unstudied, Tupí was seriously proposed as the new official language to replace Portuguese. Gonçalves Dias, the first great popularizer of Indianist poetry, himself authored a dictionary of Tupí, published in 1857.

With the coming of age of literary Romanticism, the Indian became a symbol of Brazilian national aspirations.[11] He was transformed into a literary prototype having little connection with his actual role in Brazilian history. Like the Indian of James Fenimore Cooper, the Indian of Brazilian Romanticism was a sentimental literary symbol who offered no threat to the comfort of his readers. The parallel with Cooper was clearest in the novels of José de Alencar.[12] The Negro usually appeared in Romantic literature in stock roles such as the "heroic slave," the "suffering slave" or the "beautiful mulatta." The free man of color, who existed at every level of Brazilian society, was conspicuously ignored by the Romantic authors.[13] The contrast with the agonized attempts of later writers—Sílvio Romero, Euclides da Cunha, Graça Aranha—to come to grips with Brazil's ethnic reality could hardly be greater.

This, then, was Brazil in 1865. It was, as summed up by the literary historian Antônio Cândido, a Jesuitical traditionalism supported by an agrarian economy and a "Romantic" ideology.[14] It had its more distant roots in the clericalism and agrarianism of Portugal. This tradition, resting on a weak church, had been greatly altered by the Enlightenment in the late eighteenth and early nineteenth century—bringing into the traditional culture a dose of political liberalism, thus producing the Brazilian hybrid of a liberal monarchy.

THE RISE OF A REFORM SPIRIT

The most immediate cause of a change in national mood was the Paraguayan War (1865–70), which stimulated many of the Brazilian elite to re-examine their nation. Even the Emperor called it "a good electric shock." The war dragged on and finally it took the aid of Argentina and Uruguay for Brazil to overcome Paraguay—a much smaller and poorer nation—and the effects of this drawn-out conflict on the Brazilian Empire were extensive. Brazil's ineptitude in initial mobilization for the war forced many civilians to wake up to their country's lack of modern facilities in such basic areas as education and transportation.[15] It also embarrassed the military, arousing in officers a consciousness that led them to become a powerful political pressure group after the war. Furthermore, when the Emperor refused a Paraguayan offer to negotiate a peace in 1868 (in the face of the war's general unpopularity in Brazil) he permanently alienated an important political faction and precipitated the founding of the Brazilian Republican party in 1870. Finally, the war dramatized Brazil's shortage of able-bodied freemen. The lack of acceptable volunteers for the Army necessitated the recruitment of slaves, many of whom proved to be good soldiers. They were given their freedom in return, and many became regular soldiers.[16] This, in turn, had an important secondary effect, because in 1887–88 the Army was asked to assume responsibility for hunting runaway slaves. The result was a contradiction, as Army officers had seen the value of ex-slaves when given their freedom. This anomaly, combined with growing doubts about slavery in principle, made Army officers more receptive to abolitionist and Republican ideas after the war.

All these changes wrought by the extended fighting in the Plata basin were reinforced by the penetration of ideas from abroad. Brazil, Puerto Rico, and Cuba were the only slave territories in the Americas after the United States abolished slavery in 1865. Meanwhile political and economic liberalism was moving from triumph to triumph in France and England.[17]

Change was also overtaking the social and economic structure. Urbanization was beginning to produce a social group not directly tied to the agrarian sector. Although class differences pro-

duced by urbanization were still minimal in the late Empire, and
although economic, political, and family links between the city
and the plantation remained very close, change was in the air.
Many young men of the 1870's were ready to challenge the established political system and culture. Some were soon absorbed
into the establishment structure, but others continued to criticize. A number of these younger men came from their fathers'
plantations. Others came directly from urban backgrounds. By
the decade of the 1880's they were caught up in the converging
tide of abolitionism, anticlericalism, and republicanism.

Political developments were the most obvious harbingers of
change. In 1868 the Emperor dismissed his Liberal party Prime
Minister, Zacarias. The occasion was a disagreement over the
conduct of the Paraguayan War. Pedro II then requested the
Conservatives, who had only a minority in Parliament, to form
a new government. The Conservatives were happy to cooperate.
They immediately called a new election and came back with a
majority produced by a degree of manipulation excessive even
under the lax electoral standards of the day. The radical wing of
the Liberal party, already highly sensitive to what they alleged
to be the Emperor's "tyrannical" behavior, responded by split-
ting off to found the new Radical Liberal party in 1868 (their
manifesto appeared in 1869), dedicated to radical political reforms that would include strict controls over crown powers. Two
years later (1870) another group of dissidents went farther, founding the Republican party.

Although neither group included more than a small minority
of the political elite (with the Republicans concentrated in São
Paulo), they did represent a break with the conciliatory political
culture on which the monarchy was based; and they appeared to
constitute a direct challenge—posed in the language of democratic secularism—to the entire structure of hierarchy and privilege inherited from the colonial era.[18]

These political tremors were accompanied by new intellectual
stirrings.[19] Beginning in 1868 a group of ambitious students, who

shared little respect for tradition, coalesced in Recife.[20] Their acknowledged leader was Tobias Barreto, a student who graduated
from the Law Faculty in 1869.[21] For the following ten years Recife was the center of a small but self-confident cadre of young
intellectuals. Barreto, who had taken a schoolmaster's post in the
interior of Pernambuco, commuted regularly to Recife. He continued to be a leader among the young graduates and students,
spreading the ideas of German materialist philosophy, of which
he had become an avid student. Sílvio Romero, a young polemicist from Sergipe who had done his secondary schooling in Rio,
was another energetic and influential member of this group
(which he later labeled the "Recife School"). Other members,
all to become prominent in Brazilian intellectual life, were Franklin Távora, a novelist, Araripe Júnior, a literary critic, and Inglês
de Sousa, another novelist (who transferred to the law school in
São Paulo to finish his degree).

Positivism, evolutionism, and materialism were studied intensely. Comte, Darwin, and Haeckel were all read, along with
Taine and Renan. During the first few years the spell of Romanticism was not quite broken, but by the early 1870's Sílvio Romero and Tobias Barreto had launched a fierce campaign against
Indianism and Eclecticism.[22] The Recife School entered a new
phase when Tobias Barreto finally won a chair in the Faculty of
Law in 1882, which he occupied until his death in 1889. From
this prestigious position, he exercised a strong influence over yet
another generation of students—among whom were Artur Orlando, Clóvis Beviláqua, Graça Aranha, Fausto Cardoso, and
Sousa Bandeira. By the 1880's the defenders of traditional thought,
or even of an up-dated militant Catholicism, were badly outnumbered in Recife.

Although Recife was one of the earliest, and remained one of
the most influential centers of the new critical mentality, intellectual unrest soon appeared elsewhere. The province of Ceará became another center of intellectual innovation in the north. Some
younger men who had studied in Recife started their own move-

ment in Ceará's capital of Fortaleza in 1874. Their leaders were Rocha Lima, Capistrano de Abreu (later to attain fame as Brazil's first modern historian), and Araripe Júnior, the literary critic.[23]

This new critical spirit was by no means limited to the north, however, as products of the Recife School often later claimed. In the rest of Brazil the break with traditional ideas was identified with the spread of Positivism.[24] The first Positivist Association was founded in Rio de Janeiro in 1876. The following year Miguel Lemos and Teixeira Mendes journeyed to Paris where their involvement deepened from philosophical sympathy to religious commitment. In 1881 they founded the Positivist Apostolate, which declared its loyalty to the Pierre Lafitte faction of European Positivists.

Positivism made rapid inroads among the young cadets at the military academy in Rio, where the doctrine was spread by the officer-professor, Benjamin Constant (Botelho de Magalhães).[25] Positivism was getting a similar boost from other teachers, such as Antônio Carlos de Oliveira Guimarães, a lecturer in mathematics at Colégio Pedro II, the most prestigious secondary school in Rio. Both Constant and Guimarães were founding members of the Positivist Society in 1876. In contrast to the Brazilian Apostolate, however, they adopted the doctrinal position of E. Littré, Lafitte's rival for the loyalty of the divided Positivists in Europe.[26]

One cannot understand the influence of Positivism in Brazil without remembering that it attracted followers of widely varying degrees of commitment.[27] At one extreme there were the orthodox religious Positivists, organized into a formal church in 1881 (the "Positivist Apostolate");[28] they eventually became so rigid they expelled their own Mother Church in Paris. At the other extreme were Brazilians who read Comte, or more often his popularizers, and sympathized with his general interpretation of the importance of science and the passing of religion without accepting his schematic theories of historical inevitability and his detailed formulae for social engineering. Between these two extremes were the "heterodox" Positivists, such as Luís Pereira Barreto, who accepted Comte's historical theories but rejected the religion founded in his name and institutionalized in Rio de Janeiro. It was Pereira Barreto, a São Paulo physician, who published in 1874 the first Brazilian treatise written from a systematic Positivist position.[29]

Positivism proved influential in Brazil because it appeared at the moment when the traditional mentality was most vulnerable. Critical younger minds were ready for a systematic rejection of the Catholicism, Romanticism, and Eclecticism associated with the agrarian monarchy, Clóvis Beviláqua, a product of the Recife School, explained in the 1890's how Positivism had served a unique function:

> Previously Brazilian philosophy, as represented by Mont' Alverne, Eduardo França, Patricio Muniz, etc., went its way in isolation from the progress achieved in the old world. It seemed to us that Positivism was the best system to rescue our thought from this depression, because only Positivism contained a strong and coherent structure to pose against the Catholic structure that was dissolving.[30]

Furthermore, Positivism came from France, the country whose culture enjoyed greatest prestige among lettered Brazilians. It was logical, if ironical, that intellectual rebels should have used Comte to attack their elders' slavish imitation of Victor Hugo.

No less important, Positivism became quickly identified in Brazil with applied science, which was just gaining respectability among the elite. Brazilians studying mathematics or engineering in Rio in the 1860's met teachers who argued that the philosophical doctrines of Comte were the logical application of science to society. Such ideas led many students toward Positivism; and a number of these graduates of the military school and the Polytechnic School went on to become leading Army officers and engineers.[31] Even when they stopped short of becoming orthodox Positivists in later years, they often remained sympathetic to Positivist ideas and antipathetic to the Catholic humanistic culture which they had heard criticized by their teachers.

Positivism also had an appeal for those members of the elite who wanted economic development without social mobilization. Regarding the mass of their population as "ill-prepared" for full participation in society (because of illiteracy, inferior racial background, etc.), they could find in the authoritarian aspect of Positivism a model for modernization which rationalized the continued concentration of power in the hands of the elite. Comte's emphasis on the family as the basic social unit was another attractive idea for those Brazilians interested in modernization but worried by the strong emphasis on the individual (thereby possibly undermining the family) in European liberal thought.[32]

Finally, the orthodox Positivists were among the most diligent propagandists to be found in the late Empire. Their Church began publishing pamphlets and "annual circulars" in 1881. Its members contributed generously to the Church's educational mission—one of Positivism's prime tenets—and gained converts, or at least publicity, because they were willing to work hard at selling their doctrine in an era of few well-organized propagandists. Later Positivist enthusiasts often overstated the impact of their doctrine as such, but one cannot dispute the great influence of systematic philosophical Positivism in the training of engineers, Army officers, and medical doctors beginning in the 1870's. These men were exposed to a scientific dogma that challenged the entire structure of existing privilege in politics (monarchy), economics (slavery), religion (established Christian Church), and education (neglect of the sciences and the official sponsorship of religious instruction).

The new ideologies of progress and science were strong and attractive medicine for young minds in a nation whose social structure and mental heritage could hardly have been more different from the scenes of material progress in western Europe and North America. As Pereira Barreto, the Paulista Positivist, wrote in 1878 to José Bonifácio (moço), one of the political patriarchs:

Your Excellency has been living in the clouds—you have clung to them and neglected earthly business. Your generation was all for literature and the imagination; ours is all for science and reason. Other times, other temperaments.[33]

ABOLITIONISM

It was in this atmosphere that the movement for abolition[34] finally gathered momentum.* Opposition to slavery took a long time to become an important political force in Brazil. A few isolated voices had called for gradual abolition earlier in the century. The most famous was José Bonifácio Andrada e Silva, a patriarch of Brazilian independence.[35] Few took notice, however, of his courageous proposal for total abolition in 1825, and rare was the Brazilian who wished (or dared) to oppose the slave trade, which continued at a high rate until British pressure finally forced its liquidation in 1850.[36] With the supply of new slaves finally cut off and with manumissions, the slave population steadily decreased. Remarkably enough, slavery ceased to be a live political issue for a decade and a half.

The calm was broken in 1866, once again after pressure from abroad. A group of French abolitionists appealed to the Emperor, asking that he use his great powers to end slavery in Brazil. In his reply Pedro II made the first official government commitment to abolition by noting that total emancipation was only a matter of time. He promised that as soon as the pressure of the Paraguayan war permitted, his government would "consider as an object of first importance the realization of what the spirit of Christianity has long since demanded of the civilized world."[37]

The war with Paraguay gave the occasion for a first step toward abolition. In an effort to recruit troops quickly for the campaign, as mentioned above, the hard-pressed Army accepted slaves into

---

* A fuller discussion of race relations in the late Empire and early Republic will be given in Chapter 2. Emphasis here is on the basic ideas underlying the abolitionist campaign.

its ranks. Aware of the apparent contradiction of slaves fighting alongside freemen, the Imperial government decreed in November 1866—shortly after replying to the French abolitionists—that slaves serving in the military would be given their freedom unconditionally. In the last year of the war the Conde d'Eu, son-in-law of Emperor Pedro II and commander of the Brazilian fighting forces, successfully forced the provisional Paraguayan government to issue a decree immediately abolishing slavery in that country.[38]

When the war was over, as the Emperor had promised, the government tackled abolition at home. Significantly, there was still no abolitionist movement. Liberal writers such as Tavares Bastos had already called for gradual abolition. So did the Liberal party manifestoes of 1868 and 1869. Yet there was no organized pressure group campaigning on the issue; nor was one to appear until the end of the 1870's.

It is worth noting that the Republicans said nothing about slavery in their founding manifesto of 1870. Unlike the Liberal reformers, whose statements invariably included calls for abolition (usually gradual), the Republicans chose to equivocate on slavery. They were playing politics on abolition in order to maximize their appeal to the slaveholding planters, especially in the fast-growing coffee province of São Paulo. This tactic continued as official party policy until final abolition in 1888, although it provoked many bitter arguments at the local level and led to some local Republican organizations unilaterally affiliating with abolitionist causes.[39]

And an effective tactic it turned out to be. The Republican party reaped the political rewards of the eclipse of royal authority. While the Liberal party continued its role as the perennial inspirer of reform, it never enjoyed the fruits of victory. The three great abolitionist bills, for example, were all passed by Conservative governments. Meanwhile the Republican party gained a fateful advantage.

The first legal step, well before the formation of the abolitionist movement as such, was taken by the cabinet of Viscount Rio Branco (1871–75). In 1871 Rio Branco guided to passage the "Law of the Free Womb," which declared that all children subsequently born of slave mothers would be free. (This bill proved distinctly less effective than advocates had hoped, because if the master did not wish to accept the government's indemnity payment for the child at age eight, he still had the option of retaining the "freeborn" child under his authority—i.e., in de facto slavery—until the age of twenty-one.)

It was not until 1879 that any national politician dared call for immediate and total abolition. The initiative came from Jeronymo Sodré, a medical professor and deputy from Bahia, who was not otherwise notable for his political leadership.[40] In that same year a man of greater promise entered Parliament as a deputy from Pernambuco. He was Joaquim Nabuco, the elegant son of a planter family and soon to become the leader of a rapidly growing abolitionist movement.[41] Emancipation societies sprang up in every major city. By 1883 the abolitionists had merged their efforts in a national campaign. They concentrated on two fronts: demanding liquidation of the legal basis of slavery, while at the same time mobilizing donations for voluntary manumissions.

Both goals were eventually achieved, but only after another five years. In 1884 the provinces of Ceará and Amazonas succeeded in voluntarily manumitting all slaves within their borders. In 1885 the Parliament passed the Sexagenarian Law, unconditionally freeing all slaves over sixty-five years old, while conditionally freeing those between sixty and sixty-five (they had to render three more years' "service" to their masters). By 1887 slavery was being undermined from every direction. Slaves were fleeing their masters, the Army had refused to hunt them down, and the judges began ignoring the owners' claims.[42]

The third and final abolition bill, which granted immediate and total emancipation on May 13, 1888, was the work of a Conservative cabinet led by planters (primarily from São Paulo) who had previously fought to preserve slavery. At the last minute they saw that replacement of slave by free labor was inevitable and could even be beneficial because free laborers would be less expensive and more efficient than slaves. Furthermore, to manage the final step to abolition would leave the planter elite in control of the government, thus preventing the rise to power of long-time abolitionists who might harbor radical ideas such as land reform."[43]

Most of the intellectuals caught up in other liberal movements, such as Republicanism and anti-clericalism, finally became abolitionists. In the 1880's, for example, most of the politically conscious students in the law faculties (and therefore, by definition, spokesmen for the future governing elite) were ardent abolitionists as well as supporters of either Republicanism or the radical wing of the Liberal party. Even those abolitionist leaders who chose not to attack the monarchy per se, such as André Rebouças and José do Patrocínio, subscribed to the liberal doctrine in virtually all its political and philosophical particulars. Rebouças read John Stuart Mill, and Joaquim Nabuco confessed in his autobiography that he owed his political inspiration to Bagehot.[44] Luiz Gama, a fiery mulatto lawyer and pioneer abolitionist from São Paulo, commended to his son's attention two books: the *Bible* and Ernest Renan's *Life of Jesus*.[45] He was thus recommending an amalgam of traditional religion and theological liberalism. Even the pseudonyms used by the abolitionists showed their longing for the Anglo-American model of liberalism: Rui Barbosa called himself "Grey," Nabuco used "Garrison," and Gusmão Lobo "Clarkson."[46]

The active abolitionists could be divided into two groups. As Nabuco noted in his memoirs, there was a "pioneer" group composed of José do Patrocínio, Ferreira de Menezes, Vicente de Souza, Nicoláu Moreira, and João Clapp. These men were primarily propagandists, relying upon emotional arguments; their forum was the press and speakers' platform. Skilled at arousing fervor in their audiences, some (like Patrocínio) came close to preaching revolution. The other principal group—led by Nabuco,

André Rebouças, Gusmão Lobo, and Joaquim Serra—was composed of moderates whose aim was manipulation of parliamentary opinion.[47]

Nabuco was the leading theoretician among the abolitionists. He wrote one of the first manifestoes—published by the newly founded Anti-Slavery Society (Sociedade Contra Escravidão) in 1880.[48] There the liberal rationale stands out as the heart of the abolitionist message. Slavery had made Brazil a shameful anachronism in the modern world, out of step with the "progress of our century." The moral condemnation of Europe and North America weighed heavily: "Brazil does not want to be a nation morally isolated, a leper, expelled from the world community. The esteem and respect of foreign nations are as valuable to us as they are to other peoples." It was no good arguing that only twenty years ago slavery was still readily accepted in the United States: "Social morality doesn't have to wait for us. . . . To isolate oneself is to condemn oneself."

Slavery, furthermore, was "a tree whose roots invariably sterilize the physical and moral ground they touch." It was inherently corrupting to all Brazil, since "man is free neither when a slave nor when a master." It corrupted family morals, demeaned the value of labor, and reduced religion to a "superstition." Worst of all it covered the land with a "network of feudal realms, where the master is the tyrant of a little nation of men who dare not face him." Brazil, he said, could never progress until it expunged slavery: "What we visualize is not simply the emancipation of the slave, but the emancipation of the nation; it is the development of free labor which must be the responsibility of this generation." Only then could Brazilians work to "found a free country, uniting around a common flag—emancipation of the soil."

Nabuco developed his abolitionist arguments further in O Abolicionismo (1883), which soon became a classic of the movement. In it he repeated many of the arguments of the 1880 manifesto, but the battles since 1880 had given him greater skill in combining humanitarian with practical arguments. Along with the familiar moral injunctions went the claim that continued slavery inhibited Brazil's development according to the liberal capitalist model—because it "prevents immigration, dishonors manual labor, delays the appearance of industries, promotes bankruptcy, diverts capital from its natural course, keeps away machines, and arouses class hatred." Only by abolishing slavery could Brazil enjoy the "miracles of free labor" and "work creatively for the benefit of humanity and the advancement of South America."[49] Nabuco took the position—differing not only from Republicans but many members of his own Liberal party—that abolition was the most urgent item on the docket of liberal reform.

From the beginning Brazilian abolitionists were heavily indebted to foreign opinion. The slave trade had ended only after three decades of British pressure which culminated in a virtual blockade by the Royal Navy in 1850. And it was an appeal by French intellectuals in 1866 which had triggered the government's first formal commitment to abolition. Many of the younger generation, in fact, testified that it was foreign censure of Brazil which galvanized them into action. For Manuel Vitorino, for example, later to be governor of Bahia and Vice President of the Republic, "one experience made me politically militant—my trip to Europe showed me just how far they were slandering us and how our reputation bedevilled us, the fact that we were a country that still had slaves. After returning home [in early 1881] my abolitionist feelings became insistent and uncompromising and on this issue I never again conceded."[50]

And the abolitionists struggled to mobilize even greater foreign pressure on their countrymen. In 1880 Nabuco solicited the American Minister, Henry Hilliard, for an opinion about slavery in Brazil. Hilliard readily complied, arguing for abolition and the replacement of slave with free labor. His enthusiasm, notably indiscreet for a diplomat speaking on a domestic issue, delighted the abolitionists. They capitalized on their propaganda opportunity, all the greater since Hilliard himself had been a slaveholder and Confederate soldier before he saw the error of his ways and the "happy transformation in the condition of the people in the great agricultural region when slavery formerly existed."[51]

French intellectuals remained a favorite weapon which the abolitionists used against the Brazilian government at every opportunity. In 1884 José do Patrocínio wrote Victor Hugo, pleading with him to intervene personally with Pedro II. Patrocínio's action was remarkable for two reasons—first, that he should have thought Hugo capable of such influence (perhaps he was considering the Emperor's exaggerated admiration for Hugo); second, that he should have thought it within Pedro II's power to bring abolition. Could it have been a gross overestimation of the crown's power, which liberals, after all, hoped to limit? Patrocínio—the passionate orator who sought to rouse the masses to action—apparently succumbed to the wishful thinking of an elitist, longing for the Emperor to realize the liberal vision in a single benign gesture.[52]

This practice of appealing for foreign help made the abolitionists vulnerable to the charge of being un-Brazilian. And indeed, at every stage of the campaign the defenders of the status quo tried to undermine their abolitionist opponents by questioning their patriotism. In 1871, for example, José de Alencar, the Romanticist author who was also a Conservative deputy from Ceará, ridiculed the "proclamations of European philanthropy" that produced "obeisances to foreign opinion." Alencar thought many other reforms (such as "emancipation of the vote") were more important than abolition—even gradual abolition as proposed in the Law of the Free Womb (passed in 1871). But he added pointedly, "these essential interests of the country [i.e., the reforms he thought most important] do not have a French voice to say to someone, 'Sir, by this act your name will acquire everlasting fame.' "[53]

The abolitionists were also charged with endangering Brazil's basic interests for the sake of arousing cheers in foreign capitals. One witty slavocrat argued as late as 1884 that all had been well in the slave fields until the "wolves came from the city," and "whispered into their [i.e., the slaves'] ears the new ideas from the Court. They told them . . . of the hopes that European wise men have of seeing slavery abolished in Brazil, come what may, by the next centennial of the discovery of America [i.e., 1892]."[54]

The abolitionists, in their turn, tackled these charges explicitly. At the elaborate banquet attended by virtually all the leading abolitionists in honor of the American Hilliard (whose analysis had proved so obliging) the principal Brazilian speaker, Nabuco, went out of his way to rebut the charge of "foreign intervention." The Brazilian government itself, he said, had more than once found it worthwhile to respond to "foreigners'" demands (as in the Emperor's reply to French intellectuals' 1866 appeal for abolition). And the government itself had even intervened in another country when the Brazilians chose to abolish slavery in Paraguay!

"This moral support which we [abolitionists] derive from world approval honors us and we seek it. No liberal cause can ever be debated in any country without the liberal forces in every other country organizing for its support." Nabuco made a conspicuous salute to the official American diplomatic representative as an ally in the cause. Pronouncing him an honorary member of the Anti-Slavery Society, Nabuco said Hilliard was in Brazil "just as Benjamin Franklin was in France—on the eve of a liberal revolution."[55]

What did the abolitionists think of the issue of race, as distinct from slavery? They were unavoidably aware of the racist theories pouring in from North America and Europe, although their full implications were not yet perceived. Nabuco, for instance, left no doubt that his goal was a whiter Brazil. He was honest enough to say that had he been alive in the sixteenth century, he would have opposed the introduction of African slaves, just as he now opposed the plan for "Asiatic slavery," referring to a current proposal to import Chinese workers to replace the slaves. In Nabuco's view, it was a shame the Dutch had not remained in Brazil back in the seventeenth century. Although he carefully explained that the great Dutch contribution was "freedom of trade and freedom of conscience," the ethnic implications seemed unmistakable: "Our social evolution was delayed by the quick end of Dutch rule."[56]

The abolitionists were, however, very ready to take a position on whether a liberal society was possible if a large part of the population was non-white. According to the abolitionist manifesto of 1880 (written by Nabuco):

> If a nation can progress only by using the forced labor of an extra-legal caste, then it is a mere first approximation of an independent and autonomous state. If a race is able to develop in a latitude only by making another race work to support it, then that race has not yet attempted to acclimatize. Traditional Brazilians think that a Brazil without slaves would quickly perish. Even that result would be better than a life that can be maintained only by undermining national character and humiliating the country. If abolition should mean suicide, then humanity would be rendered a service by those incapable of surviving on their own. At least they would have the courage to leave to the stronger, heartier and braver, the incomparable heritage of a land that they could not cultivate and where they could not survive.

To this remarkably frank appraisal Nabuco added an optimistic conclusion:

> Instead of being suicidal, ending slavery would be a provident and just act. It would summon forth new qualities in our national character and launch the nation on an epoch of progress and free labor, which would be the true period of our definitive development and our real independence.[57]

Although worried about the "ethnic factor," the abolitionists shared the predominant Brazilian belief that their society harbored no racial prejudice. The debates over the abolitionist bills reveal the prevalence of this belief among all political factions. In 1871, for example, Perdigão Malheiro, a deputy from Minas

Gerais and a noted authority on slave law, condemned what he considered to be unjustified slurs on Brazil's racial harmony. "Since Negroes came to Brazil from the African coast there has never been that contempt for the African race to be found in other countries, especially the United States." Slavery had become less pernicious, especially since 1850, he argued. Color prejudice in Brazil? "Gentlemen, I know many individuals of dark skin who are worth more than many of white skin. That is the truth. In the schools, higher faculties, and churches do we not see good colored students alongside our distinguished men? In Parliament, government, the Council of State, the diplomatic missions, the Army, and the public offices do we not see men whose skin is more or less dark, men of the *mestiço** as well as the African race?"[58]

This was the accepted view among the elite: Brazil had escaped race prejudice. As Nabuco wrote in *O Abolicionismo*: "slavery, to our good fortune, never embittered the slave's spirit toward the master, at least collectively, nor did it create between the races that mutual hate which naturally exists between oppressors and oppressed." Furthermore, recent experience had shown that "color in Brazil is not, as in the United States, a social prejudice against whose persistence no character, talent, or merit can prevail."[59] Unlike in the United States, abolitionists in Brazil were seldom forced to discuss the question of race per se, because the defenders of slavery virtually never resorted to theories of racial inferiority. Their North American counterparts had earlier been forced to struggle with claims of Negro racial inferiority at the same time they faced political and economic arguments in defense of slavery.

Nonetheless, Brazilian abolitionists did talk about the role of race in history. Most foresaw an "evolutionist" process, with the

---

* The Portuguese term *mestiço* means "mixed blood," which can be any mixture of racial backgrounds, including Indian, African, and European. It should not be confused with the Spanish term *mestizo*, which has entered English with the primary meaning of a European-Indian mixture.

white element gradually triumphing. They were also prepared to accelerate this "evolution" by promoting European immigration, which they favored for two reasons. First, Europeans could help fill the labor shortage resulting from the elimination of slave labor, all the more necessary since the rate of reproduction of the free colored population was thought to be insufficient to meet the labor needs. Second, European immigration would help to speed up the "whitening" process in Brazil. Nabuco was startlingly forthright on this point. What the abolitionists wanted, he explained in 1883, was a country "where European immigration, attracted by the generosity of our institutions and the liberality of our regime, may constantly bring to the tropics a flow of lively, energetic, and healthy Caucasian blood, which we may absorb without danger. . . ."[60]

Other abolitionists, who also believed in "whitening," described the process more euphemistically. José do Patrocínio, a mulatto, argued that Brazil was more blessed historically than the United States: "We have been able to fuse all races into a single native population, because Portuguese colonization assimilated the savage races instead of trying to destroy them, thus preparing us to resist the devastating invasion of race prejudice."[61] Here was white predominance described in the more polite terms of "fusion."

Nowhere did the abolitionists' belief in "whitening" become clearer than in their reaction to the Chinese worker proposal. A group of planters and politicians who saw the inevitability of total abolition proposed in the 1870's that Brazil should import Chinese laborers to replace black slaves. This was not a new idea, having been proposed as early as the reign of Dom João VI (1808–21). In 1870 it had arisen again and was hotly debated among the members of the Society to Aid National Industry (Sociedade Auxiliadora da Indústria Nacional). The backers of Chinese labor were notably apologetic. They wanted only "temporary" workers, *not* colonizers who would "become a permanent part of our society." Their objective was merely a "means of transition" to a "system of completely free labor" when "measures on immigration, hygiene and religious education can produce their fruits and render superfluous Chinese cooperation."[62]

Although the proposal was rejected by the Society, it did not die. During the 1870's it reappeared among the many ideas for meeting the labor shortage, although very few who urged immigration could bring themselves to consider favorably the Chinese. Menezes e Souza, the persuasive author of an 1875 report urging government measures to attract immigrants, went out of his way to denounce the Chinese. Brazil needed "new blood," not "old juice" from "degenerate bodies." He based his racism on "anthropological truth," which had established that the "Chinese race bastardizes and makes our race degenerate."[63] Such a view, incidentally, was at least semi-official, since his book had been written as a formal report to the Minister of Agriculture.

The Chinese labor proposal surfaced again in the late 1870's, proposed by a group calling itself "the Society for Importing Asiatic Workers of Chinese Ancestry."[64] Their idea became a subject of major debate when the leader of the Liberal Government, Viscount Sinimbú, ordered an official study of Chinese immigration into the United States. The investigation was entrusted to Salvador de Mendonça, who was then the ambitious and successful Brazilian Consul General in New York. Mendonça soon became an enthusiastic supporter of Chinese immigration. His memorandum, later expanded into a book published by the Brazilian government, praised the Chinese as "intelligent, frugal and industrious workers." Since they would come from Canton, "where the climate is tropical, they would quickly adapt to Brazil," just as they had already adapted to Cuba and the mines of the United States.[65]

Mendonça knew the prejudices of his Brazilian audience. Like the earlier advocates of Chinese immigration, he wanted the Asian workers only "temporarily," to provide some continuity of labor supply "between the African and the European." The Chinese could not be considered as permanent immigrants because they "don't learn to love the land to which they migrate," aside from the fact that he considered them "suspicious, disloyal, lying, and lustful."[66]

Such official support for an "investigation" of the practicalities of Chinese immigration made the question a subject for full-scale discussion. Once again it was attacked on racial grounds. Joaquim Nabuco was incensed at the Prime Minister's willingness to consider importing Chinese. Nabuco argued that there was no real demand for them in Brazil. A wave of Chinese immigration would, he said, "pervert and corrupt our race even further."[67] However limited the immigration, Nabuco argued, Brazil would inevitably become "mongolized, just as it was Africanised when Salvador Correa de Sá brought over the first slaves."[68]

Although Nabuco regarded the Chinese as racially inferior as he did the Negro, he thought they lacked the Negro's capacity to be assimilated in Brazil. On the contrary, since the Chinese could survive in "the worst of conditions," they were fated to "occupy" any country where they gained a foothold.[69] In sum, Nabuco opposed the Chinese "ethnologically because they will provoke race conflict and degrade our present population; economically because they will not solve the labor shortage; morally, because they will introduce into our society that leprosy of vices that infects all cities where Chinese immigration occurs; politically, because instead of freeing labor it will only prolong the present low moral level of labor and at the same time help to preserve slavery."[70]

As we saw above, Nabuco started from the assumption that Brazil should be "improving" herself eugenically. By this logic, importing the Chinese would be a step backward. In the parliamentary debate where Nabuco questioned the "civilizing" value of the Chinese, one deputy supported him, "We must raise the moral level of this country," to which another replied, "both things are needed: morality and workers." The Chinese did not fit into this picture. As another deputy explained, "the Negro improves himself, but the Chinaman is impossible."[71]

Despite this opposition, all the planters did not give up hope of importing Chinese laborers. As the slave population dwindled and European immigrants failed to appear, a planter group entered into direct negotiations in 1883 with a shipping company director, who proposed to supply them with Chinese. The abolitionists' loud opposition undoubtedly contributed to the failure of the scheme, which never gained the necessary cooperation from the Chinese. Furthermore, the English government, with the Royal Navy at its command, had threatened to intervene to prevent the scheme.[72] The controversy over Chinese immigration had forced many Brazilians, however, to make clear their racial views. What emerged was a strong commitment to a progressively whiter Brazil.

EUROPEAN THOUGHT AND DETERMINIST DILEMMAS

Abolitionist thought, like all reform thought in Brazil, grew out of the nineteenth-century European liberalism that had accompanied the Industrial Revolution, rapid urbanization and economic growth. These changes had been made possible, in turn, by the application of science and technology. European faith in liberalism seemed justified by European economic prosperity. In Brazil, however, liberalism came as a result of intellectual trends per se rather than any profound economic change. Although cities were growing rapidly after 1850, there was no comparable leap in Brazilian economic development. The Brazilians were applying liberal ideas, therefore, in a social context not significantly different from the world of their fathers.[73]

As the major European powers grew stronger economically and politically, and as they increased their dominance over more parts of the non-European world, European thinkers began to produce explanations for greater economic success. Their intellectuals offered "scientific" reasons for Europe's success. These apologias for European superiority were exported to Latin America along with European liberalism, and their juxtaposition created an uncomfortable paradox for the thinking Brazilian.

Such ideas emerged after the prestige of natural science (largely a European creation in its modern form) had buttressed Europe's intellectual authority. The argument was made that northern Europeans had achieved superior economic and political power because of their heredity and their uniquely favorable physical environment. In short, northern Europeans were the "highest" races and enjoyed the "best" climate, which carried the implication that darker races and tropical climates could never produce comparable civilizations. Some of these writers explicitly ruled out the possibility of civilization in an area that lacked European conditions. Not coincidentally, their analysis was directed at the area that had succumbed to European conquest since the fifteenth century: Africa and Latin America. Thus an expanding Europe found a scientific rationale for its political and economic conquests.[74] For our analysis it does not matter that in their popularized form these ideas were grossly oversimplified and often distorted. A great many people did, in fact, subscribe to them.

One of the best-known such writers was the English historian, Henry Thomas Buckle (1821–62), whose multi-volume *History of Civilization in England* (1857–61) contained a clearly stated philosophy of climatic determinism.[75] In eight pages Buckle analyzed the rainfall, topography, hydrographic system, and wind patterns of Brazil. Never having visited the country, and lacking almost any genuinely scientific studies for evidence, Buckle had to rely on travel accounts, which he cited copiously. His description of Brazil sounded much like the Romantic stereotype: "so rank and luxuriant is the growth that Nature seems to riot in the very wantonness of power." He went on to describe the "tangled forests," and "birds of gorgeous plumage." Unfortunately, however, "amid this pomp and splendor of Nature, no place is left for Man. He is reduced to insignificance by the majesty with which he is surrounded." Brazil came in for special censure in Buckle's survey of civilization. "Nowhere else is there so painful a contrast between the grandeur of the external world and the littleness of the internal. . . . And the mind, cowed by this unequal struggle, has not only been unable to advance, but without foreign aid it would undoubtedly have receded. For even at present, with all the improvements constantly introduced from Europe, there are no signs of real progress. . . ."[76]

It is unlikely that many Brazilian intellectuals read all of Buckle's ponderous work, but they certainly knew his eight-page indictment. Hardly a Brazilian social thinker for the next sixty years could avoid strugggling with this kind of pessimistic view of Brazil's potential, and they often referred explicitly to Buckle.

Another deterministic doctrine with a long history, racism, was also brought to the surface in a new form by European writers, of whom Arthur de Gobineau (1816–82) was a prominent example. Shortly before Buckle published the *History of Civilization in England,* Gobineau published his *Essai sur l'inégalité des races humaines (1853–1855).* It was read less widely in Brazil than Buckle, but Brazilians were very familiar with the basic ideas of racism which Gobineau expressed.

Racial determinism had already been politically endorsed in English North America, where separation of the "superior" and "inferior" races was a well-institutionalized system. Brazil, however, had been a multi-racial society for too long for strict segregation along biracial lines to be a practical possibility. Brazil's historical racial balance had led to widespread miscegenation, touching even the oldest families. But this fait accompli of social history did not prevent Brazilian social thinkers from worrying about the effects of racial mixing. Brazil was the largest single New World colony in which the black percentage of the population had been over 50 per cent for so long. The black population in the United States never approached 50 per cent of the total population, even in the South (although it did in a few individual states).

Unlike Buckle, Gobineau actually went to Brazil, although after his *Essai* was published. As an ambitious diplomat with political aspirations, he thought of Brazil as a professional dead end, as well as living proof of his theories. From the moment he was assigned there as French Minister (landing during the carnival celebrations of 1869), he detested the country. He thought it a cultural backwater and a constant health hazard. He despised the Brazilians, whom he regarded as irretrievably sullied by miscegenation.[77] And he was terrified that he might contract yellow fever before he saw France again (not unjustifiably—there was an epidemic in 1869–70).

His aesthetic sense was offended by "a population totally mulatto, vitiated in its blood and spirit, and fearfully ugly."[78] He announced that "not a single Brazilian has pure blood because the pattern of marriages among whites, Indians and Negroes is so widespread that the nuances of color are infinite, causing a degeneration of the most depressing type among the lower as well as the upper classes." Gobineau did not hesitate to draw sweeping conclusions, noting in an official report on slavery that native Brazilians were "neither hard-working, active, nor fertile."[79]

The last point became central to Gobineau's analysis of Brazil's future. Although the climate and natural resources were favorable, he thought the native population was destined to disappear, due to its genetic "degeneracy." By a curious bit of arithmetic, he calculated that it would take "less than two hundred years . . . to see the end of the descendants of Costa-Cabral [sic] and the emigrants who followed them." The only way to avoid this dénouement was for the existing population to "fortify itself through joining with the higher value of the European races. . . ." Then the race would "revive, public health would improve, the moral temperment would be reinvigorated, and the best possible changes would occur in the social condition of this admirable country."[80]

None of this long-range philosophizing could soften the Frenchman's fury at having been relegated to a South American backwater. His letters reveal an unrelieved contempt for his colleagues of all other nationalities, but his harshest words were reserved for the Brazilians. "Everyone is ugly here, unbelievably

ugly, like apes."[81] His only consolation was his friendship with
the Emperor. He echoed Buckle's description of an empty land:
"Except for the Emperor there is no one in this desert full of
thieves."[82] Gobineau's frustration even spilled over into his personal conduct. He quarreled frequently, culminating in a wild
street brawl with the son-in-law of a Brazilian Senator. In 1870
he was recalled, on the insistence of his good friend the
Emperor.[83]

Other foreign observers also reminded Brazilians of the implications of racist doctrines. José Ingenieros, the Argentine philosopher (1877–1925), influenced the Brazilian elite with his confused doctrines of the racial inferiority of non-whites.[84] Louis
Couty was another foreigner who was very frank. A Frenchman
who knew Brazil well, Couty was especially interested in the coffee-growing provinces of the Center-South. He collaborated
closely with Brazilian reformers such as Viscount Taunay and
other leaders of the Imperial Society for Immigration. In 1884
Couty published a book about Brazil with the title "Sociological
Sketches." In the Preface he stated his racial views unambiguously: "I attempt to prove that the settlement by enslaved Africans has produced all Brazil's difficulties and I indicate that the
settlement by freemen from Europe is the only possible solution."[85] There is no evidence that any of Couty's important Brazilian friends attempted to refute his unilateral interpretation of
Brazilian history.

Perhaps the most famous indictment by a foreign visitor to
Brazil was that of Louis Agassiz, who came to Brazil in 1865 on
a scientific expedition, and three years later (with his wife) published an account of their trip. "Let any one who doubts the evil
of this mixture of races, and is inclined, from a mistaken philanthropy, to break down all barriers between them, come to Brazil.
He cannot deny the deterioration consequent upon an amalgamation of races, more wide-spread here than in any other country in the world, and which is rapidly effacing the best qualities
of the white man, the Negro, and the Indian, leaving a mongrel

nondescript type, deficient in physical and mental energy."[86] Agassiz concluded his book with an attempt to pay tribute to his Brazilian friends, who were soon able to read his book in a French translation.[87] He acknowledged their "susceptibility to lofty impulses and emotions, their love of theoretical liberty, their natural generosity, their aptness to learn, their ready eloquence." But he could not avoid alluding again to race and climate, as he added: "if also I miss qualities of the Northern races, I do but recall a distinction as ancient as the tropical and temperate zones themselves."[88]

THE AGONY OF A WOULD-BE NATIONALIST:
SÍLVIO ROMERO

A careful reading of Brazilian social thought before abolition leaves little doubt that Brazilians skirted over the problems posed for their nation by deterministic theories of race. Yet there were a few exceptional thinkers who struggled with issues that took the majority of their literate countrymen many more years to face. This chapter will end with a discussion of the liberal reformer who struggled as honestly and continuously as any with questions of race and environment—Sílvio Romero (1851–1914).[89]

In what follows we shall analyze Romero's thought on race and environment before 1889. His views in this period were worked out primarily between 1869 and 1881, and then summarized in the major work of his career, *História de Literatura Brasileira*, which first appeared in 1888.[90] His views after 1889, which underwent little basic change on the question of race, will be discussed in later chapters.

Romero earned his principal reputation as a literary critic. He followed a sociological approach to literature, arguing that race and environment were the keys to understanding artistic creations. He described himself as a Social Darwinist, and although harboring reservations about some of Spencer's ideas, thought they were the best guide for understanding history.[91] An incorrigible polemicist, he often contradicted himself in order to score a debating point.[92] Yet his inconsistencies had another more significant explanation—the fate of Brazil, as analyzed within the analytical framework of Social Darwinism, was not a comfortable issue for speculation.

He did, however, have one unswerving conviction: Brazilians had to master current scientific doctrines and apply them to their country. And he never surrendered his emotional commitment to his country, however depressing his conclusions became. The assumption from which he started was that any nation is the product of an interaction between the population and their natural habitat. The nation's specific character and culture was a product of long-term adjustment. How long? Romero's estimate varied. The implications of any estimate were serious because they inevitably reflected upon Brazil's status and future.

Romero tackled the question of environmental determinism directly, pronouncing Buckle's verdict on Brazil as "hard words but essentially correct."[93] Although contesting specific points, he thought Buckle should be read in Brazil, and he printed in translation virtually the entire eight-page section on Brazil from the *History of Civilization in England*. This appeared both in a series of articles printed in the *Revista Brazileira* in 1879–80 and in his *História da Literatura Brasileira*—undoubtedly helping to publicize the indictment.[94]

Romero thought that Buckle had overdrawn his analysis—his theory being "too cosmographic."[95] He "divides civilization into two great branches: European and non-European; in the former, man's energy prevails over nature, while in the latter one finds the contrary. The distinction is capricious."[96] Furthermore, he found Buckle misinformed about the facts of geography and climate in Brazil. Brazil had no huge mountains (as Buckle had suggested); it suffered from drought rather than excessive rain, just as impassable jungle was less serious than the semi-barren interior.[97] Nature's products had long been thought to be vaster in Brazil than anywhere else, "which is an advantage, say [Bra-

zilian] patriots; which is a hindrance, says Buckle; which is an
error, say I."[98]

Romero had no doubt that the Brazilian habitat was seriously
debilitating. The oppressive heat and periodic drought helped
to make Brazilians "listless and apathetic."[99] He cited approvingly a handbook of hygiene which listed the supposed physical
consequences of man's residence in the tropics—languid blood,
slow digestion, and oversensitive skin. The physical condition of
the Indian supposedly "proved" the enervating influence of the
climate, where fevers and diseases were common. Romero quoted
this depressing description at length and pronounced it "more or
less exact" for Brazil. He added "we have a morbid population
which for the most part leads a short, sickly, and unhappy life."[100]

Did Romero think this baneful influence of climate irremediable? Apparently not, because he flatly rejected the determinism of Buckle. Furthermore, he appreciated the importance of
diet and hygiene as instruments in helping man to adapt to the
tropics. He could not, of course, know of the impending discoveries in the field of contagious diseases and the treatment of
parasites, so the tone of his discussion was equivocal.

Romero worried more, however, about race. He began by accepting the basic idea of a hierarchy of races, often using the
phrase "ethnographic scale" and referring to "inferior" and "superior" races. At the same time, he was skeptical enough to see
some of the inconsistencies in racial thought—noting that the
definition of race itself was vague, and that the "historic races"
(including the Aryan) "had experienced the most complete miscegenation."[101] These qualifications did not save him from repeating many of the current European theories about Indian and Negro inferiority.

Romero saw Brazil as the product of three racial streams—
white European, black African, and indigenous Indian. The
views he expressed about each of them were hardly encouraging.
Of the particular white strain ("Greco-Latin") that came to
Brazil—via the Portuguese—he held the same view as the Roman-
tics who popularized cultural Nationalism, namely, that it was

inferior to the "Germano-Saxon" branch. He reminded his coun-trymen that "the robust peoples of the North, led today by the English and the Germans," had the historic role of "invigorating the blood and ideas of Latin, Celtic and Iberian peoples."[102] The Indian he regarded as "certainly the lowest on the ethnographic scale."[103] Of a low cultural level, they had barely managed to in-fluence Brazilian culture. The African he described as "defeated on the ethnographic scale." He quoted Wilberforce approvingly on the inherent inferiority of the black compared to the white man, and repeated the familiar if ill-founded argument that blacks had never created a civilization.[104]

Having described these ethnic elements Romero argued that the particular character of Brazil was due to a mixture of the three. "The Aryan race, combining here with two totally dif-ferent races, has contributed to the creation of a *mestiço* and creole sub-race distinct from the European. . . . It helps little," he said in 1888, "to discuss whether this is good or bad. It's a fact and that is enough."[105]

There were no pure racial types left in Brazil, he argued, and even when there were, no *pure-blood* Negroes or Indians had ever become "notable" in Brazilian history.[106] Yet the product of cen-turies of miscegenation showed widely differing degrees of in-fluence by the three elements. Whites had predominated, be-cause their culture had been more developed, the Indians had been annihilated by war and disease, and the African was brutal-ized by slavery. "The result is easy to discern: The white man, the unfeeling perpetrator of so many crimes, took what he could from the red man and Negroes, and then threw them away like useless objects. He was constantly helped in the process by the *mestiço*, his son and his collaborator who ended up replacing him, assuming his color and his power."[107] Romero thought the African strain had contributed much more than the Indian to the new race, going so far as to describe it as a "robust, civilizing agent," which had helped the new race adapt to the tropical climate.[108]

To the hard question of whether race mixture had been beneficial his answer varied. Just as in the case of climatological determinism, the scientific arguments he needed in order to write a definitive rejection of racist determinism did not yet exist. In 1880 he wrote: "we are a people descended from the degenerate and corrupt branch of the old Latin race, to which were added two of the most degraded races in the world—the coastal Negroes and the American redskins. . . ." The result? "The senility of the Negro, the laziness of the Indian, the authoritarian and miserly talent of the Portuguese had produced a shapeless nation with no original or creative qualities."[109] At other times he felt more hopeful. In the same year (1880) that he published the preceding statement, he challenged Brazilians to study their real culture and not some artificial creation of the Romantic Indianists. "In this great work of civilization there are no privileged races or continents; there is only the privilege of creative effort."[110]

At heart, of course, Romero was uncertain. "If it is true that the mixture of diverse peoples guarantees vigorous growth, then no one can offer greater advantages than the Brazilian."[111] The conditional clause epitomizes his uncertainty. He was unflinching in declaring that miscegenation was at the center of Brazilian history. But his conclusions about its significance depended upon his estimate of the current progress in Brazil and his natural tendency to confuse historical analysis with predictions about the future. His equivocation was hardly surprising. Scientific thought about hybrids was changing rapidly in Romero's day. European science tended to denegrate human mixed bloods as weak and potentially sterile. Romero thought this was probably nonsense, but did not yet have any scientific basis for saying so.

His racial views became most intense when he talked of Brazil's future.

> My argument is that future victory in the life struggle among us will belong to the white. But the latter, in order to achieve this victory in the face of the hardships of the climate, will have to capitalize on the aid the other two races can furnish, especially the black race

with which it has mixed most. After having rendered the necessary help, the white type will continue to predominate by natural selection until it emerges pure and beautiful as in the old world. That will come when it has totally acclimatized on this continent. Two factors will greatly contribute to this process: on the one hand the abolition of the slave trade and the continuous disappearance of the Indians, and on the other hand European immigration![112]

In other contexts he saw the final result as less than pure white.

The proverbial tendency of . . . the mulatto to pass for white when his color permits the illusion is well known. We have virtually no purely Aryan families. Presumptive whites abound. Within two or three centuries perhaps this ethnic fusion will be complete and the Brazilian *mestiço* well defined.[113]

Elsewhere:

The future of Brazilian people will be an Afro-Indian and Latino-German mixture if, as is probable, German immigration continues alongside Portuguese and Italian.[114]

Romero's vision of the future depended very much on whether he thought the existing racially mixed population was psychologically stable or not. We have already noted his inconsistency on this point. In 1880 he was cautious: "The two great agents of transformation—nature and the mixture of diverse peoples are still at work, and the result cannot yet be determined with certainty."[115] Elsewhere the same year he noted, "the three races among us have not yet disappeared into the combination of a single type and this process will be very slow. Meanwhile the mixture of colors and a confusion of ideas remains our inheritance."[116] By 1888 he was more confident. "If the Brazilian people as we see them today do not constitute a single compact and distinct race, they have the elements to develop forcefully and take on an original character in the future. Perhaps we shall yet represent in America a great cultural and historical destiny."[117]

2 Racial Realities and Racial Thought after Abolition

On May 13, 1888, Princess Isabel, acting for her ailing and absent father, signed the law that abolished all slavery and gave no compensation to the masters. This final triumph owed more than a little to the pragmatic flexibility of the slaveholders. Antônio Prado, one of the wealthiest planters in São Paulo, for example, supported unconditional liberation in May 1888, although he had opposed outright abolition as late as 1887. The prosperous planters of the south were already looking to Italian immigrants as their labor source; and with final abolition inevitable, the landowning classes were astute enough to realize that presiding over the last act would enable them to keep political control.

NATURE AND ORIGINS OF BRAZIL'S MULTI-RACIAL SOCIETY

As the more perceptive men of property had foreseen, abolition did not bring the economic and social transformation expected by the more naïve abolitionists.[1] Brazil was still a predominantly agrarian economy when abolition came. Its paternalistic system of social relations prevailed even in the urban areas. This system of social stratification gave the landowners (who were white —or occasionally light mulatto) a virtual monopoly of power— economic, social, and political. The lower strata, including poor whites as well as most free coloreds, were well accustomed to submission and deference. This hierarchy, in which social classification correlated highly with color, had developed as an integral part of the slave-based colonial economy. But by the time of final abolition it was *not* dependent upon slavery for its continuation.

Exactly when the dependence ceased is a question that remains to be researched. The important point here is that the majority of Brazilian planters, especially those in the prosperous coffee regions of Center-South Brazil, came to understand that abolition need not endanger their economic and social dominance. This analysis proved correct. The newly freed slaves moved into the paternalistic multi-racial social structure that had long since taught free men of color the habits of deference in their relationships with employers and other social superiors. It is within this context—termed "pre-industrial" by the French sociologist Roger Bastide—that race relations proceeded after abolition.[2]

Nineteenth-century Brazil already exhibited a complex system of racial classification. It was pluralistic, or multi-racial, in contrast to the rigidly bi-racial system of North America.[3] The half-million slaves who were freed in 1888 entered a complex social structure that included free men of color (of every shade). Skin color, hair texture, facial, and other visible physical characteristics were the determinants of the racial category into which a person would be placed by those he met. The apparent wealth or status of the person being observed, indicated by his clothes or his immediate social company, also influenced the observer's reaction, as indicated by the Brazilian adage "money whitens"— although the instances observed usually applied to light mulattoes.[4] The sum total of physical characteristics (the "phenotype") was the determining factor, although perception of this might vary according to the region, area, and observer. Brazil had never, at least not since late colonial times, exhibited a rigidly bi-racial system. There was always a middle category (called

mulatto or *mestiço*) of racial mixtures. The strict observation of
color-based endogamy, which became sanctified by law during
the 1890's in the United States, had never existed in Brazil.

The fact that Brazil had escaped the rigid application of the
"descent rule"—by which ancestry, not physical appearance (unless one "passes" for white), determines racial classification—
should not be overemphasized.[5] Origin could still be thought important in Brazil. Upwardly mobile mixed bloods often took great
pains to conceal their family background. And such behavior sug-
gests that a mulatto, whose phenotypical features had given him
his desired social access, felt insecure enough to believe his mobility would have been endangered by having his social status
redefined because of his family origin.[6] But the mulatto can be
said to be the central figure in Brazil's "racial democracy," because he was granted entry—albeit limited—into the higher social
establishment. The limits on his mobility depended upon his
exact appearance (the more "Negroid," the less mobile) and the
degree of cultural "whiteness" (education, manners, wealth) he
was able to attain. The successful application of this multi-racial
system required Brazilians to develop an intense sensitivity to
racial categories and the nuances of their application.[7] Evidence
of the tension engendered by the resulting shifting network of
color lines can be found in the voluminous Brazilian folklore
about the "untrustworthy" mulatto.[8]

What were the origins of this multi-racial system? It is especially important for those who know only a rigidly bi-racial society to appreciate how a racially pluralistic society could have
emerged in Brazil.

Demographic ratios offer one clue. Brazil already had a large
number of freemen of color before final abolition. Slaves probably outnumbered freemen (white and colored) in Brazil in the
seventeenth century; and whites were never in a majority anywhere in Brazil, until immigration markedly altered the racial
balance in several states of the South and Center-South.[9] The
free colored population had apparently grown very rapidly in the

TABLE 1

Brazilian Slave Population Compared to Total Population,
by Region, 1819 and 1872

Region*	Total Population		Slave Population		Slave Population as Per cent of Total Population	
	1819	1872	1819	1872	1819	1872
North	143,251	332,847	39,040	28,437	27.3	8.5
Northeast	1,112,703	3,082,701	367,520	289,962	33.0	9.4
East	1,807,638	4,735,427	508,351	925,141	28.1	19.5
South	433,976	1,558,691	125,283	249,947	28.9	16.0
Center-West	100,564	220,812	40,980	17,319	40.7	7.8
Total Brazil	3,598,132	9,930,478	1,081,174	1,510,806	30.0	15.2

* Provinces included in each region are as follows: North: Amazonas, Pará; Northeast: Maranhão, Piauí, Ceará, Rio Grande do Norte, Paraiba, Pernambuco, Alagoas; East: Sergipe, Bahia, Espírito Santo, Rio de Janeiro, Côrte (City of Rio de Janeiro, now state of Guanabara), Minas Gerais; South: São Paulo, Paraná, Santa Catarina, Rio Grande do Sul; Center-West: Goiás, Mato Grosso.
Sources: For 1819—Arthur Ramos, "O negro no Brasil: escravidão e história social," Pedro M. Arcaya et al., Estudios de Historia de América (Mexico City, 1948), p. 159. For 1872—Brazil, Directoria Geral de Estatística, Recenseamento do Brazil Realizado em 1 de Setembro de 1920 (5 vols.; Rio de Janeiro, 1922–30), 1, 414.

nineteenth century. In 1819 the total population of approximately 3.6 million was slightly under one-third slave (see Table 1), probably only about 10-15 per cent of the total population being free colored. During the intervening half-century the free colored population grew to 42 per cent of the total population, while the slaves dwindled to less than 16 per cent. And by 1872 there were almost three times as many free as slave among the colored population.

The existence of this large free class of color created models for free colored existence. By the time of final abolition Brazil had already had long experience with millions of free colored; and it had had an even longer tradition stretching into earlier centuries of upward mobility by a small number of free colored.[10] There were also established patterns of movement from slavery to freedom. It is plausible that a long-standing shortage of skilled and semi-skilled white labor in colonial Brazil forced the European colonizers to legitimize the creation of a category of freemen of color who could perform these tasks.[11] The same process probably continued into the nineteenth century.

Differential fertility was a second factor at work in helping to create the multi-racial system. The rate at which different racial groups replace themselves obviously has great influence on the pattern of race relations—rapidly increasing groups becoming a progressively larger share of the total than those that are dying out.[12] The slave population in the United States, for example, grew at a relatively rapid rate during the nineteenth century. Census figures showed that it increased at an average rate of about 23 per cent each decade between 1830 and 1860;[13] and since the slave trade in the United States had ended in 1808, the increase could be accounted for only by a net natural increase among the existing slave population.

In Brazil, however, the trend had apparently been just the opposite, at least before the end of the slave trade in 1850.[14] Such a phenomenon was apparently common in those slave economies that continued to depend upon the slave trade[15]—where the low fertility rates of slaves have been traced to distorted sex ratios (sharp excess of men over women) and high rates of morbidity and mortality.[16] Yet one would have expected these factors to disappear in Brazil after the end of the slave trade in 1850, with the native-born blacks exhibiting a fertility ratio similar to the general population, as indeed occurred in the United States.

Such did not turn out to be the case. Even allowing for the inaccuracies inherent in the Brazilian data (such as classifying

mixed-blood children differently from their mothers), demographers have concluded that the black population reproduced at
a slower rate after abolition than the mulatto and the white.
Spot checks suggest that this trend (considering here free
blacks, not slaves) can be traced back at least to the early nineteenth century.[17] Parenthetically, one may note that this lower
fertility rate for blacks apparently contributed significantly to
the "whitening" process, whose promotion became the heart of
the Brazilian racial ideal that will be described below. The
causes of this low fertility rate remain a matter for conjecture.
One of the likeliest hypotheses is the disadvantage in mating en-
countered by black women.[18]

The relative absence of sectionalism in Brazil was another factor that helped produce a multi-racial system. Slavery became a
regional institution in the United States, whereas it was truly national in Brazil (see Table 1). The economic center of Brazil
shifted away from the sugar-producing Northeast as a result of
the gold and diamond booms of the Center-South in the eighteenth century, then continued southward with the coffee boom
of the nineteenth century. As a result, by the nineteenth century
every major geographical region had a significant percentage of
slaves among its total population. In 1819, according to one unofficial estimate, no region had less than 27 per cent slave out of
its total population (see Table 1).

By the time the abolitionist campaign began, the national
slave population was concentrated—from the standpoint of absolute numbers—in the three major coffee-growing provinces of
São Paulo, Minas Gerais, and Rio de Janeiro. But seen as a percentage of the over-all population within each region, slaves continued to be distributed throughout the Empire at a remarkably
uniform rate. In 1872, when slaves made up 15.2 per cent of
the national population, no region had 7.8 per cent of its total
population still in slavery, and the highest ratio was only
19.5 per cent (see Table 1). Although several provinces did manage to achieve total abolition four years before the final national

law of 1888, race relations did not become the plaything of regional politics. No province could claim that its economic interests or its social structure had been undermined by the imposition of force from another region of the country. Obviously there must have been regional variations in race relations during the eighty years since abolition. The evidence to date, however, does not show the variations to be great enough to prevent our assuming a high degree of similarity over time and space in Brazil —at least for purposes of studying racial thought since 1870.[19]

The final fact is that the free colored played an important role long before total abolition in Brazil.[20] Free coloreds had succeeded in gaining a considerable occupational mobility—entry into skilled occupations and even occasionally prominent positions as artists, politicians, and writers—while slavery was still dominant *throughout* the country. These economic and social opportunities enjoyed by free coloreds furnish proof that the multi-racial pattern of racial categorization was well established before final abolition.

Although this pluralistic scale of social classification had given Brazil a flexibility notably lacking in some other ex-slave societies such as the United States, it is essential to realize that the multi-racial society nevertheless rested on implicitly racist assumptions. The "caucasian" was considered to be the natural and inevitable summit of the social pyramid. The white European represented the ideal "somatic norm image"[21]—the phrase coined by H. Hoetink to designate the most socially prized physical characteristics. Brazilians generally regarded whiter as better, which led naturally to an ideal of "whitening," articulated in both elitiest writings and popular folklore.[22]

Interestingly enough, the ideal seems to have been realized in practice, as can be seen in Figure 2.1. There was a rapid increase in the "white" population of Brazil between 1890 and 1950. As defined by the official census, the percentage of whites grew from 44 per cent in 1890 to 62 per cent in 1950. The concomitant decline in the colored population was sharpest in the mulatto cate-

percentage   FIGURE 2.1
of total   *Brazilian Population by Color, 1872-1950*
population

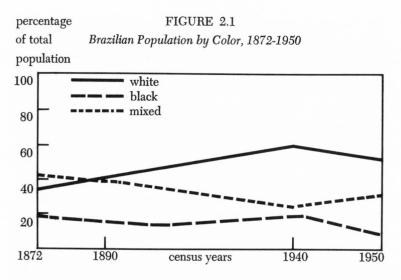

Source: Brazil, Instituto Brasileiro de Geografia e Estatística, Conselho Nacional de Estatística, *O Brasil em Números* (Rio de Janeiro, 1966), p. 25.

gory between 1890 and 1940, falling from 41 per cent to 21 per cent, although it rose to 27 per cent by 1950. Admittedly, the census figures must be viewed with caution. The definition of racial categories must have varied according to the historical era of the census, the instructions given the census taker, and the social attiutdes prevailing among census takers and respondents. It is known, for example, that in the most recent period for which a comparison is possible, 1940 and 1950 (race was omitted from the census in 1970 and 1960 data remain unpublished), there were sharp discrepancies in the instructions given census takers.[23] Furthermore, one must assume that the social definitions of racial phenotypes changed over time. Even allowing for these factors, however, we cannot escape the conclusion that there has been a whitening of the population in the last hundred years, for which there are several reasonable explanations.

First, there was immigration, which was overwhelmingly white—since 1890 3 million Europeans have settled in Brazil.

Second, there is empirical evidence in the census figures for the city of São Paulo (where, by the 1920's, observers were documenting a "Negro deficit") to support the conclusion that the black population had a low rate of net natural increase. This low reproduction rate can be accounted for by several factors. The slave imports (ending in 1850—although some slaves arrived as late as 1852) were largely male; and this, as long as it lasted, created a continuing sexual imbalance and a resulting low birth rate in the colored population. The miserable living conditions of most of the colored population must have further depressed the survival rate of their children—confirmed in the vital statistics for the city of São Paulo.[24]

There is a final explanation for the whitening effect: the way in which miscegenation occurred. If Gilberto Freyre's portrait is to be believed—and there is much corroboration from other sources—we may assume that white males must have fathered many mixed bloods, thereby increasing the proportion of lighter skinned offspring in the next generation. The ideal of whitening, as well as the traditionalistic social system, helped to prevent dark-skinned men from being such active progenitors because females, wherever possible, had powerful conditioning to choose lighter partners than themselves. In short, the system of sexual exploitation which gave upper-class (indeed, even lower-class) white men sexual license, helped to make the social reality conform increasingly to the ideal of "whitening."[25]

Brazilians found this apparent lightening of the population reassuring, and their racial ideology was thus reinforced. Since miscegenation had worked to promote the declared goal, white genes "must be" stronger. Furthermore, during the high period of racist thought—1880 to 1920—the "whitening" ideology gained scientific legitimacy, because racist doctrines came to be interpreted by Brazilians as supporting the view that the "superior" white race would prevail in the process of racial amalgamation.

The immediate aftermath of abolition had seemed to confirm the die-hard slavocrats' prediction that abolition would bring social disruption.[26] Thousands of slaves left their plantations and sank into subsistence agriculture wherever they could find land on which to squat, although soon many were eager to rejoin the rural work force and sought out their former masters. Others migrated to the cities, which were ill-prepared to receive an influx of unskilled labor. Some joined street gangs, whose members (*capoeiristas*) practiced a form of physical assault based on kicking, and terrorized the cities. Derived from Africa, it made them more than a match for any street opponent who was not heavily armed. This immediate threat to "law and order" confirmed the worst fears of many members of the elite, who found it less uncomfortable to worry about urban criminals than the social consequences of abolition. It was less the actual number of freedmen who left the countryside than the dramatization of the process that influenced public policy. Police forces were increased, and the *capoeira* gangs became the special target of repressive penalties in the new Penal Code of 1890, including expulsion from the country. Such violence reinforced the image of the black as a backward, anti-social element, thus giving the elite a further incentive to work for a whiter Brazil.

The unskilled who went to the cities to look for work found few opportunities. In the south they had to compete with immigrants, who were often much better equipped to survive in the urban capitalistic world. In the north, on the other hand, there were few job opportunities for anyone owing to the lagging economy. Thus the lower-class Brazilian, which included the vast majority of those dark in color, found it very difficult to rise economically. This failure confirmed the elite's conception of him as a drag on national development.

Although Brazilians often talked of their lack of racial prejudice, there were reports in the Brazilian press of alleged discrimination against blacks or dark mulattoes. The incidents involved those official Brazilian institutions likely to have contact with foreigners. The *Correio da Manhã* complained in 1904 that blacks were excluded from serving as guards at the Teatro Lírico, a famous theater in Rio. In 1906 an editorial alleged discrimination against both blacks and mulattoes in the recruitment of the Guarda Cívica, or state militia, of São Paulo. This was said to be in preparation for the arrival of a French Army training mission, whom the Paulistas did not wish to offend. The *Correio da Manhã* writer ridiculed such an attitude, reminding his readers of the distinguished roster of Brazilian mulattoes, including Tobias Barreto and André Rebouças. Even Rodrigues Alves, President of the Republic and a former Governor of São Paulo, was rumored to have Negro blood.[27]

The Navy, which had a reputation for recruiting only white officers, was the scene of several incidents. In 1907 black sailors were allegedly excluded from a naval mission that sailed to the United States. The government was accused of attempting to present Brazil (in Europe and the United States) as a white country, a charge obviously not unfounded.[28] In a similar incident, the Navy supposedly screened black sailors out of the crew which manned the ship where visiting Argentine General Roca was entertained.[29] The Navy had earlier experienced racial rebuffs in the United States: In 1905 a Brazilian cruiser anchored in Norfolk, Virginia, where some of its officers were refused lodging on the grounds that they were Negro—especially galling in view of the Navy's apparent attempt to keep the officer corps white. Ambassador Joaquim Nabuco made vigorous protests. This unpleasant contretemps in Norfolk may have influenced the later attempts to screen naval crews headed for the United States.[30]

VARIETIES OF RACIST THEORY FROM ABROAD

The nineteenth century had witnessed two contradictory movements in thinking about race. On the one hand, abolitionist movements triumphed throughout the North Atlantic world and finally even in the South Atlantic. Yet at the very time that slavery was receding under the impact of economic change and moral pressure, European thinkers were articulating systematic theories of innate racial differences. The era that produced Wilberforce also spawned Gobineau. Racism, which has been defined as "a rationalized pseudo-scientific theory positing the innate and permanent inferiority of nonwhites," became a formidable theory.[31] Such a systematic body of racist thought did not yet exist in the Europe of 1800. By 1860, however, racist theories had achieved the blessing of scientific theory and the full acceptance of cultural and political leaders in the United States and Europe. Over the course of the century, three principal schools of racist theory emerged.[32]

One was the ethnological-biological school, which gained its first systematic formulation in the United States of the 1840's and 1850's.[33] This "American school of ethnology" argued that human races had been created in the form of different species, a theory known as polygeny. The ethnographers Samuel Morton, Josiah Nott, and George Glidden published tomes of "evidence" (skull measurements of Egyptian mummies, etc.) to prove that the human races had always exhibited physical differences. They offered, in effect, a new version of the long-standing polygenist hypothesis about human creation. The basis of their argument was that the assumed inferiority of the Indian and Negro races could be correlated with their physical differences from whites; and that these differences were a direct result of their creation as separate species.[34] The theory gained important support from Louis Agassiz, the eminent Swiss-born zoologist at Harvard who became the most famous scientific supporter of polygeny in America. Agassiz believed that the creation of separate species among animals had been required by the differing "zoological provinces" on earth, leading to the implication that the distinct species (or races) of *genus homo* could be attributed to the distinct climatic regions where they dwelled. Since the initial assumptions labeled the white race as superior in mental and social qualities (such as "civilization building"), white superiority was thus given scientific basis as fact.

The American school's polygenist hypothesis was soon laid to rest by Darwinian theory. But the weight of scientific evidence they compiled, indicating permanent physical—and, by implication, mental differences—proved very lasting. For the next fifty years scientists continued to produce elaborate tables of cranial measurements, skeletal structure, and disease histories, broken down by what were assumed to be scientifically definable "races." Virtually all such attempts rested on the assumption that physical differences could somehow "prove" the existence of other differences—what later would be termed "cultural." The popularizers of the ethnological-biological school were using the instruments of a new science—physical anthropology—to give a scientific basis to pre-existing prejudices about the social behavior of non-whites, as were other researchers who purported to find evidence for black mental inferiority in the results of their IQ tests. The ethnological-biological school, in short, offered a scientific rationale for the subjugation of non-whites (whether in legal servitude or not soon became immaterial).

Although the ethnological-biological version of racist thought received its earliest systematic formulation in the United States, it soon spread to England and Europe, where it gained powerful adherents; and it was primarily by way of these European converts that it reached Brazil. The small number of ethnographers and anthropologists active in Brazil during the years between 1870 and 1914 were principally in contact with French and German scientists. But one leading representative of the "American School" did have a direct influence in Brazil—Louis Agassiz. His *Journey in Brazil* was widely quoted in Brazil and gave much currency among the elite to the ideas of inherent racial differences and mulatto "degeneracy."

A second body of racist thought to emerge in the United States and Europe proved equally influential in Brazil. It was the historical school (well represented by Gobineau—discussed above). These thinkers also started with the assumption that sharply differing human races could be distinguished, with the white race permanently and inherently superior. But they relied primarily upon historical evidence, taking for granted that permanent physical differences had been established by the ethnographers and anatomists. Thomas Arnold, Robert Knox, and Thomas Carlyle in England, for example, interpreted history as the successive triumphs of the creative races, of which the Anglo-Saxon was pre-eminent. Gobineau and lesser known proponents of the historical school helped spread the message in Europe that race was the central factor in history.

The historical approach to racism received a further nuance in the cult of the Aryan. Propounded by such prophets as Houston Stewart Chamberlain, Aryanism became virtual dogma in Germany after the Franco-Prussian war (1870–71). Its unverifiability gave the myth a flexibility that made it easily adaptable also to England, where a belief in Anglo-Saxon superiority became the counterpart to Aryanism. This theory—that the Aryan (or Anglo-Saxon) had reached the highest level of civilization and was therefore destined, by nature and history, to gain increasing control over the world—was supported by elaborate historical monographs. Apparent exceptions to the view that non-Aryans had never produced a culture worthy of the name were accounted for by the most intricate explanations of probable Aryan participation. It need hardly be added that the definition of "Aryan" remained elusive, beginning as a linguistic category but soon being understood to mean "white native Northern European." It was also easily translatable as "Nordic," which some of its adherents preferred.

The third school of racist thought was Social Darwinism. Although it differed importantly from the earlier ethnographical-biological school described above, the two theories in the end proved reconcilable. On scientific grounds, Darwin's thesis could be accepted only by discarding the polygenist hypothesis, because Darwin argued for an evolutionary process that, by definition, began with a single species.

Darwinism could, however, be used by the polygenist racists

if they modified their theory. If evolution toward higher forms of natural life resulted from the "survival of the fittest" in a competition of varying species and varieties, it was logical to assume that different human races had gone through a similar process. In the historical process the "higher" races had been proved to predominate, making the "lower" races doomed to dwindle and disappear. Agassiz himself never accepted Darwinian theory, but most other proponents of the ethnological-biological school did so relatively quickly. As a careful student of American race-thinking notes, "the essence of polygenist thinking about race was preserved in a Darwinian framework."[35] Social Darwinists described blacks as an "incipient species," making it possible to continue citing all the evidence—from comparative anatomy, phrenology, physiology, and historical ethnography—that had previously been offered in support of the polygenist hypothesis, while at the same time providing a new scientific respectability for racist theory.

Taken together, these three schools of racist thought influenced all Brazilians who bothered to think seriously about race. Brazil lay vulnerable, like the rest of Latin America, to racist doctrines from abroad. It could hardly have been otherwise, since these doctrines were a vital part of the North Atlantic civilization so fervently and uncritically admired by most Latin American intellectuals before 1914. The more that Brazilians read the latest ideas from Europe the more they heard about the inferiority of the Negro and Indian. This was especially true at the turn of the century when the Brazilian preference for French culture led them directly to popular racist writers such as Gustave Le Bon and Vacher de Lapouge.[36]

The theory of Aryan superiority, at least in good part, was widely accepted as historical fact by the Brazilian elite between 1888 and 1914. Some theories of "Aryanism" were vague enough to include virtually all Europeans as "Aryans," although the subtleties of the Nordic versus Celtic distinction were awkward for a Brazilian. The vogue of northern European superiority led some Brazilian writers to endorse the theory of "Latin degeneracy"—reflected in the frequent descriptions of the Portuguese as the least progressive Europeans, given to improvidence, immorality, and indolence.[37] This denigration of the Iberian appealed to nationalists who held strong anti-Portuguese feelings, but proved inconvenient for nationalists who also feared "Anglo-Saxon" intervention or domination. Most often, however, the latter did not bother to disown the Aryan theory, but simply pleaded with their countrymen to wake up to the Darwinian struggle being imposed by American or northern European incursions, and represented by large investments or immigrant colonies.[38] The application of the Aryan theory to the African caused no trouble, however, because in this context "Aryan" could be readily translated into "white." Brazilians readily repeated the charge that the Negro had never built any great civilization, citing English and European reports of the "primitive" African social structures with which white colonial governors had to cope.

Social Darwinist works, in particular, had great influence in Brazil. Virtually every Brazilian social thinker before 1914 grappled with Social Darwinism. One finds constant citations of such figures as Spencer, Le Bon, Lapouge, and Ingenieros (the Argentine racist philosopher).[39] The Brazilians usually accepted Social Darwinism in principle, trying only to work out its implications for *their* national situation. But everywhere they turned, Brazilians found the prestige of "civilized" culture and science arrayed against the African. Like the dinosaur, the Negro was doomed to extinction, or at least domination, by the "stronger" and more "civilized" white races. How could a mere Brazilian argue with evolution?

RACIST THEORY IN BRAZIL

Brazilians did not argue with evolution.[40] Their social reality, however, was different enough from North America—let alone

Europe—to force them to find some way to make it consistent with the theories being preached. Brazil was already a multi-racial society. Unlike the United States, there was no institutionalized color bar. Also unlike the United States, instead of two castes (white and non-white), there was a third social caste well recognized in Brazil—the mulatto.

The free man of color in Brazil was already establishing a clear place in society during the late eighteenth century, while their counterparts in the United States were facing the systematically discriminatory system (laws in the South, customs in the North) that effectively prevented their entering the established economic or social order.[41] As a result, there was no tradition in Brazil of supressing nonwhites within a rigidly bi-racial caste system, and racist thought could not therefore be used to buttress such a system.

This contrast is nowhere clearer than in attitudes toward miscegenation. Americans and northern Europeans found racial intermarriage to be anathema. Although the practical question hardly arose for Europeans, for Americans it was an issue of deep significance. Americans could not avoid the historical reality that miscegenation had frequently occurred under slavery. But they could draw comfort from the fact that the mulatto offspring were rigidly relegated to the "Negro" caste. These mixed bloods were then regarded as lost to the superior race—a process which, if miscegenation were practiced on any large scale, could mean a serious threat to the numerical dominance of the "superior" race. The resulting fear of "mongrelization" was a direct result of this possibility, and was an important part of the profound psycho-social fear in the American attitude toward racial cross-breeding.[42]

At their most extreme, polygenists had argued that mulattoes must be sterile, since the laws of zoology taught that any animal produced by the union of parents of different species would be unable to bear offspring.[43] Yet human "mixed bloods" were obviously not infertile. Since even the most fervent polygenist could hardly ignore the evidence of mulatto fertility, he usually fell back on arguing that after a single generation one of the original "pure" races would predominate, thereby eliminating the cross-strain. Such theories continued to be advanced in England and the United States in the 1850's and 1860's, despite abundantly contradictory evidence from the West Indies and elsewhere.[44]

The polygenists' theory of mulatto infertility (or later-generation infertility) gained few adherents in Brazil. Perhaps it was so clearly contradicted by social reality that it proved impossible to assimilate. Certainly it struck too close to home. It was one thing to claim that whites (or Aryans) were superior and blacks inferior, but quite another to add that any mixture of the two was inherently pernicious. "Pure" white Europeans and North Americans could contemplate miscegenation as a problem of no immediate relevance to their societies—although to make such an attitude plausible Americans had to enforce, by legal segregation, a two-caste social structure. Brazilians had no such choice. Their society was already multi-racial, and the middle caste was precisely the social category for whom the flexibility of Brazilian racial attitudes was most important. To have accepted the description of it as "degenerate" or infertile would have threatened an established and accepted feature of Brazilian society. It would also have cast a shadow over more than a few members of the elite itself. In fact, miscegenation did not arouse the instinctive opposition of the white elite in Brazil. On the contrary, it was a well-recognized (and tacitly condoned) process by which a few mixed bloods (almost invariably light mulattoes) had risen to the top of the social and political hierarchy.

Sílvio Romero's writing in this period reflects well the inconsistencies that the juxtaposition of domestic mores and imported theory made hard to avoid. During the late Empire, he had been one of the first to argue for recognizing Brazil as the product of miscegenation. He had even predicted a happy outcome for its future ethnic evolution. In 1904 he rejected a description of Brazil by Teófilo Braga, the Portuguese intellectual and political leader, whom he thought to have underestimated the role of the *mestiço*.[45] Yet in 1906 he classified himself as believing, along with Gobineau, Ammon, Lapouge, and Chamberlain, that the blond dolichocephalic peoples of northern Europe were superior to other men. His formula for improving Brazil was to increase the influx of Germans, who were to be spread throughout the country so that they could absorb Brazilian culture and accept the authority of the Brazilian government.[46] In 1912 he was still praising Gobineau for his "admirable, genius-like vision" and the "wise words that merit every consideration," and (in a violent polemic) was carried away to the point of endorsing an extreme version of the theory of mulatto degeneracy. He claimed that "the most competent naturalists" had "demonstrated that races which were too different seldom tend to cohabit, and, when they do, they either fail to breed, or produce infertile bastards after the second or third generation." He included extensive citations from Lapouge's account of the biological corruption of the "primitive Gaullic aristocracy" by such Latin intrusions as the armies of Julius Caesar.[47]

It is not surprising that little rigorous analysis of racial theory came from Brazil itself in this period. There were no higher faculties except law, medicine, and engineering; and without a university structure it was difficult for would-be scientists to find a base of operations. (This relative absence of organized social science was common throughout Latin America before World War I, but Brazil was especially backward in organizing universities.)

Physical anthropology was one of the earlier recognized disciplines, in part due to the stimulus of a series of important expeditions by foreign scientists, frequently German. In 1876 a laboratory of experimental physiology was founded in connection with the Museu Nacional in Rio de Janeiro. The original director, Ladislau Neto, organized a "Brazilian Anthropological Exposition" in 1882, a first for his country. He and the colleague who succeeded him as director in 1895, João Batista de Lacerda, both concentrated on the Indian, using the latest European techniques of cranial measurement. But the museum lacked the funds for field expeditions. Such trips continued to be the virtual monopoly of foreign visitors, especially Germans and Scandinavians, whose published works furnished important ethnographical and linguistic information.[48] Another center of physical anthropology appeared when the Museu Paulista was founded in 1893. Its founder and first director was Herman von Ihering, an immigrant German zoologist.[49] The limited research there also centered exclusively upon the Indian, and a similar situation prevailed at the Museu Paraense, located at the Amazon port city of Belém and founded by an immigrant Swiss, Emílio Goeldi, in 1885.

Together the three museums were the only centers devoted to anthropological research and writing. All suffered from inadequate budgets. Equally important for the history of racial thought, none had devoted any attention to the African in Brazil. The "primitive" peoples studied were the remote Indian tribes. The African "immigrant" and his Afro-American progeny aroused no scientific interest among their staffs. *

The first scientifically respectable ethnographic study of the Afro-Brazilian by a Brazilian came not from the museums but from a medical professor at the prestigious faculty of Bahia. In the early 1890's Nina Rodrigues, a young mulatto doctor, won a chair there. By the end of the decade he had distinguished himself as the pioneer in two fields: Afro-Brazilian ethnology and legal medicine. Neither was recognized as a field of inquiry when he began, but his efforts helped lay the foundations in Brazil for both. Although he died in 1906 at the age of forty-four, he had already published many scientific papers as well as founding

---

* Save for Melo Moraes Filho at the Museu Nacional, who performed pioneering work in collecting Afro-Brazilian folklore (Museu Nacional, *João Bastista de Lacerda: Comemoração do centenário de nascimento, 1846-1946*, Rio de Janeiro, 1951, 14-15). The principal publication from Melo Moraes Filho's work was [Alexandre Jose de] Melo Moraes Filho, *Festas e tradições populares do Brazil*, Rio de Janeiro, 1901.

the Revista Médico-Legal. He was in close contact with like-minded researchers abroad and enjoyed membership in such groups as the Médico-Legal Society of New York and the Société Medico-Psychologique de Paris. By the time of his death he had become a highly respected figure in Brazilian scientific circles.[50]

Nina Rodrigues, then, was the first researcher to study African influence systematically. He attempted a careful cataloguing of the precise African origins of the slaves brought to Brazil, and he tried, without the advantage of any first-hand knowledge of Africa, to identify the primary linguistic groups. He collected photographs and drawings of Brazilian objets d'art of African origin, and was also engrossed in the question of how the Africans had been assimilated in their new home. Throughout his work he stressed the importance of distinguishing clearly among major regions of Brazil when discussing the assimilation of the African.

Rodrigues and his work will be dealt with in some detail below because his scientific commitment led him, although he was a mulatto himself, into being the most prestigious doctrinaire Brazilian racist of his era. He was widely read by those seriously interested in race, and he gained great distinction; but his views remained outside the Brazilian mainstream. While few of his Brazilian contemporaries could deny concern over what Rodrigues called "this sphinx in our future—the 'Negro problem' in Brazil,"[51] few were in danger of adopting racist ideas as systematically doctrinaire as his.[52]

Rodrigues explained to his readers that the inferiority of the African had been established beyond scientific doubt. In 1894 he dismissed the "sentimental" notion that a "representative of the inferior races" could attain in intelligence "the elevated level attained by the superior races" as "hopelessly condemned in the face of modern scientific knowledge."[53] By 1905 he was willing to grant that scientists could not agree on whether Negro inferiority was inherent or transitory. Even if the transitory hypothesis were true in theory, he concluded, European civilization was progressing too fast for it to be tested in practice.[54]

Rodrigues did not hesitate to follow the implications of his racial doctrines, saying (one feels with a certain relish) that his personal feelings had nothing to do with scientific theory—particularly since he had a "lively sympathy" for the Brazilian Negro.[55] At the same time as his pioneering ethnographical research was generating data based on oral testimony (primarily from Bahia), he was applying the theory of racial inferiority directly to his work in legal medicine—voicing the view, with few apologies, that inherent racial characteristics affected social behavior and should therefore be taken into account by lawmakers and police authorities. In 1894 he published a book proposing that the penal responsibility of the "inferior races" could not be equated to that of the "civilized white races." Although a few individuals might prove exceptions, especially mixed bloods, they always had the potential to regress. He therefore recommended that Negroes (by which he meant blacks) and Indians be judged to have only "attenuated responsibility," which would apparently be a rather child-like status. Mixed bloods, not surprisingly, presented him with a problem. He got around it by dividing them into three subgroups—(a) the superior type (fully responsible, presumably including Rodrigues himself); (b) the degenerates (some partially responsible; the rest totally irresponsible); and (c) the socially unstable types who, like blacks and Indians, would bear only "attenuated responsibility."[56] Nowhere did Rodrigues explain *how* these graduated categories were to operate, or *who* was to decide the racial classification of any individual citizen. In fact, the very subdivision of categories for the mixed blood illustrated their absurdity, because the middle "castes" included precisely those Brazilians for whom the language or racial categories was most elastic. One suspects that racial distinctions might well have depended on the desire of the relevant officials to punish the accused.

In any case, Rodrigues produced a full-blown theoretical justification for considering the ex-slaves to be incapable of "civilized" behavior. Even worse, he assumed away any possible rights of the inferior: "Aryan civilization is represented in Brazil by a small minority of the white race, which in turn has the task of defending it, not only against anti-social acts—crimes—by its own members, but also against the anti-social acts of inferior races, whether they be true crimes as defined by these races or manifestations of the conflict—the struggle for existence between the superior civilization of the white race and the crude civilization of the conquered or subjugated races."[57] Not a word about the right of the "inferiors" to be protected from anti-social acts by their superiors. Here was a vision of Brazilian society which was authentically racist—human beings were to be judged according to their supposed racial classification. Rodrigues had gone farther in his acceptance of foreign racist theories than most other members of the Brazilian elite. Significantly, however, his proposal had no influence on those responsible for the revision of Brazil's penal code in 1890. And he lamented this lack of responsiveness from legal authorities and legislators.

Genetics was not yet a well-developed science before Rodrigues' death in 1906, and respected scientists still argued over whether cross-breeding among different "races" produced "vigorous hybrids" or physical degenerates. Rodrigues leaned toward the latter position. He cited Agassiz as an authority on miscegenation, thereby associating himself with the most distinguished North American theorist of mulatto degeneracy. Elsewhere he cited José Verissimo's description of "degraded" mestiços in the Amazon valley, and Ladislau Neto (Brazilian ethnographer and Director of the Museu Nacional until 1893) on the supposed "atavism" of mixed bloods. Rodrigues did not go as far as Agassiz in condemning the mixed blood, but he flatly contradicted the commonly held view that miscegenation had helped the white race to adapt and survive in tropical northern Brazil. Negro influence, he said, would "forever constitute one of the causes of our inferiority as a people";[58] and nothing could halt the "elimination of white blood" in that region. Miscegenation had merely slowed it down. Rodrigues particularly opposed the "unjustifiably" optimistic view of most Brazilians toward the *mestiço*'s "social value," writing a series of technical papers on such topics as "Pathological Anthropology: The Mestiços" (1890), "Miscegenation, Degeneracy, and Crime" (1898), and "Physical and Mental Degeneracy Among Mixed Bloods in Warm Lands" (in progress at the time of his death). This, of course, put him in opposition to the commonly accepted belief among the elite—that miscegenation would sooner or later lead to a white Brazil:

> I don't believe in the ethnic unity or quasi ethnic unity of the Brazilian population, either now or in the future, as accepted by Dr. Sílvio Romero. I don't believe in the future spread of the Luso-African *mestiço* throughout the country. I consider it improbable that the white race will succeed in imposing itself as the predominant type in the entire Brazilian population.[59]

Rodrigues worried especially about the north of Brazil. Although the whitening process might in fact succeed in southern (temperate) Brazil, he thought the tropical north was doomed —leading him to fear the possibility of a Brazil racially divided between the white south and the *mestiço* north.[60] Interestingly enough, he turned to climatic determinism to clinch the point. "Tropical" climes, he said, were "inhospitable to the white." A posthumous paper, although characterizing the Portuguese as "routinized and unprogressive," considered two factors more important in Brazil's development. One was the "strong barrier to the white" posed by the tropical climate; the other was the "vast degree of miscegenation which, by delivering the country to the *mestiços*, deprived it for a long period of the supreme direction of the white race. And the latter was the guarantee of civilization in the United States."[61]

It is interesting to note that, despite his acceptance of racist theory, Rodrigues thought it very important to distinguish Brazil's ethnic situation from that of the United States. Even in the

1890's, anyone discussing the "Negro problem" in Brazil was vulnerable to the charge that he was applying an American paradigm where it had no basis in reality. Rodrigues was sensitive to this charge and attempted to refute it. The scientific theories of racial inferiority had nothing to do with the American slaveholders' defense of slavery, he argued (thus revealing his assumption that Brazilian readers might reject any racist ideas if they could be associated with the United States). Because the United States enjoyed several advantages Brazil conspicuously lacked—a "surplus" of whites and an absence of tropical climate —American debates over the "Negro problem" could hardly apply to Brazil. Yet it was significant that he could never satisfactorily explain why the degree of race prejudice among Brazilian whites was so "much less than it is said to be in the United States."[62]

The brand of doctrinaire racism expressed by Nina Rodrigues came out in statements of prominent officials, such as Joaquim Murtinho, the Minister of Industry, Transportation and Public Works, who (in his 1897 ministerial report) rejected any attempt to take the United States as a model for industrialization "because we don't have the superior aptitudes of their race. . . ."[63] It was also filtered through the pens of second-rate social thinkers and minor propagandists in the subsequent decade, as can be seen in the address given by the class orator, Hermann Soares, at the 1913 graduation of the Recife Law Faculty. Little known thereafter, Soares gave an unoriginal address which serves as a typical synopsis of the early twentieth century Brazilian qualifications to doctrinaire racist theory.

"The Latin race has no perseverance, no character, no energy," he argued.[64] This was the familiar theory of Latin degeneracy, which had become a corollary of the historical school of racist thought. "The English and North Americans are peoples predestined to make great conquests" because they are "descendants of another race." Brazil could never attain the "highest levels of development, unlike North America," because of her origins. That sorry history began with colonization by the Portuguese, "a people in decline."

This was a view often stated by intellectuals. In 1914, for example, a writer using the pseudonym of "João Grave" declared that "the Latin race, creator of civilizations and guide to humanity, felt exhausted of its vital fluid."[65] Alcides Bezerra, a minor literary critic, explained that he believed in the "superiority of northern men over the Latin races when it comes to practical abilities." The "Aryan race" was the "lord and master of the world by virtue of its enviable spiritual qualities," and, therefore, "modern civilization has to model itself after the English and North American examples."[66]

To resume Soares' portrayal, events worsened as the colonizers mixed with the "indolent though shrewd" natives, then mixing further "with those unfortunate arrivals from Africa . . . descendants of the Negro race, bereft of intelligence or character, like all the sons of uncivilized Ethiopia." He quoted Le Bon on the "perpetual anarchy" that inevitably arises in countries afflicted with "an excessive number of mixed bloods." (Le Bon, in turn, had cited Agassiz on the "degeneracy produced by the miscegenation which has taken place more extensively in this country than in any other.")[67] *But*, said Soares, "the Brazilian character is not completely lost" if his countrymen would adopt the system of American education, "which has elevated that country to the highest pinnacles." American schools were producing "the qualities of character we lack," qualities that made America a country where "there is no place for the weak." By copying these schools, Brazil might be able to govern "with an iron hand," which Le Bon had suggested as the only antidote for "the anarchy reigning in our country."[68]

This contradiction in terms was typical and was followed by more. Soares noted that "the Negro race has never done anything in support of any idea—it exists in ignorance without energy and without a will." (Significantly, he did not describe these defects as inherent or irremediable.) Furthermore, he saw the "absorp-

tion of the Negro race by the white" to be "a great danger for the
security of our country" because "the greater the number of
mixed-bloods in a country the greater the degeneracy of the
country's population"; and yet Soares condemned the "terrible
humiliation" suffered by Negroes in America, "living under the
constant threat of terror" or "ending up being lynched." Americans treated Negroes "as if they are not even human beings,"
when, in fact, "they are doubtlessly adaptable to all that country's advancements and to its astonishing civilization."[69]

After all this, Soares turns out to be endorsing the usual
"whitening" ideal for Brazil, i.e., the man of color can be elevated—but only by a great investment of effort. The acculturation process, in his view, can transform the Negro element, if the
"civilized" force were given enough time. They also must have
enough leverage—that is, the number of people to be "whitened"
culturally must not exceed the "civilizing" capacity of the "civilized." He did not hazard a guess as to the critical ratio. . . .

"WHITENING," THE BRAZILIAN SOLUTION

The Brazilian theory of "whitening" has already been mentioned.
Coming to be accepted by most of the Brazilian elite during the
years between 1889 and 1914, it was a theory peculiar to Brazil.
Seldom stated as a "scientific" formula and certainly never embraced in Europe or North America, it is worth explaining here
in some detail.

The whitening thesis was based on the assumption of white
superiority—sometimes muted by leaving open the question of
how "innate" the inferiority might be, and using the euphemisms
"more advanced" and "less advanced" races. But to this assumption were added two more. First, the black population was becoming progressively less numerous than the white for reasons
which included a supposedly lower birth rate, higher incidence
of disease, and social disorganization. Second, miscegenation was
"naturally" producing a lighter population, in part because whiter

genes were stronger and in part because people chose partners lighter than themselves. (White immigration, of course, would reinforce the resulting white predominance.)[70]

Obviously the optimistic conclusion to this racial analysis rested on another key assumption: that miscegenation did not inevitably produce "degenerates," but could forge a healthy mixed population growing steadily whiter, both culturally and physically. That assumption was given scientific blessing by the Director of the Museu Nacional, João Batista de Lacerda, who was the only Latin American to deliver a paper ("The Métis, or Half-Breeds of Brazil") at the First Universal Races Congress in London in 1911.[71]

In his paper, Lacerda first disposed of the theory that facts regarding hybridity in animals ("Galton's deductions") could be applied to humans. He then described the effects of the historical process of miscegenation between Africans and Europeans in Brazil (the Indian went unmentioned). His tone hardly has a modern ring. He pronounced mixed bloods as "obviously inferior to the blacks" as "agricultural laborers" and as having "little power to resist disease"; where their superiority lay, in his opinion, was that they were "physically and intellectually well above the level of the blacks." The whitening thesis was supported in the following manner:

> Contrary to the opinion of many writers, the crossing of the black with the white does not generally produce offspring of an inferior intellectual quality; and if these half-breeds are not able to compete in other qualities with the stronger races of the Aryan stock, if they have not so pronounced an instinct of civilization as the latter, it is nonetheless certain that we cannot place the *métis* at the level of the really inferior races.

Having thus disposed, in his fashion, of the scientific case against mixed bloods, Lacerda then went on to support his argument with a description of the major role they had played in Brazilian history. Here his tone became less condescending. Their influence, he said, had even increased as the "new regime [i.e., the Republic proclaimed in 1889] opened the door to all talent," thus enabling "many able mulattoes" to enter "the highest political offices" and the "highest branches of the administration." Furthermore, interracial marriages (between mulattoes and whites) "are no longer disdained as they formerly were, now that the high position of the mulatto and the proof of his moral qualities have led people to overlook the evident contrast of his physical characters, and his black origin is lost sight of in the approximation of his moral and intellectual qualities to those of the white."

Lacerda even went so far as to assert that in Brazil the "children of métis have been found, in the third generation, to present all physical characters of the white race." Some of them, he admitted, "retain a few traces of their black ancestry through the influence of atavism . . ." but "the influence of sexual selection . . . tends to neutralize that of atavism, and removes from the descendants of the métis all the characteristic features of the black race. . . . In virtue of this process of ethnic reduction, it is logical to expect that in the course of another century the métis will have disappeared from Brazil. This will coincide with the parallel extinction of the black race in our midst." The latter process had a special explanation. Since abolition the blacks had been "exposed to all kinds of destructive agencies and without sufficient resources to maintain themselves." Now "scattered over the thinly populated districts," they "tend to disappear from our territory."

Martím Francisco, a prominent Republican politician and writer, agreed with Lacerda's timetable. He wrote in his diary during a trip abroad in 1913 that although the Negro had been indispensable in Brazil's agricultural growth the "caucasian blood" was "stronger" and therefore was now "dominating the Ethiopian. . . . It will win out within a century, and will later conquer the Indian." For evidence he drew on observations in his home state: "In São Paulo, for example, thanks to the climate and a number of other anthropological factors, Negro blood disappears in the fifth generation."[72]

Lacerda's paper was criticized, however, by Brazilians who were incensed over his timetable—because his estimate of a century was too long! In 1912 he replied to these critics—showing, in fact, how little he really differed from them. He noted that the Haitian representative, "a dark Negro and an educated man," had praised his paper, as had W. E. B. DuBois, a *mestiço*. Having thus established sympathy from members of those races doomed to extinction in Brazil, he then pleaded that it could hardly be a mistake to point out the existence of race mixture at home. He had been quoted out of context, he claimed, regarding the time span of a century for total whitening. Although his reply did not state that whites *were* already a majority, he implied as much. At the end of his pamphlet he triumphantly produced statistics furnished him by Edgar Roquette-Pinto, Professor of Anthropology at the Museu Nacional. Although the census of 1890 showed the population to be only 44 per cent white, Roquette Pinto's figures for 1912 (unofficial) listed the white population as exactly 50 per cent. This, coincidentally, was the minimum figure Lacerda's critics demanded. (There is no way to check accuracy of these figures, since the next census, taken in 1920, was not broken down by race.) Later, the 1940 census showed the white population to be 63 per cent of the national total. Using Roquette Pinto's statistics further, Lacerda produced multi-colored bar graphs projecting Brazil's racial composition up to the year 2012. During the intervening century the white population would supposedly rise to 80 per cent, while the Negro fell to zero, the *mestiço* to 3 per cent (from an estimated 28 per cent in 1912), and the Indian rose to 17 per cent (from an estimated 13 per cent in 1912).[73]

Brazilians were encouraged in their whitening ideology in this period by foreign visitors, such as Pierre Denis, who published in 1909 a widely read travel account of his stay in Brazil. He devoted a chapter to the "Negro populations," characterizing them as "indolent" and "irregular in their work." He found the "economic and moral inferiority of the Negro population in Brazil to be irrefutable." Ravaged by alcoholism and a "total lack of hygiene," they did not multiply "as their extreme fecundity would lead one to expect." His conclusion must have reassured proponents of a whiter Brazil: "Doubtless it would be an exaggeration to predict their [the Negroes'] imminent extinction. Nonetheless, it is probable that they are not growing at the same rate as the other elements in the Brazilian population. Their role in Brazil can only decline; they will never have decisive influence on the destiny of the country."[74]

His book was enthusiastically reviewed in Brazil by Tobias Monteiro, the prominent Republican journalist and former presidential aide. Monteiro reprinted Denis' conclusion on the Negro almost verbatim, adding not a critical word. Since the reviewer had generally praised Denis for his accuracy and insight, it is logical to conclude that Monteiro shared the author's view of the Brazilian Negro's present and future.[75]

Another foreign visitor who described the whitening process approvingly was the former American President Theodore Roosevelt, who had undertaken a scientific expedition with Colonel Rondon into the interior of Mato Grosso in 1913–14. Roosevelt wrote an enthusiastic article about the disappearance of the Brazilian negro in *Outlook* magazine in 1914, which was translated and published on the front page of *Correio da Manhã,* an influential Rio daily. He noted that:

> In Brazil . . . the idea looked forward to is the disappearance of the Negro question through the disappearance of the Negro himself —that is, through his gradual absorption into the white race.
> This does not mean that Brazilians are or will become the "mongrel" people that they have been asserted to be by certain writers, not only French and English, but American. The Brazilians are a white people, belonging to the Mediterranean race, and differing from the northern stocks only as such great and civilized old races as the Spaniards and Italians, with their splendid historic past, differ from these northern stocks. The evident Indian admixture has added a good, and not a bad, element. The very large European immigration of itself tends, decade by decade, to make the Negro blood a smaller element of the blood of the whole community. The Brazilian

of the future will be in blood more European than in the past, and he will differ in culture only as the American of the North differs.[76]

On this issue at this time, Sílvio Romero was once again in a minority. In his view, Lacerda's paper was vulnerable because of its "optimism" in estimating only a century for the triple disappearance of the Negro, the Indian, and the *mestiço*. And he was contemptuous of Lacerda's other critics: "Our representative came to truly optimistic conclusions and even then he couldn't escape the fury of this aristocratized, Europeanized pack of present-day patriots. What a comedy!"[77] He was appalled at his countrymen's overoptimism in assessing Brazil's progress in whitening. Commenting on the uproar provoked in the Brazilian press by a Belgian's report that she had seen Negroes and mulattoes even in the larger cities in Brazil, he noted sarcastically, "Suddenly the country has aryanized itself."

In his *História da Literatura Brasileira* (1888) Romero had estimated three or four centuries for the whitening process. Now he thought it would take "some six or eight, if not more" for Indians and Negroes. Furthermore, he had decided the mixed bloods would never disappear. "One would have to be completely ignorant of anthropology and ethnography not to know, first, that fundamental racial characteristics persist, and second, that *mestiços* crossbreed whenever they are in contact." The *total* disappearance of the Indian, Negro, and *mestiço* could occur, Romero argued, only if all future breeding included one very light (if not white) partner. There were no statistics in Romero's analysis. He argued from his own impressions and reading. Always the maverick, it was true to his polemical style for him to question any conclusion once it had become the established view.[78]

COMPARISONS WITH THE UNITED STATES

A well-established way to explain Brazilian "whitening" was to contrast Brazil with the United States. As we saw above, even a relatively doctrinaire racist thinker such as Nina Rodrigues was nervous lest he be thought to be likening Brazil to the United States. People espousing more optimistic racial views enjoyed making the comparison. Batista de Lacerda put it this way:

> While the Portuguese did not hesitate to mix with the Negro to the extent of begetting a mixed offspring, the Anglo-Saxon, more jealous of the purity of his lineage, kept the Negro at a distance, and merely used him as an instrument of toil. It is a curious and remarkable fact that neither the lapse of time nor any other factor has been able to alter this early attitude of the North Americans, who keep the black race separated from the white population down to our own days. Brazil acted differently. The whites there set up a race of métis that is scattered today over a vast extent of its territory.

Lacerda's description of the United States was, of course, non-sense. Whatever the supposed difference in racial attitudes, Americans had freely practiced miscegenation. In 1850 the Negro population of the United States was officially listed as 11 per cent mulatto, and by 1910 it was 21 per cent. And one should remember that American census-takers were probably less generous in their application of the mulatto category (as opposed to black) than their Brazilian counterparts would have been.[79] No slave society in the Americas failed to produce a large mulatto population. It was not the fact of miscegenation but the recognition or non-recognition of the mixed bloods as a separate group that made the difference. In discussing the United States, Lacerda confused the system of legal and social segregation with supposed racial purity—actually referring to mixed bloods as a "race." In fact, white American society had simply pushed its mixed bloods back down into the "Negro" category.

Lacerda's faith in whitening led him even further in his comparison in the pamphlet replying to the critics of his 1911 paper. In the United States, he reasoned, the Negroes had been "expelled" from the general white community and thus forced to organize their own institutions in order to protect themselves. In their segregated state they also proved to be prolific and given to family life. Thus it was implied that the Negro element was increasing, or at least remaining stable, although no statistics were given. In Brazil, on the other hand, Negroes were disorganized, "without any kind of initiative, lost on unmarked roads like animals strayed from the fold"—making it happily inevitable that the Brazilian Negro should disappear.

The comparison with the United States was an awkward one for Brazilians. If whitening were the answer to the "race problem," then why was the United States not better situated, since its white population was already such a numerical majority? Nina Rodrigues had pointed toward this question when he noted that a white "surplus" existed in the United States. But most Brazilian analysts preferred, like Batista de Lacerda, either to imply that miscegenation had hardly occurred in America, or that subsequent segregation had rendered impossible any future dilution of the African element. Lacerda's conclusion was typical of most of his contemporaries: "In Brazil the race problem is being resolved without effort or difficulty, while today in the United States it still presents that country's statesmen with an insoluble problem, clothed in difficulty and danger."[80]

Another comparison came from the pen of Manuel de Oliveira Lima, a widely read essayist and historian who was a career diplomat and spent the decade of the 1890's in Washington, D.C. He subsequently published a book about America, the first chapter of which was entitled "The Negro Problem." In it he sketched events since the Civil War, noting that "today one must confess that the Negro in America is incontestably an evil." He then concentrated his analysis on the South, referring to it as similar to the Brazilian north. Looking back on slavery, Lima claimed that the fate of the American slave had been "infinitely worse than in Brazil." The difference was due to "the greater weakness for emotion among the Latin race and to its lesser disdain for inferior races." American planters lived in constant fear of slave insurrections, "which never much worried planters and plantation owners

in Brazil" (thereby rewriting Brazilian history).[81] Lima suggested that the key to subsequent developments was the relative racial balance of the population. Blacks could "improve in an
atmosphere of whites." But the American South had too many
blacks (although its percentage was notably lower than the Brazilian northeast!), and therefore "only white immigration" along
with a migration of blacks from the South to elsewhere in the nation could restore its former prosperity. He did add that Brazil
also needed more immigrants, especially in view of the "relative
mental backwardness and enervation of the colonizing race."
Such immigration would help to "correct the extreme miscegenation begun by the Portuguese" and would "reinforce the actual
supremacy of the whites," who still face the danger of being
"drowned by the spreading of inferior races."[82]

Oliveira Lima's analysis was typical of his era in several respects. First, he traced the contrast he found in race relations between countries to alleged differences in slave treatment, for
which no proof was offered and which was in turn explained
as a reflection of national character. Second, a passing concession
was made to Aryanism by admitting the backwardness of the
Latin colonizers. Third, the Negro was described as inferior but
redeemable—under white tutelage and through miscegenation.
Fourth, a racial balance was stressed, to be aided by increased
white immigration. The over-all tone was optimistic, implying
that Brazil's more flexible national character made possible a harmonious whitening solution to the "Negro problem"—a path probably closed to Americans because of their rigid racial prejudices.
Brazil could never prohibit intermarriage because the "indul-
gence of our attitudes and the carelessness of our customs prevents us from hostility toward the Negro on any level, even race
mixture."[83]

Brazilian reviews of Lima's book centered on his discussion of
race. Two will be quoted here as evidence that his views were
generally held. They differ from him and from each other only in
terms of how optimistic they thought they should feel. José Veríssimo, the noted literary critic, praised the work and added: "I am

convinced, as is Sr. Oliveira Lima, that western civilization can only be the work of the white race, and that no great civilization can be built with mixed peoples. I even tend to believe that the United States owes its rapid and steady development to its ethnic purity. But I wonder if obtaining it a century ahead of time was worth the sacrifice of millions of human beings. . . ." So much for the United States Civil War.

> There is no danger, as Sr. Oliveira Lima implies, that the Negro problem will arise in Brazil. Before it could arise it was already resolved by love. Miscegenation has robbed the Negro element of its numerical importance, thinning it down into the white population. Here the mulatto, beginning with the second generation, wants to be white and the white man, harboring no illusions and with some insignificant exceptions, welcomes, esteems, and joins with him. As ethnographers assure us, and as can be confirmed at first glance, race mixture is facilitating the prevalence of the superior element. Sooner or later it will perforce eliminate the Negro race here. This is obviously happening already. And when immigration, which I think is Brazil's principal need, increases, it will, through the inevitable mixtures, accelerate the selection process.[84]

Medeiros e Albuquerque, another well-known literary critic who reviewed Lima's book, also assumed Negro inferiority and the possibility of a whiter Brazil. He did doubt, however, that the "fusion" which had absorbed so much of the African element had produced a stable element. "One does not so easily suppress profound organic characteristics. The skin is the least important. What is not in the skin may be in the blood, the nerves, the brain. . . ." He had no doubt that Brazil would become lighter and that millions of immigrants could finish the job. But he worried whether the result would leave anything that could be called Brazilian identity. "It remains to be seen" whether "there will be anything left that will correspond historically to what is known as the Brazilian people."[85]

The insistent vision of a whitened Brazil also appeared in fiction. Afrânio Peixoto's highly successful novel, A Esfinge (The Sphinx: 1911), reflected in its dialogue the racial concerns of the

Rio elite. Toward the end of the novel an older man reassured his young countryman that their land was fortunate to have been colonized by the Portuguese, without whom Brazil would lack the "beautiful Latin genius." (This rejection of Aryanism reflected Peixoto's own pro-Portuguese position.) He went on to explain that the Indian and the Negro had contributed much to his country's history, but "these sub-races tend to disappear once the white race is reintegrated into exclusive possession of the land." Then came the belief in fusion: "The Portuguese had another advantage—cross breeding with the Negro, thereby eliminating it with the successive infusions of white blood."

"The slow fusion of still imperfect mixtures, the repeated cultural selection, the forced discipline of social organization will make this mass into a strong, happy, and healthy population because the dominant traits are good. Today's promising beginning will produce a strong-willed, sensitive, and intelligent people worthy of this land and the time in which they live." The inevitable comparison with America followed. "In another three hundred years, we will all be white. I don't know what will happen to the United States, if their Saxon intolerance allows the compact nucleus of their twelve million Negroes to grow in isolation."[86]

The comparison between Brazil and the United States did not escape visitors from North America. Some were very favorably impressed by the Brazilian solution to the ethnic problem. The whitening ideology caught the attention of an American, Clayton Cooper, who published an account of his visit to Brazil in 1917. He noted that "a new experiment among nations" was under way, "different from anything known either in the United States or in any other European nation in its colonization of people with color different from their own." An "attempt is honestly being made here to eliminate the blacks and browns by pouring in white blood. It is claimed that one factor in this process is the natural selection of the female species to choose a mate lighter in color than herself." He further reported that "certain parts of Southern Brazil where comparatively few of the negroid or dark skinned types are found, are cited as examples of the progress already made toward this daring and unprecedented accomplishment." "Many of the most highly cultured Brazilians will tell you that this country will reveal one day to all the world the one and only method of racial inter-penetration, the only one that will prevent racial wars and bloodshed." Even the biology, for Cooper, was reassuringly obvious: "It seems to be a clear case of Lamarck and Darwin's selective process. If for purely social reasons a certain type becomes fashionable, all marrying drifts that way, and finally that type prevails in the race."

Finally came the same kind of comparison so common to Brazilian observers of his own country: "Although probably the average American would express his satisfaction over the fact that our civilization places many obstacles in the way of the development of such a principle in the United States, not to recognize the seriousness of the motive of the Brazilians in this vital mixture of the races is unfortunate."[87]

Theodore Roosevelt had a similar reaction, and reported it in detail that bears citing at length:

> The great majority of the men and women I met, the leaders in the world of political and industrial effort and of scientific accomplishment, showed little more trace of Negro blood than would be shown by the like number of similar men in a European capital. Yet not only is there in some classes a considerable infiltration of Negro blood, with a corresponding tendency of the pure Negro type to disappear, but this process is regarded with hearty approval by the most thoughtful statesmen of the country. Their view, so different from our own, can perhaps best be expressed in the words of one of these very statesmen, himself of pure white blood, who said to me substantially:
>
> "Of course the presence of the Negro is the real problem, and a very serious problem, both in your country, the United States, and in mine, Brazil. Slavery was an intolerable method of solving the problem, and had to be abolished. But the problem itself remained, in the presence of the Negro. . . .
>
> "Now comes the necessity to devise some method of dealing with it. You of the United States are keeping the blacks as an entirely

separate element, and you are not treating them in a way that fosters their self-respect. They will remain a menacing element in your civilization, permanent, and perhaps even after a while a growing element. With us the question tends to disappear, because the blacks themselves tend to disappear and become absorbed. . . .

"The pure Negro is constantly decreasing in numbers, and after two or more crosses of the white blood the Negro blood tends to disappear, so far as the physical, mental, and moral traits of the race are concerned. When he has disappeared, his blood will remain as an appreciable, but in no way a dominant, element in perhaps a third of our people, while the remaining two-thirds will be pure whites. Granted that this strain will represent a slight weakening in one-third of our population, the result will be that in our country two-thirds of the population will have kept its full strength, with one-third slightly weakened, while the Negro problem will have entirely disappeared. In your country all the white population will have been kept in its original race strength, but the Negro will remain in increased numbers and with an increased and bitter sense of his isolation, so that the problem of his presence will be more menacing than at present. I do not say that ours is a perfect solution, but I regard it as a better solution than yours. We and you have to face two alternatives, neither of them without drawbacks. I believe that the one we Brazilians have chosen will in the long run, from the national standpoint, prove less disadvantageous and dangerous than the one you of the United States have chosen."[88]

The elite's faith in "whitening," so perceptively described by Teddy Roosevelt, continued during the first two decades of the Republic.[89] Seen through the prism of the whitening ideology, Brazil seemed to have the best of both worlds. It had avoided the bitter racial divisions of the United States, said to have been caused by the rigid prejudices of the Anglo-Saxons—a trait supposedly absent in the more libidinous Latin Portuguese. Yet Brazil was now eliminating the inferior racial element through natural black attrition and what José Veríssimo euphemistically described as "love." So it was argued that the Brazilians would escape the determinist trap of Buckle and Agassiz in a steady ascent toward whiteness. By denying, implicitly or explicitly, the absoluteness of racial differences, this explanation offered a convenient escape from the gloomy conclusions of rigorously racist thought. Furthermore, the whitening ideology squared with one of the most obvious facts of Brazilian social history—the existence of a large "middle caste," generally called "mulatto." Within this category there were enormous variations, ranging from socially prestigious figures who could be described only as "mulatto" in the most intimate circles, to underworld criminals who would have fitted Nina Rodrigues' suggested penal category of "degenerates."

By any objective physical characteristics it was nonsense to refer to such a single category as "mulatto." Yet the Brazilians consistently did so, and their belief in such a category was an essential part of their race thinking. Given the experience of their multi-racial society, the whitening thesis offered Brazilians a rationale for what they believed was *already* happening. They borrowed racist theory from Europe and then discarded two of that theory's principal assumptions—the innateness of racial differences and the degeneracy of mixed bloods—in order to formulate their own solution to the "Negro problem." Not the least of its attractions was the sense of relief—sometimes even of superiority—it gave them when comparing their racial future to the United States.

To imply that *all* members of the Brazilian elite espoused the racial views described as the "whitening ideal" would, of course, mislead. Nonetheless, in the period between 1889 and 1914 the great majority undoubtedly did hold these views. A few, such as Nina Rodrigues, adopted the doctrinaire racist theory that differences were innate and that the process of whitening would not triumph, at least, in all parts of the country. A few others, including some German immigrants living in the southern states, held rigidly racist views and tried to segregate themselves from the native-born population. Finally, there were a few thinkers, to be analyzed later, who completely rejected the frame of reference of scientific racist theory in their search for a more authentic definition of Brazilian nationality.

3 Politics, Literature, and the Brazilian Sense of Nationality Before 1910

We have seen how race became an issue in the Brazil of the early Republic, and how thinking Brazilians tried to achieve a tenable compromise in their struggles with racial determinism. This chapter will discuss the connection between Brazilians' feeling about their national identity in this period, and the prevailing views on race that they could not avoid.

Around the turn of the twentieth century a country was likely to measure its sense of national identity and, therefore, self-confidence in two ways. The first was its ability to achieve political stability, and the second was its relative development of an authentic national literature.* The meaning of the former was clear—the ability of a country to change its party in power, or even its form of government, without violent political upheaval. Brazilians identified coups with the "laughable" banana republics of Spanish America—a cautionary example they wanted to avoid. The meaning of an authentic national literature was not satisfactorily spelled out in this period, although we shall struggle with certain implicit definitions as this chapter proceeds.

As measured by both these indices, Brazil, in the eyes of its literate citizens in this period, left much to be desired. This chap-

---

* A third measure, not considered here, was the degree of economic development.

ter traces the forms the resulting discontent took, and then argues that the pervasiveness of this discontent led perceptive critics to connect the issue of race with the troubling lack of success as measured by these two indices.

THE POLITICAL REALITIES OF THE NEW REPUBLIC

In late nineteenth century terms, political stability was often correlated with constitutional government. This section will, therefore, outline the principal political events and trends witnessed by Brazil in this period.[1]

The first decade of the Republic witnessed regional revolts (Rio Grande do Sul, 1893–95), military rebellion in the capital city (Naval Revolt of 1891 and 1893–94), a stock-market crash (1892), severe inflation, and the repeated suspension of civil liberties—hardly the ideals urged by the liberal reformers of the late Empire. The two-party system of the Empire—unrepresentative though it may have been—was replaced by a network of one-party political machines in each state. The Liberal and Conservative parties disappeared as recognizable organizations, and the deputies elected to the Constituent Assembly in 1890 were primarily Republicans. This monopoly was later relaxed when some high electoral offices went to politicians who had been prominent non-Republicans during the Empire (as was the case of Afonso Pena, Governor of the State of Minas Gerais from 1892 to 1894 and President of the Republic from 1906 to 1909). Even then, however, the power to nominate such men lay with the state Republican organizations. Electoral politics therefore became a contest for power *within* the Republican ranks of each state. On the national scale it became a game of negotiation among the Republican chiefs of the most powerful states—São Paulo, Minas Gerais, Rio de Janeiro, Bahia, Pernambuco, and Rio Grande do Sul.[2]

There was a sharp contrast between the ideal of free representative government and the socio-economic realities in most of the country, especially the rural areas. The movement to widen the franchise—which had begun in the late Empire—dramatized this contrast, as vote fraud became common in the 1890's. A nominee of the official party could not fail to win election, unless a dissenting faction of the party challenged the official slate. Such a challenge meant—in many areas—the use of force or blatant promises (or both) to win the favor of the local authorities charged with counting the ballots. The resulting system was labeled by subsequent writers as *coronelismo,* a reference to manipulation by local bosses who were often simply referred to as the *coronel* (or "colonel," an informal label used to describe local political strong men). In the few economically developed and urbanized states electoral competition was usually more open. In São Paulo, for example, it was possible eventually for a dissident Republican faction to found an independent party. Even in such states, however, *coronelismo* usually prevailed in the rural areas.[3]

Violence was not uncommon. Hired gunmen were sometimes used to eliminate rival candidates or political leaders, especially in the Northeast. In states where Republicanism had never taken firm root, the local Republican party simply furnished a new stage for the struggle between rival clans that had previously fought under the label of Liberal and Conservative. Under the system of one-party representation, the clan that was "out" could gain power only by seizing control of the Republican machinery from the incumbent clan.

Politics on the national level also took on a different complexion from the imperial period. The new Constitution provided for an elected President, following the American model. The ballot for President and Vice-President was national, thus requiring the state party leaders to reach agreement on official nominees. In a one-party system, failure to achieve such agreement often led to bitter conflict.

Thus the political structure of the new Republic rested on a largely boss-ridden local system and a tenuous national alliance of state leaders. It did not produce the open, rational political competition that liberal reformers of the late Empire had visualized. It would be wrong to conclude, however, that outstanding men were never elected. The state machines nominated and elected many intelligent and eloquent politicians. Individual local bosses were proud of their ability to mobilize the electorate for a representative whose rhetoric may well have been incomprehensibly sophisticated to many of the voters recorded in his support. Nonetheless, such politicians were left at the mercy of the men with power, who could (and did) dump them unceremoniously when circumstances dictated. A number of men of intellect had this experience—including Sílvio Romero, José do Patrocínio, Gilberto Amado, and Coelho Neto.

The overthrow of the Empire and the proclamation of the Republic in November 1889 occurred with so little social upheaval that one is tempted to classify it as a typical Latin American palace coup. The consolidation of the new Republic proved more traumatic. Less than a year after a Constituent Assembly had approved a new constitution in 1891, constitutional rule gave way to military dictatorship. The first President, General Deodoro da Fonseca, quarreled with the Congress (which was the Constituent Assembly wearing a new hat) that had elected him. Like Emperor Pedro I, who quarreled with the Assembly that drafted the previous Constitution (of 1824) and then haughtily dismissed its members, General Deodoro closed the Congress in retaliation. But he soon fell ill and was unable to contain the diverging Republican forces. He resigned in favor of another general—Vice-President Floriano Peixoto. Floriano ruled from 1891 to 1894, suppressing, without visible emotion, the many enemies of the new Republic.

He had his work cut out for him. By 1891 the Emperor's loyalists—without any encouragement from the deposed monarch—had organized a conspiracy to restore the Empire. They included among their number many intelligent, wealthy, and politically experienced men such as Visconde de Ouro Preto, who headed the last imperial cabinet (June-November 1888). Although they

had no opportunity to organize a broadly based political movement, the monarchists harassed the government throughout the
1890's, attempting to run congressional candidates (whom the
government disqualified) and unleashing a stream of propaganda
against the Republic and its leaders. The Republican dissidents
also posed a threat to Floriano. Rebel opposition movements
emerged in the states of Rio Grande do Sul, Paraná, and Santa
Catarina. Rebels arose even within the military. In 1893 units of
the Navy revolted, with some rebel leaders, such as Admiral Saldanha da Gama, proclaiming their monarchist loyalties. Brazil's
credit in London plummetted. Her bonds could be sold only at
huge discounts. Floriano ruled by decree, freely suspending civil
liberties in order to suppress critical publications and speeches.
Federal power managed to prevail, as the revolts were stamped
out.

To the surprise of many, the Army leadership showed little desire to prolong their rule. Power passed to an elected civilian in
1894—Prudente de Morais, the first of a succession of Presidents
from the prosperous state of São Paulo.[4] Floriano had succeeded
in establishing firm Republican authority throughout the country, and that seemed enough for the military—and for the world
of international finance. Prudente reaped the political rewards of
Floriano's rule. Brazil's credit rating rose in London, making possible negotiations for consolidation of the high-interest short-term
debt, which was achieved in 1898.

Nonetheless, armed revolts continued. A prolonged rebellion
against federal authority occurred in northern Bahia in 1896–97
where Antônio Conselheiro led an uprising of backlanders, later
immortalized by Euclides da Cunha in Os Sertões (see below).
It became the most serious threat to Prudente's government,
largely because the government misjudged the situation disas-
trously. As a severe test of prestige for both the government and
the Army, it led to a wave of hysteria against the monarchists, favorite scapegoats of Republican politicians when under pressure.
The wave increased in 1897, when the Minister of War was as-

sassinated by a dissident soldier.[5] The government chose the opportunity, whether through misinformation or malice, to impose censorship and condone street violence against the monarchists. A state of siege was voted by the Congress, giving Prudente de Morais emergency powers which he promptly used against dissidents of every stripe. The revolt was finally crushed, and the turn of the century began a decade of relative political calm.

President Campos Salles (1898–1902) fared much better than his predecessor. He was also a Paulista, thus cementing the dominance of that fast-growing state in national Republican politics. The Paulistas sent their third successive President to Rio de Janeiro when Rodrigues Alves was elected in 1902. It appeared that the Republican chiefs had discovered the secret of wielding power and transmitting it effectively.

The working alliance among the principal state leaders (dubbed the "politics of the governors") was evident when a prominent politician from Minas Gerais, Afonso Pena, was elected President in 1906. Pena won virtually uncontested, coasting to victory on the understanding that it was time for São Paulo to give way to the second most powerful state. Like Rodrigues Alves, Pena had been an active politician during the Empire. Both were progressive, dynamic administrators by the standard of the day. Both attempted to apply the Republican formulae of liberal constitutionalism that had suffered such sharp attack in the 1890's. Both were notably successful.

The Republican presidential system seemed at last to be working. Economically and financially Brazil also grew stronger. She continued to be the world's leading coffee producer, although plagued by overproduction. A valorization scheme begun in 1906 made possible a manipulation of the world market (primarily by foreign brokers) that shielded Brazilian producers from violent market fluctuations. It also began a long-term government (state and later federal) program of surplus coffee purchases and stockpiling. The net result was to guarantee a minimum profit margin for the efficient coffee growers, located primarily in Minas Gerais and São Paulo. These states, in turn, were the linch pins of Republican politics. Brazil's exports were boosted by the boom in natural rubber, on which she had a monopoly until the rubber from the English-owned plantations in the East Indies reached the world market in 1912. Equally important, the foreign debt had been consolidated in 1898 when the Campos Salles government succeeded in negotiating a "funding loan" in London. With her foreign credit rating restored, Brazil could hope to attract foreign investment and increased trade.[6]

But all the principal features of the Republican system remained—low political mobilization, frequent manipulation and fraud in elections, one-party government, and a high degree of decentralization. States enjoyed the power to contract foreign loans and impose taxes on goods exported abroad. The most powerful, such as São Paulo and Rio Grande do Sul, maintained state militia that were often larger and better equipped than the national Army units within their borders. In short, the national political system was overshadowed at many points by the growth of state power. Such a trend was hardly surprising since the opportunity for such growth had been a principal Republican demand during the Empire. It was urged passionately by the Paulistas, who capitalized most quickly on the new autonomy during the early Republic. The Monarchists had exaggerated the threat of dismemberment, but they had correctly seen that national government was bound to suffer at the expense of local power.

POLITICAL CRITICISMS OF THE NEW REPUBLIC

Although political stability appeared to have been achieved between 1898 and 1910, thereby giving satisfaction and relief to the worried elite, they had been deeply disturbed by the upheaval of the 1890's. Criticism of the new political order for failing to provide stability came from Republicans, Monarchists, and political visionaries. Among the latter the Jacobins were the most intransigent.

They were alarmed over what they saw as the erosion of Brazilian nationality. Their attention was also on the political arena, and they soon found a convenient scapegoat—the Portuguese. Anti-Portuguese feeling had repeatedly surfaced in Brazilian history, just as similar sentiments about their mother countries had arisen in all the other New World colonies. Brazilian independence in 1822 had aroused nationalist feeling against Portugal, which was then transformed into the more diffuse nativism of the Romantic movement. Yet Lusophobia did recur, usually in the form of resentment against the control over commerce held by the Portuguese in virtually every Brazilian city. There had been a virulent outbreak of Lusophobia in Recife as recently as 1872–73, when Eça de Queiroz' unflattering portrait of the Brazilian in his novel, As Farpas, had outraged Pernambuco.[7]

One group of political radicals founded the journal O Jacobino, primarily as a vehicle of anti-Portuguese propaganda.[8] The reason for its title, which was soon attached to all the radical nationalists: "A century ago Jacobinism in France succeeded in consolidating the Republic against internal attacks from reactionary factions and in driving off the nation's soil those invading armies which had allied to restore royalty and clerical rule." Now only "violent methods" and "energetic methods" such as those of the French Jacobins could save Brazil from "the torpor in which the country has languished since its accidental discovery by the Lusitanians."[9] In its inaugural issue the paper proclaimed that "we hate and combat the Portuguese colony, which is corrupting us and destroying our existence by monopolizing everything and sacrificing our population."[10]

The Jacobins soon found a flame to fan. In the naval revolt of 1893 certain rebels had been evacuated on vessels of the Portuguese Navy, which had promised the Brazilian government that the fugitives would be deposited only in Portuguese ports. The ships docked in Montevideo, apparently because of mechanical difficulties, where the rebels were allowed to alight, making it relatively easy to return to Brazil across the border of Rio Grande do Sul. When the news arrived in Rio de Janeiro, crowds attacked Portuguese-owned shops and businesses. This popular outburst was abetted by the inflammatory editorials of O Jacobino, whose editor Deocleciano Mártir, it must be admitted, was described by a contemporary as "half-crazy, impulsive, emotional in the extreme, walking with a crutch often used as a weapon since he was always mixing into street fights."[11]

The delirium was furthered by other propagandists, such as Aníbal Mascarenhas, who edited O Nacional, another (more moderate) Jacobin paper. It fought the "great naturalization" included in the 1891 constitution (which provided that all aliens resident in Brazil would automatically become Brazilian citizens unless they filed an explicit waiver), a measure that significantly benefited the large Portuguese colony. Here Lusophobia was being mobilized against one of the most liberal provisions of the new Constitution. O Nacional also advocated protection for national industry, and the "gradual nationalization" of commerce, industry, and property.[12] The impassioned loyalty to Floriano's battle against the foreigners extended down into the high schools, where one student remembered years later having been an "enthusiast of the Iron Marshal."[13]

The most famous of the Jacobins was Raul Pompéia, the novelist and poet. He was active in the Jacobin Club of Rio de Janeiro and a fanatical supporter of Floriano. In 1893 he wrote an Introduction to Rodrigo Octávio's schoolbook on "national holidays." The book itself revealed a concern with building a national consciousness through attention to commemorative days. Although Octávio's text was rather bland, Pompéia's Introduction was a bitter attack on foreign economic interests, especially the Portuguese. The historical role of Pedro II was dismissed as having been "preoccupied with looking good in Europe" and "forever turning his back on his country." Pompéia's real target was foreign capital: "The great nerve centers for our interests are in London or Lisbon. In any case, not here. As a political economy we are pitifully spineless." Thus the "gangrene of foreign mercantilism" and of "enervating cosmopolitanism" was eroding what was left of the country. These foreign interests were well represented in Brazil, he argued. They were behind the constant public campaigns launched under "the guise of vain formulas of liberalism against any of the measures, steps or energetic precautions that have brought about the economic and financial salvation of other states."

Pompéia ended with an onslaught against the Portuguese commercial community. Although he never named the nationality explicitly, no Brazilian reader could have failed to know the context. To the action of "this party" he attributed "the sickness of the Brazilian public spirit. . . . Our blind sociological analysts prefer to investigate obscure and depressing metaphysics or national character when they could acknowledge the obvious and simple reality."[14]

Extreme anti-Portuguese feeling did not last long. Although Floriano's government broke off diplomatic relations with Portugal in 1894 after the Portuguese Navy ships allowed the fugitive Brazilian rebels to disembark in Uruguay, relations were re-established in 1895 and the Portuguese sent as their Ambassador the poet Tomás Ribeiro, who proved a very effective conciliator in Brazil. The Jacobin press bitterly fought the resumption of relations, but to no avail. Floriano had left the presidency, Raul Pompéia had committed suicide in 1895, and the foreign economic interests he had fought were now profiting from the new stability in Brazil.[15]

LITERATURE, INTELLECTUALS, AND
THE QUESTION OF NATIONALITY

The second measure often used in this era to gauge a country's development was the degree to which it had attained a unique national culture. For most Brazilian intellectuals this meant literature. Music, dance, painting, sculpture, folk art—none of these were, rightly or wrongly, given the same weight. Now that we have installed a new political system, the argument went, and now that we have abolished both slavery and the monarchy, we must be becoming a more autonomous country. Where, then, is our national literature?[16]

At the outset of our period, Machado de Assis (the leading literary figure of his generation) spelled out, in a way that is instructive, the challenge of developing a national literature. In a brief essay in 1873 he surveyed the state of Brazilian writing and concluded that a Brazilian literature did not yet exist. He thought the achieving of literary independence would take a long time—more than a generation or two—although the process, in his opinion, was probably already under way. He upbraided those writers who simply threw in the names of local birds and flowers (thinking they were thereby being Brazilian). Although the "majestic scenes of American nature" offered great possibilities for the poet and novelist that must be handled with "imagination," Machado posed the perennial dilemma of the artist— how to develop nativist themes while at the same time remaining universal in appeal. Their task, charged Machado, was to "question Brazilian life and American nature." He condemned the late Romantic excess of equating the Indian with the authentic Brazilian, but he did concede that the customs of the interior best preserved the national traditions.[17]

Machado's challenging but vague dicta omitted any consideration of the connection between, on the one hand, Brazil's political and social development and, on the other hand, its literary evolution. (Later critics stressed this connection.) It is significant that he makes no positive definition of what a *national* literature might mean. In fact, he makes no significant mention of popular culture and its usefulness as a source for writers, nor does he anywhere suggest that Brazilian writers investigate Brazil for themselves.

In this connection, it is most significant that Machado de Assis was himself writing sophisticated urban literature. Since Brazil was (and has remained, at least until the 1960's) basically a rural society, the paradox is clear. How could Brazilian writers struggle with the task of making their writing more Brazilian? One way to do this was to describe the flora and fauna (this was only done in a romanticized, obligatory way). The other was to pick up the legends or language of popular culture and use them in their writing. In the period before World War I the literary establishment failed to do the latter. Only a few writers even tried, but the critics largely ignored or downgraded them.*

Between 1889 and 1910, Brazilian literature did not in fact experience any significant innovations. With few exceptions (such as the novelist, Lima Barreto, who had little success with the public or the critics before his death in 1922), writers avoided depicting the real conditions of many aspects of Brazilian life, either in the city or the countryside. And there was little innovation in language or artistic form (with the exception of the Symbolist movement in poetry, which was ostracized by the literary establishment). In short, there was little evidence that an independent, original literary culture was developing. The following section is concerned with the various reactions to that fact.

* Valdomir Silveira wrote short stories using the colloquial language of the *caboclo* in the interior of São Paulo. Writers from Rio Grande do Sul, such as Alcides Maya and Simões Lopes Neto, produced a regionalist literature reflecting the gaúcho traditions of Brazil's southernmost state. Afonso Arinos did this for the state of Minas Gerais in his short stories and plays and Melo Moraes Filho gathered popular literature from all over Brazil (Alfredo Bosi, *História Concisa de Literatura Brasileira*, São Paulo, 1970, 232-40; Antônio Cândido, *Literatura e Sociedade*, São Paulo, 1965, 136; Ronald Dennis, "Brazilian Literary Nationalism Among the Critics, 1870-1900," Ph.D. dissertation, University of Wisconsin, 1972, 102-12). They and the few others like them made little impact on the predominant trend, which continued to be set by the European-centered writers of Rio de Jaeniro. Oral tradition and popular culture is another source of "national" literature, growing out of lower-class social experience and existing independently of the formal writers and literary critics. In Brazil of this era it had its own vitality. The legends and folk tales of this popular culture were later to be seen as a prime expression of an original Brazilian culture and were a source of inspiration for the Modernist Movement that erupted in 1922. This tradition can exist, of course, independently of formal literary criticism, and did.

A week after the proclamation of the Republic, a group of writers addressed a manifesto to the Provisional Government, warning their new leaders that "Brazilian literature will not prostrate itself at your feet, as at the throne of Augustus or Louis XIV. . . ." Terming themselves "a factor in the development of this country and an element in the . . . progress in . . . the Republic they helped to found," they expected of the government "only justice and liberty—justice for our labors and liberty for our thought." The proclamation ended on an optimistic note: "The country is spreading its wide wings in the direction of a land studded with progress. Literature will embark on the flight to accompany it closely."[18]

The upheavals of the 1890's produced recurrent waves of censorship. It was a sharp contrast with the Empire of Pedro II, which, for all its failures, had preserved a remarkable degree of personal freedom for the elite. The small number of intellectuals had enjoyed freedom of the press and speech.

Despite these vicissitudes, the literary world of the early Republic succeeded in institutionalizing itself. During the reign of Pedro II, the outlets for intellectual life had been very restricted. There was the Emperor's favored but very limited *Instituto Histórico e Geográfico Brasileiro*, where papers were read in solemn sessions presided over by Pedro II himself. There were the newspapers of a few major cities—Rio de Janeiro, Recife, São Paulo, Pôrto Alegre. There were the law faculties in Recife and São Paulo.

It was not until the early years of the Republic (1897) that Brazil's first official literary institution was founded—the *Academia Brasileira de Letras,* although in the 1890's there were the scattered informal meeting places in Rio de Janeiro: the office of the *Revista Brasileira* (which the critic José Veríssimo had been instrumental in reviving in 1895), the *confeitarias,* and writers' homes, with Coelho Neto's residence being a favorite. The original proposal for the Academy had quickly gained the blessing and active support of Machado de Assis, Brazil's most famous man of letters, although its effective founder was Lúcio de Mendonça. The first Secretary was Rodrigo Octávio. Its organization followed the French model, with chairs for forty "immortals." The composition of the Academy reflected the establishmentarian character of culture in the Brazilian belle époque. The founding members were the scions of late imperial liberalism. They saw themselves as the creative minority upholding cultural standards in a South American outpost of European civilization. But what kind of a culture could it be? How would the European inspiration express itself in this New World setting? At heart this was the perennial question faced by any new nation that sought to apply liberalism: would it necessarily be accompanied by the uncritical importation of another culture?

It was most common for the topic of Brazil's cultural originality to arouse an equivocal response from intellectuals of the early Republic. Such was evident in the speech by Joaquim Nabuco on the occasion of the founding of the Academy of Letters in 1897. As the General Secretary of the new institution, Nabuco delivered an intellectual valedictory. He noted that Brazil had not yet produced a "national book, even though I think that the Brazilian soul is defined, delineated and expressed in the works of its writers; it is simply not all in one book." With the charge that Latin American writers were merely imitative, Nabuco agreed:

> We are nothing more than conductors of electricity, and journalism is the battery which sends that continuous current through our hearts. . . . If we were simply conductors, there would be no harm in that; after all, what can undersea cables feel? We are, however, wires endowed with a consciousness which prevents the current from passing from one point to another without being felt, and which gives us all down the line the constant shock of these universal transmissions. . . .

Nabuco ended on a note of confidence:

> The founding of the Academy of Letters is the affirmation that in literature, as well as in politics, we are a nation which enjoys its

own destiny, its own distinct character, which can be directed only
by itself, while developing its originality from its own resources,
desiring and aspiring only to that glory which can be produced by
its own genius.[19]

What signs were there that Brazil had demonstrated any "genius" of her own? Nabuco's autobiography (published in 1900)
sounded less optimistic.

> We Brazilians—and the same can be said for the other American
> peoples—belong to America merely on a new and fluctuating layer
> of our mind, while we belong to Europe on all the stratified levels.
> As soon as we acquire the least culture, the latter predominate over
> the former. Our imagination cannot fail to be European, that is, to
> be human. . . .

This tension led to the "most terrible of instabilities" which grew
out of the fact that "in America the landscape, the life, the hori-
zon, the architecture and everything around us lacks a historical
dimension and a human perspective, while in Europe we lack a
homeland. . . ." The result? "On one side of the ocean you sense
the absence of the world, on the other, the absence of a country.
The feeling in us is Brazilian, but the imagination is European."[20]

Graça Aranha, a diplomat and prominent figure in the literary
establishment, added to this picture a concern over the cultural
influence of European immigrants. Delivering a lecture in
Buenos Aires in 1897 entitled "Literature Today in Brazil" he
noted:

> We are a new people and we have not yet assumed an authentic
> historic identity. We know we are the product of different races. We
> are also certain that we are not simply a mixture of Portuguese, In-
> dian and African. These basic elements in our make-up are being
> disturbed daily by the arrival of other forces on our soil. The na-
> tional type cannot establish itself with the diverse mixtures which are
> sapping it. The Brazilian character remains an unknown.[21]

In the early twentieth century, even when they remained at
home, Brazilians promoted a culture that was heavily imitative of

Europe. There was an overriding desire to demonstrate that Brazil was a worthy outpost of European civilization. It was assumed that the élite could speak and read French fluently. Principal literary newspapers centered their attention on intellectual life in Paris. The *Gazeta de Notícias,* for example, ran an elaborate four-page illustrated story on Bastille Day, 1907, with portraits of Rousseau, Marat, and Victor Hugo, along with a large photograph of the key to the Bastille. In the same year Olavo Bilac, the prince of poets in the Brazilian belle époque, exulted over the sympathetic reception given the French politician Paul Doumer by a Rio audience: "This audience, familiar with the French language . . . listened to Sr. Paul Doumer with an instinctive receptivity [*simpatia*] that would not be duplicated for a lecturer of any other nationality. Our soul is still, and I believe always will be, an extension of the French soul."[22]

In 1910, the Rio newspaper *O País* reviewed enthusiastically a book on progress in Brazil by the Frenchman Baron de Anthouard, noting: "Brazil is morally linked to France, from whose books she has learned, whose art she finds fascinating and whose history she knows and loves. There is no country in a better position to develop a formidable area of influence in Brazil than France. . . ."[23] Monteiro Lobato, the prominent writer-publisher who was born in 1882 in the interior of the state of São Paulo, confessed (in a letter to Godofredo Rangel in 1915) that practically all his reading of literature before the age of twenty-five had been in French: "I can count on my fingers the number of books I read in our language before that age: a little Eça [de Queiroz], about five volumes of Camilo [Castelo Branco], half of Machado de Assis. Plus Euclides [da Cunha] and the newspapers."[24]

For the representative Brazilian writer Paris was the center of civilization, the spiritual home he longed to visit. A few went to London, preferring its different world of aristocratic culture (*not* the middle-class culture that was in fact typical of the Victorian era), or Berlin, where the wave of science seemed irresistible.

For Brazilians, especially the traditionally minded, Portugal was a sometime mecca. But only the most loyally Lusitanian Brazilian could find in late nineteenth century Lisbon a sufficiently satisfactory atmosphere for the life of the mind. Portugal usually turned out to be a stopping place en route to Paris.

The very instruments of culture in the Brazilian belle époque passed through European hands. In book publishing, just as in many other spheres, the lifelines of Brazilian culture still ran to the Old World. There were, for example, only a few major book publishers in Brazil before 1914. The principal house was Garnier, a French-owned firm that printed most of its books in Paris.[25] Books were usually distributed directly from Paris and Lisbon to the few scattered outlets in the ports.

The decade after 1900 was a period of intense literary activity that produced relatively little literature of lasting value. Perhaps the style of the era inhibited the serious and innovative artist. In retrospect the literary historians can find no convenient label for these years: "post-Symbolism" or "post-Parnassianism" say some; others call it "pre-Modernism." In either case the belle époque is defined in terms of what came before or after. No single school or style sets it off.[26]

Machado de Assis, the undisputed lion, had entered his final phase. Still the master of his unique style, he was no longer breaking new ground, although he remained the most honored living writer. Other novelists and short story writers such as Coelho Neto and Gonzaga Duque sold well in their own day, but their literary reputations have not fared well subsequently. They catered to the tastes of their immediate audience—primarily the ladies of Rio and São Paulo—thereby earning royalties but losing the esteem of later critics.[27] The literary high point of the era came in 1902 with the publication of two widely read works— Euclides da Cunha's *Os Sertões* and Graça Aranha's *Canaã*— works that will be analyzed in later sections. The era was rich in minor writers, some of whom could command a wide audience, such as João do Rio, Afrânio Peixoto, and Medeiros e Al-

buquerque. It was also an era for chroniclers and gossip colum-
nists, such as Figueiredo Pimentel, who edited the column "Bin-
oculars" in *Gazeta de Notícias*.[28]

The short-lived prosperity and stability of the belle époque also
made possible the emergence of a pretentious cultural atmosphere in Rio de Janeiro. The clique that gained prominence made
a mockery of the Brazilian "genius" that Nabuco had envisaged
in his inaugural address at the Academy. The motto of the
novelist-critic Afrânio Peixoto—"Literature is society's smile"—
seemed to many contemporaries to epitomize the era.[29] A successful writer in that atmosphere was Medeiros e Albuquerque,
who, in 1901, enthusiastically reviewed the latest literary accomplishments of his fellow Academy members. Having described
their works in superlatives, he concluded that while "others give
Brazil their labor and intelligence in the spheres of commerce,
industry and agriculture, we shall also contribute our effort."
Then followed the rhetoric: "In skies so vast . . . new stars will
yet be born. Perhaps we shall be the least brilliant in the constel-
lation that shines for our country. But we shall struggle and labor
to increase its greatness in our own field."[30]

Medeiros' idea of such labor revealed itself in his lectures at
the National Music Institute in 1905–6. His topics were "Kisses,"
"The Foot and the Hand," and "The Dead," all of which he
treated in a manner calculated to amuse his listeners. As the author confessed, few could be surprised at the "frivolity" of his
lectures, least of all his sponsors, since Medeiros himself "knew
perfectly well from the beginning that I could only say things of
obvious frivolity."[31]

Men of minor talent gravitated to the salons of Rio. One of
the least inhibited was Elysio de Carvalho, a young aesthete who
had married wealth, thus enabling him to buy handsomely bound
editions of European classics.[32] He complained that Rio had pitifully few salons where one could find "a suave atmosphere of
things intellectual, of good music and delicate perfumes." The
best was presided over by the Countess Sylvia Diniz, "who can

. . . evoke the mists of London, the landscapes, heights and snows of the Alps, the radiant beauty of the gardens and parks of Paris, the superb magic of Venice. . . ."[33] Such figures as Medeiros e Albuquerque and Elysio de Carvalho rivalled each other in catering to their wealthy countrymen's need to imitate continental "sophistication."

No writer better personified the elegance of the belle époque than Paulo Barreto, better known by his pen name of "João do Rio." This literary gadfly, who admired and translated Oscar Wilde, was an unrivaled apologist for the cultural patina of the Avenida Central—Rio's principal thoroughfare, built during President Rodrigues Alves' renovation of Rio de Janeiro. Since the turn of the century João do Rio had produced a stream of newspaper columns, chronicling the manners of the Rio literati. A dandy who was said to emulate Oscar Wilde in more than literary taste, he was Rio's most talented social journalist. Elysio de Carvalho dedicated one of his volumes to Paulo Barreto, "the most extraordinary chronicler of our lecheries, our perversions, our madnesses, our sensualities, . . . and our grotesque vanities. . . ."[34] Later, Carvalho called him "the ironic, paradoxical and cruel observer of our times."[35] It was the latter quality that helped to produce so many enemies for the aggressive dandy with a mordant intelligence. As one contemporary remembered, "João do Rio had no friends. Everyone attacked him. Everyone detested him. They claimed he had nothing, not even talent, which, in actual fact, was the most robust and fertile of his generation." Why such hostility? "He lived by his pen, sowing the wind. Naturally he harvested storms."[36]

One is tempted to look deeper for the explanation of his enmities. Many of his contemporaries must have resented the accuracy with which he depicted their world of bookstores, theaters, and cafés. He described in eloquent detail the well-dressed senhoras and the illiterate stevedores, the spoiled rich sons and the street urchins. The contrasts were all the sharper for the subtlety with which they were drawn. He winced at the pretentions of

the newly "civilized" Rio, of which he himself soon became a familiar symbol. "Let's have coffee? My boy, that's not civilized!
Let's have tea instead." So the city, "like the men, laid out avenues, adopted foreign names, ate French-style and lived French-
style." The local snobs could be recognized at a glance because
they "pretended not to be Brazilian." The middle class copied
them "and the poor, influenced by this bizarre sense of inferiority,
have the same view."[37] Here was the "terrible instability" Nabuco had described, taken to a new extreme.

Most Brazilian intellectuals were acutely aware of how imitative their culture was. And, as noted above, they made a close
connection between literature and nationality. Their self-
awareness was evident in the collection of interviews published
by João do Rio in 1908. Thirty-six writers, including most of the
major literary figures of the belle époque, gave their views on the
state of their literature. Virtually every respondent frankly recognized Brazil's dependence upon French models. One symbolist
poet bemoaned the "deplorable paralysis" of present-day literature, adding that "we expect the New Idea to arrive aboard the
next transatlantic French steamer," and "it arrives much the
worse for wear at the hands of imitators without talent," added
Duque Estrada. None of the writers thought Brazil had yet
achieved a literature of her own. Olavo Bilac's explanation was
typical: "We are a race in formation, and diverse ethnic elements
are still struggling for supremacy. There can be no original literature if the race is not yet formed. . . ." Medeiros e Albuquerque
thought Brazil "a nation which is forming anarchically," so that
"no one knows where it is headed," and Raymundo Correia believed that "only in ninety years could I say for certain what the
result will be."[38]

One of the best-selling authors was equally frank. "What do
we have that is original?" asked Coelho Neto, "Nothing." "The
Brazilian character is hiding in the backland [sertões]. The cities
are denationalizing on the pretext of civilizing. We buy everything abroad—from bread to battleships, from clothes to books.

Even our views are imported."[39] Writers such as Sousa Bandeira
and Medeiros e Albuquerque were honest enough to recognize
that literature, and even literacy, was the prerogative of a tiny
minority.[40]

In a few cases the authors dismissed even the possibility of a
uniquely Brazilian literature. Medeiros e Albuquerque not only
thought his country had not yet created a national literature, he
also predicted that she would *never* have one "because by the
time we become a nationality and attain the necessary cultural
level the world around us will also have changed and we, while
using Portuguese, shall merely be expressing sentiments analo-
gous to those of civilized intellectuals . . . in France, in Japan
. . . in the entire world."[41]

Elysio de Carvalho was less subtle. Instead of professing a
long-range universal vision, he embraced the Europe of his own
day. "The Brazilian intellect is far too elementary to influence
me," he announced. Brazilian writers of the past gave him a feeling of "repulsion," while the moderns "give me nausea and pain,
above all, pain." Thus, he could assure his interviewer that "my
soul is very little Brazilian; and this is natural enough because I
am moving with the development of ideas in this century." "I am
not a Brazilian writer either by inclination or aspiration. . . . I
am supernational and I belong to the European intellectual
scene."[42]

REACTION TO INADEQUACY

Brazil was thus found wanting, and found wanting by Brazilians
themselves.[43] As we saw above, the reaction of the politically oriented was to struggle for changes in the political structure. The
reactions of the intellectuals can be divided into three groups.
The first reacted by writing that the criticism had been overdone,
and Brazil was really progressing admirably—some even went as
far as to shout that it was better than anywhere else. The second
group agreed there was something wrong, and nervously attempted to think through the relationship between their national

identity and the problem of race. Although these writers assumed the deterministic views then prevalent were basically correct, they tried to argue that Brazil would prevail and become a self-respecting member of the community of nations. Not surprisingly, the only comfort they could draw was from holding to a self-contradictory position, and not pursuing the inconsistencies in that position. The views of both these groups were well represented in the thinking of the elite. The next two sections will analyze them in detail.

The third group rejected the scientific racist assumptions entirely, arguing that Brazil was different, and if Brazilians honestly came to terms with their own uniqueness, they could build a strong nation. The last section of the chapter discusses two of the few writers who took this position. They offer evidence as precursors of a later and more enlightened view.

Turning Determinism on Its Head: The Brazilian Chauvinists: Sousa Bandeira, a literary critic, put the first, rather defensive, attitude very neatly in 1901: "The defects of our country are endemic to the era, and do not represent signs of exceptional barbarity. In the present crisis there is nothing to make us especially ashamed." He had grown weary of the critical phrase ("so banal that it had become ridiculous") that "This is not the Republic of my dreams."[44] He felt quite free to excoriate the politicians, but did not transfer any criticism to the nation itself. "With our superb natural resources and the almost inexhaustible riches we can offer the world, we have more than enough to surmount the crisis," provided that "we work with perseverance, patience and confidence in the future."[45]

Later in the Republic, Bandeira returned to this theme, proudly describing the "complete reversal" from the gloom of the 1890's which was "a republic without manners, whose early years were spent in military revolts, political intrigues, and financial deals." The "old pessimism was followed by an extraordinary optimism; the country seemed to be shaken by a mighty dionysian impulse."[46]

One of the most famous (and earliest) expressions of this new confidence was Afonso Celso's paean of patriotism, *Porque me Ufano do meu País* (Why I am Proud of My Country).[47] Thousands of schoolchildren—future members of the elite—learned from Celso's primer (published in 1901) that their country was a geographic paradise chosen by God as his favored nation for the modern age. He addressed his children (to whom the book was dedicated) in the Preface: "When you say, 'We are Brazilians!' lift up your heads, bursting with noble pride [*ufania*]. Convince yourselves that you ought to thank God every day for His having given you Brazil for your cradle."[48] Celso listed eleven reasons why Brazil was superior to any other country in the world, which included its territorial greatness, its beauty, the variety of its climate (no natural calamities), its noble national character (and the excellence of the races that made it up), and a history unmarked either by defeat or by humiliation of other peoples. "Let us have confidence in ourselves, let us have confidence in the future, and let us, above all, have confidence in God, who would not have granted such precious gifts for us to squander in vain. . . . If He has been especially magnanimous in his gifts to Brazil, it is because He has reserved for us an exalted destiny."[49]

Celso's ebullient lyric quickly became a schoolroom classic, going through seven printings by 1915, although "ufanismo" at the same time became a synonym for a naïve, romanticized patriotism. As one literary critic confessed in 1902, "I secretly exulted over this rather ingenuous manifesto" because it was "an effective antidote to the seeds of despair sown in our soil by so many illustrious hands."[50]

Celso himself left no doubt about the purpose of his book: "I presume to have demonstrated in this work that as Brazilians we have no right to despair, for it is our duty to remain ever confident. In Brazil to despair is an injustice, an act of ingratitude, a crime."[51]

A conspicuous example of "ufanism" during the belle époque

was the ecstatic reception given the aeronautical pioneer Santos Dumont when he returned home to Brazil for a visit in 1903. He had long lived in Paris pursuing his obsession with flying inventions. His tenuous tie with his homeland was indicated by the rumor that his Portuguese was less grammatical than his French. He was, however, eagerly acclaimed by the Brazilian press as proof of Brazil's scientific genius. The ceremonies in his honor were remarkable for the popular patriotism which they revealed. One might have expected a tumultuous greeting from the students in Rio or São Paulo; more surprising was the enthusiasm of popular song-writers, such as Eduardo das Neves, who wrote the lines everyone soon knew by heart:

> Europe bowed before Brazil
> Rending homage in gentle tones
> Another star shone in the sky
> As Santos Dumont appeared.
>
> He honored forever the twentieth century
> The hero who astounded all the world
> Higher than the clouds, almost God
> And Santos Dumont is a Brazilian![52]

As he toured his seldom-visited homeland, Dumont was mobbed by admirers at every stop. In the interior of the state of São Paulo, an admirer pushed a letter into his hand: "Your country's most humble and obscure citizen . . . embraces you and celebrates you as the world's greatest mind. Your invention has glorified Brazil, cradle of so many scientific luminaries. Vive Brazil! Vive Santos Dumont!" It was signed "your countryman and admirer, Joaquim Silveira dos Reis."[53]

Establishment writers were equally enraptured. Coelho Neto wrote lyrical columns describing the hero's triumphal journey.[54] Woe betide the columnist who proved "inept enough to drop from the menu the only plate presently pleasing to the public taste," for Santos Dumont is "in the spotlight" and next to him "everything fades."[55] It was as if the Brazilians were reassuring themselves that they could not be an inferior people if they had already produced an engineering genius such as Santos Dumont. There were other examples. Nilo Peçanha, who had just finished serving out the presidential term of Afonso Pena (Peçanha had been Vice-President and succeeded Pena upon the latter's death in 1909), struck a confident note in addressing his fellow countrymen at a Parisian banquet in Elysée Palace in mid-1911. Brazilians "are . . . transforming Rio de Janeiro into one of the most beautiful cities in the world." Furthermore, the country was "almost two years ahead in paying the foreign debt" and had built "the leading fleet in South America without resorting to credit." Peçanha ticked off the other accomplishments: railroad building, educational reform and the successful settlement of many border disputes.[56] The following year Rodrigo Octávio, a tireless propagandist of the belle époque, assured an audience in Geneva that his country's economic development, "now experiencing a prodigious surge," would "continue on its triumphant path" inspired by Brazil's "ever vibrant liberal spirit."[57] Octávio went so far as to describe his country (one of the largest and oldest slave societies in the hemisphere) as a "new country without history or traditions, where a new nation is rising without any aristocracy or any prejudices."[58]

Trying To Live with Determinism: It was inevitable that the historians would have to come to grips with the realities of the Brazilian's confrontation with his habitat. In the late nineteenth century an important revisionist campaign in Brazilian historiography had begun to bear fruit. J. Capistrano de Abreu (1853–1927), later considered Brazil's first "modern historian," published in 1889 a highly original study of the patterns of Brazil's colonization and settlement in the colonial era. Capistrano's study was revisionist because it emphasized much more than preceding works the importance of the interior (especially the backlands or *sertões*); it was a shift away from the preoccupation with politico-legal history of the governing clans along the coast.[59] In 1907 Capistrano went on to publish another important volume (*Capí-*

tulos de História Colonial, or *Chapters of Colonial History*),
which substituted the concept of culture for that of race, thereby
reflecting the shift in anthropological thinking that triumphed in
the United States and Europe between 1900 and 1930.[60]
Yet in his private correspondence Capistrano revealed doubts
about Brazil's future. In 1911 he wrote a friend (Mário de Alencar, the literary critic) that the "penetrating question" was
whether "the Brazilian people is a new people or a decrepit
people." Later he revealed the same kind of pessimism about Brazilian national character (although not explicitly based on assumptions of racial inferiority) when he wrote a friend that the
jaburú is "the bird that for me symbolizes our land. He has a
stout stature, thick legs, robust wings, and spends his days with
one leg crossed over the other; sad, so sad, that austere, dead, and
vile sadness."[61]
An even more famous attempt to face up to the Brazilian's interaction with his land was Euclides da Cunha's epic *Os Sertões*
(*Rebellion in the Backlands*), first published in 1902. The author's background set him off from most literary figures of the
early Republic.[62] His strong interest in mathematics and science
led him to enter the Polytechnic School, a choice far less popular
among the elite than the law faculties. He soon transferred to the
Military School, where he was swept up in the scientific reform-
ist spirit that dominated the School and captured the younger
military. He became an ardent Republican, getting himself expelled for insulting the War Minister during a visit to the School
in early November 1888.
Moving to São Paulo, he began a long association with the
leading Republican newspaper, *O Estado de São Paulo.*[63] On the
eve of the Empire's collapse in November, Euclides was a typical
young reformer, supporting the new doctrines of change and the
ideal of nationality assumed to result.[64] Aside from his impetuosity, there was little to distinguish him from most idealists of his
generation.
Immediately after the proclamation of the Republic, Euclides

successfully appealed for readmission to the Army. His Republicanism now stood him in good stead. He finished his military courses (including a stint at the Higher War College), reaching the rank of First Lieutenant in 1892. Although he remained on active duty until 1896, he never exercised command over any combat force. He became an engineer instead.

Despite the upheavals of the early Republic, he reaffirmed his republican faith in a series of articles written for *O Estado de São Paulo* in 1892. "Let's be optimistic," he proclaimed, describing the political quarrels and revolts of 1891–92 as the growing pains of a society which had suddenly leapt from a colonial existence to the status of a modern republic.[65] He repeatedly cited Darwin, Spencer, Huxley, and Comte as authorities for his Social Darwinist interpretation. Out of these "transitional" struggles would come a stronger nation and a better-defined people. Whether he meant that as a physical or psychological process was not clear. He favored (white) immigration, noting that the "intelligent and diligent" foreigner can constitute a "powerful ethnic element within the make-up which we shall soon exhibit."[66] It sounded like the whitening ideal.

Euclides' optimism was greatly tested by the troubles of the young Republic. In 1896 the rebellion led by Antônio Conselheiro erupted at Canudos, in the backlands of Bahia. Although remaining in São Paulo, Euclides wrote his own articles on the revolt (in *O Estado de São Paulo*) in March and July of 1897.[67] His accounts were so impressive that his publisher, Júlio de Mesquita, sent him to Bahia for a first-hand report, after the *sertanejos* had annihilated the first army column sent to rout them. But the artillery and fire power of the government troops eventually overwhelmed the rebels, who were massacred down to the last man. Euclides arrived in time to witness the terrible dénouement. Deeply moved by what he saw, he soon began to plan a vast work about the rebels and their struggle against overwhelming odds.[68]

He returned to the "civilized" South, took up a new and higher position with the State Department of Public Works in São Paulo, now pursuing two vocations—engineering and writing. In 1899 he began a major engineering assignment—the reconstruction of a bridge which had collapsed in the interior of São Paulo. While living on the construction site, he worked on his book about the revolt at Canudos.

By 1900 he had completed the manuscript. It now bore a Brazilian title: *Os Sertões.**The change reflected the transformation in Euclides' own thinking. He had begun by assuming, along with the rest of the reading public, that Canudos was a counterrevolution against the new republic. Once there, however, he found the causes of the rebellion to be much more complex.[69] Meanwhile, the Brazilian public continued to see Canudos as the work of superstitious, ignorant half-breeds led by a crazed, self-styled messiah. Furthermore, government incompetence had allowed the revolt to become a major political issue in Rio, with the monarchists as the chief scapegoats. The deeper implications of the uprising went virtually unnoticed. It was seen merely as another political-military threat to the new republic.[70]

Euclides' early experiences in trying to publish his book were hardly encouraging. The editors of *O Estado de São Paulo*, whose owner had sponsored Euclides' trip to Bahia, were frightened by the enormous length of the manuscript. The *Jornal do Comércio* had a similar reaction. Finally, a friend, Lúcio de Mendonça, arranged a successful contact with the publishing house of Laemmert, which specialized in scientific works, but Euclides had to subsidize the first printing himself (Laemmert assumed there would never be a second!). Throughout 1902 Euclides fretted over the proofs. Finding eighty errors in the printed edition of 2000 copies, he sat down on the eve of publication and tried to correct each one himself by hand.[71]

Convinced that his book would gain little favorable comment,

---

* It had previously borne the derivative French title "A Nossa Vendée," the title of two articles Euclides had published about the revolt before going to Canudos.

he fled to the interior of São Paulo. Notwithstanding his fears, the critical acclaim in Rio was virtually unanimous. Within weeks the book had been proclaimed a "classic" and its author acclaimed as the newest literary sensation.[72]

What kind of book was *Os Sertões*? First, it did not conform to any standard literary genre. It was not fiction since the characters and events were real. It was too long to be an essay, and it had transcended the level of journalism because of its poetic language and its drama. Loaded down with the technical vocabulary of ethnography, geology, climatology—as well as detailed descriptions of the flora and fauna of the backlands—his careful portraits of the *sertanejos* included many colloquial terms unique to the Northeast. His prose was often as difficult as the terrain he described.[73] The first quarter of the book was a long, detailed essay on the interaction of man and his environment in the *sertão*. For many readers this must have been their first look into the drought-ridden backlands. Another, longer chapter, was devoted to man in the *sertão*. Here Euclides analyzed the ethnography of the region from the standpoint of the science of his day. The remaining sections of the book described the military campaign to subdue Antônio Conselheiro's rebels.

In the early chapters he analyzed the two factors that determinists had often pointed to as Brazil's great handicaps: race and climate. He depicted realistically the scant resources and natural disasters bedevilling the *sertanejos*. Here was the inhospitable land which Buckle had tried to depict, although the problem, of course, was drought (not excessive rainfall as Buckle had thought). Worried by the great degree of racial mixture, he sought to explain the behavior of the *sertanejos* by their racial origins, repeating the doctrines common to his generation.[74] He assumed a zoological process in which race mixture would reach an equilibrium—"ethnic integration"—only after an unspecified number of generations. Such a process troubled Euclides for several reasons. First, he believed that Indian blood was a positive factor, while African blood was not. This led him to praise the mixture of Indian and white, and to denegrate the mulatto. Furthermore, he worried that much of the Brazilian population, such as the *sertanejo*, was still in an interim stage of zoological development—too "unstable" to come together as a genuine society. Euclides wrote what he revealingly called an "irritating parenthesis" in the introductory section, "Man," where he repeated the indictment of mixed blood which could be found in European sociologists such as Gumplowicz and Lapouge:

> An intermingling of races highly diverse is, in the majority of cases, prejudicial. According to the conclusions of the evolutionist, even when the influence of a superior race has reacted upon the offspring, the latter shows vivid traces of the inferior one. Miscegenation carried to an extreme means retrogression. The Indo-European, the Negro, and the Brazilian Guarany or the Tapuia represent evolutionary stages in confrontation; and miscegenation, in addition to obliterating the pre-eminent qualities of the higher race, serves to stimulate the revival of the primitive attributes of the lower; so that the mestizo [*mestiço*]—a hyphen between the races, a brief individual existence into which are compressed age-old forces—is almost always an unbalanced type. . . . The mestizo [*mestiço*]—mulatto, mameluco, or cafuso—rather than an intermediary type, is a degenerate one, lacking the physical energy of his savage ancestors and without the intellectual elevation of his ancestors on the other side. In contrast to the fecundity which he happens to possess, he shows extraordinary cases of moral hybridism: a brilliant mind at times, but unstable, restless, inconstant, flaring one moment and the next moment extinguished, victim of the fatality of biologic laws, weighted down to the lower plane of the less favored race.[75]

The revolt, pictured as a dramatic demonstration of man's potential in the *sertão*, was described on two levels. On the military level, Euclides sympathized with the insurgents. He admired their courage and skill in using their environment against the enemy—enticing the soldiers into ambushes, watching them cut to ribbons by the cacti and poisoned by trying to eat non-edible plants they had never seen before. No reader could fail to see in

Euclides' vainglorious and incompetent Army officers, directing their troops into dangerous country they had not bothered to reconnoiter, the grotesque divergence between actual field conditions and the fantasy world of the War Ministry in Rio. In the end, victory was won through sheer numbers and technology. The rebels were driven back into their utopia of Canudos and besieged with Krupp cannons. And advancing government troops slaughtered every remaining defender.

On another level, however, the book was also an indictment of the mixed blood. Euclides attributed the rebellion in large part to the emotional instability of the *sertanejos* and especially to the "atavistic" personality of the rebel leader, Antônio Conselhiero.[76] Like most of his contemporaries, Euclides lacked a satisfactory definition of race. He assumed a hierarchy of races; each of which had distinguishing characteristics. The Brazilian population, he argued, had grown from three original lines: white, Indian, and black. He further assumed that each race could by itself make up a stable society, although at different levels of civilization. The danger arose when races mixed. Such mixture produced personal and social instability. This was never substantiated with evidence. Sometimes Euclides simply assumed as much, other times he asserted it on the basis of foreign scientific authority.

Brazil thus faced the gravest of all racial problems: large-scale miscegenation. Euclides expressed the common concern of the elite in "scientific" terms. What, they wondered, was the connection between the biological process of miscegenation and the historical process of nation-building? If miscegenation created instability, how long would it take to reach equilibrium? Or was it ever to be expected? If so, what would be the result? Although he never committed himself explicitly on the course of biological evolution for all of Brazil, he implicitly foresaw an eventually homogeneous product that was something close to an Indian-white mixture. What would happen to the Brazilian nation in the interval? Could social integration occur ahead of ethnic integration?

Euclides was equivocal on these questions. To conclude that

political and economic integration had to await an ill-defined process of ethnic amalgamation would have been demoralizing. If the processes might be simultaneous, should the government and the elite attempt to direct the ethnic integration? If so, how? One answer was European immigration, which Euclides had briefly discussed. But the other side of the coin was the treatment of the native-born lower sectors, which included most of Brazil's non-whites. Euclides' portrait of the response to Canudos was a chilling reminder on that score.

Bringing these two levels of Euclides together, we see a description of the Army's incompetence, which was really a description of the elite's lack of comprehension of the interior; and we see a description of a noble, and, in some sense, justifiable struggle for freedom on the part of non-whites, which was also a description of the racial problem based on an implicit acceptance of the superiority-inferiority arguments.

Why was it received so favorably if it was both an indictment of the elite (the book buyers) and a not very optimistic description of the Brazilian backlanders? In part it may have been its scathing criticism of the Army; many intellectuals resented the military suppression of the 1890's, with its censorship and martial law. But most of the answer probably lies in the fact that Euclides was able to touch the raw nerve of the elite's guilt about the gap between their ideal of nationality and the actual condition of their country, *without* making his readers uncomfortable by questioning all their basic social assumptions.

This is borne out by the favorable reaction of the literary critics to *Os Sertões*. Virtually all the initial reviews discussed the racial question. The critics were as equivocal on the key questions as Euclides. Several agreed that the connection between ethnic and social integration was crucial. None was willing to conclude that Brazil's fate was hopeless. Only one or two were clear-sighted enough to point out the inconsistencies in Euclides' treatment.[77]

Another striking dramatization of the conflicting views of Brazilian reality (which also received an ovation) was *Canaã* (*Ca-*

naan), a novel published by Graça Aranha in the same year (1902) as *Os Sertões*. Brazil's first successful novel of ideas,[78] it was widely read and discussed between its publication and World War I, although later it came to be regarded as a mediocre literary work. Aranha's background made him an excellent example of the European-oriented intellectuals among the elite.[79] He had studied at the Law Faculty in Recife, where he was greatly influenced by Tobias Barreto, the famous proselytizer for German philosophy. Aranha retained his fascination with German culture for the rest of his life. After graduation in 1886, he served as a government attorney and judge with an assignment in the state of Espírito Santo, where he was able to witness first-hand the interaction between German immigrants and native-born Brazilians.

Like most of his generation, Aranha had been an abolitionist and a Republican, greeting the overthrow of the Empire as a cause for celebration. He became a close friend of such leading members of the Rio literary establishment as Machado de Assis, José Veríssimo, and Joaquim Nabuco with whom he collaborated on the *Revista Brasileira*. These connections apparently helped Aranha to be included among the founding members of the Brazilian Academy of Letters, despite the fact that at that time he had published only a short excerpt from his forthcoming novel. His connections also helped him enter the diplomatic service, which allowed him to live in England and western Europe from the turn of the century to World War I. It was while serving in London—as secretary to a diplomatic mission headed by Joaquim Nabuco—that he finished writing *Canaan*.

The novel was set in Espírito Santo—the central southern state where Aranha had earlier spent several months as a local judge. The plot concerned two German immigrants who discussed their reactions to the new land, and then witnessed the drama of a poor unmarried Brazilian girl who went through childbirth unattended. The baby died, and the girl was accused of murder.

The sentimental theme of a wronged maiden may have given

the book appeal for some readers, but the real drama resulted from Aranha's portrayal of the Brazilian dilemma: could a tropical land, luxuriously endowed by nature, become a center of civilization through the fusion of European immigrants and Brazilian mixed bloods? Aranha did not rely upon subtle devices. The dilemma was discussed directly in a dialogue between two immigrants which comprised all of Chapter Two. Milkau (the optimist) argued that Brazil would be redeemed and elevated by the merging of European and Brazilian blood. "Races are civilized by fusion," he argued. "It is in the meeting between the advanced races and the savage virgin races that lies the conservation of civilization, the miracle of its eternal youth." He saw this as a process occurring in Europe itself. "It is thus that Gallia became France, and Germania, Germany."[80] Milkau saw miscegenation as a positive social process that would raise Brazil's cultural and physical capacities. He was expressing the "whitening" ideal, based on the assumption that the superior race could assimilate the inferior ones. He was, in fact, articulating the Brazilian compromise with scientific racist theory.

The other immigrant, Lentz, was the pessimist. "I don't believe that from the fusion with species radically incapable may result a race efficient enough to develop civilization. It will always be an inferior culture, a civilization of mulattoes, eternal slaves always quarreling and fighting." The Negro was a degrading influence because of his "bestiality and innate servility." Progress could only come through the "substitution of Europeans for a hybrid race such as the mulattoes." Lentz saw this in a global context, since "immigration is not a simple question of esthetics" but a "complex question which affects the future of all humankind."[81] Lentz was obviously speaking for doctrinaire racist thought.

The author's sympathies lay with Milkau. Nonetheless, his dialogue gave publicity to the pseudo-scientific theory of mulatto degeneracy, with all its disastrous implications for Brazil's native-born population. Lentz was a portrait of the arrogant German or

Anglo-Saxon who believed that the undeveloped regions of the world could prosper only under a regime of strict European control. The many Brazilians who read this book must have followed the fictional debate with uneasy feelings.

Aranha had dramatized, again, several elements of racist theory in a form easily comprehensible to the elite. His treatment represented the effort of a man in close contact with the most distinguished intellectuals of his day—nearly all of whom praised *Canaan*, both as a literary work and as a thoughtful portrayal of an important social problem. None of the prominent reviewers of the book were adventurous enough to contest the racist views of Lentz, who repeated the theories of both the ethnological-biological and the historical schools. They praised Aranha's "honest" portrayal, ignoring the fact that his analysis was itself equivocal.[82]

The success of *Canaan* adds to our picture of Brazilian elite opinion. Aranha's theme *did* worry them.* Furthermore, his sympathetic presentation of the whitening ideology was accompanied by consideration of the determinist theory that would have relegated Brazil to permanent inferiority. This reflected the parallel strands of racial thinking among the elite. Finally, the elite found it easiest to visualize the native-born Brazilian, especially the mixed blood, in the terms of literary Romanticism, as an uncertain man, lost in the vastness of an overwhelming nature. The equivocal nature of Aranha's portrait was an accurate index of the uncertainty felt by a large group of those who were thinking about the Brazilian of the future.

---

* *Canaan* also appealed to Brazilians because it treated another subject (connected with race) that fascinated Brazil—the reactions of white, which meant European, immigrants. Aranha examines their views about urban versus rural pursuits, the fact that their native language was not Portuguese, and the fact that their religion (in the case of the Germans in the south) sometimes was not Catholic. In fact, the majority of immigrants turned out to be Italian, Portuguese, and Spanish, none of whom presented any major linguistic or religious barrier to assimilation.

Although they were equivocal about Brazil's basic dilemma, neither Euclides da Cunha nor Graça Aranha thought the brave rhetoric of *ufanismo* made any sense. It dissolved when one left the Brazil of Celso's romanticized waterfalls and landscapes and confronted the reality: the uncultivated land and the illiterate, diseased, superstitious, forgotten man of the interior.

Both tried to struggle with racist theory. Euclides went so far as to accept the Indian as a positive contribution, but he thought the African a liability. Aranha seemed to favor the moderate views of Milkau, but he readily included a doctrinaire racist spokesman in his fictional dialogue. The success of both books showed concern over the role of the Brazilian in his land. Could the nation hold together in the face of settlement by non-assimilated superior immigrants and dehumanizing treatment of the native-born Brazilian in the interior?[83]

Rejecting the Frame of Reference: Most of the Brazilian elite could be classified as following the two intellectual positions just described. A few lonely souls, however, were forward-looking and free thinking enough to reject the entire framework of determinism as the means for explaining either Brazil's present condition or as grounds for being pessimistic about the future. Two of these dissenters will be discussed here—Manoel Bomfim and Alberto Tôrres.[84] Both were ahead of their time in rejecting doctrines of inherent differences among races. And both argued that Brazil's escape from her relative backwardness could be achieved only by a careful analysis of the *historical* causes of her current condition.[85]

Bomfim's major work was published in 1903. Tôrres' two major books were published in 1914, but were in fact collections of newspaper and magazine articles published over the preceding years, which reflected Tôrres' analysis of his observations of Brazil *before* he resigned as a Supreme Court Justice in 1909. These two men can be regarded therefore as contemporary with the writers discussed in earlier sections. They were not widely acclaimed in this period, which is evidence that the elite was not ready to break away from the established assumptions. Brazilians of a later era would come to recognize their worth.*

Manoel Bomfim was a physician-essayist, born in the Northeastern state of Sergipe, educated at the Medical Faculty in Bahia, and later active in the newspaper and magazine world of Rio de Janeiro. In 1897 he was called upon to judge a competition of manuscripts for a new school textbook on the history of America. Writing his report on these manuscripts stimulated him to prepare a comprehensive analysis of the causes of Latin American backwardness, which he finished in Paris in 1903.[86]

Bomfim was eager to admit the *relative* backwardness of Latin America, in which he included Brazil. He described Latin American countries as riddled by vices inherited from the colonial era —a get-rich-quick mentality, lack of scientific or empirical tradition, combined with an overly legalistic culture, deep-seated political conservatism, and an absence of social organization.

Once the leaders of Europe, the Spanish and Portuguese had degenerated in the modern era, according to Bomfim, failing to participate in the scientific revolution and becoming mere hangers-on of the industrializing powers. They developed a parasitic character which was transmitted to the lands they colonized in the New World—parasites causing their host to suffer a distorted development of its various natural functions.

In essence, Bomfim's explanation for this pathological condition was based on history and national character. The latter was traced back to the character of the Iberians on the eve of colonization and to the colonization itself, which, unlike the English in North America, was merely "predatory." What he rejected was the then-current European stereotype of Latin America—coun-

---

* Tôrres' reputation, in particular, grew rapidly after 1917, and his influence must be attributed as much to the effect of his personality on a small group of followers as to any of his writings. He gathered around him bright young men such as Oliveira Vianna and Carlos Pontes. They went on to exercise great influence and to attribute their inspiration to Tôrres, which greatly increased his later reputation, somewhat in the manner of Tobias Barreto's disciples.

tries peopled by "a few million lazy, rowdy, barbaric, degenerate mixed-bloods who consider themselves masters of immense and rich territories and have the nerve to call themselves nations."[87]

He tackled all three of the leading schools of racist thought, beginning *ad hominem*. Where did the theory of "inferior races" come from? "That theory is nothing less than a despicable sophism of human egoism, hypocritically masquerading as cheap science, and used in a cowardly manner for the exploitation of the weak by the strong."[88]

He then documented the logical inconsistencies and faulty empirical basis in racist doctrine. As for the biological arguments, he could find no evidence for the alleged inferiority of mixed bloods—a racist corollary of great importance because its validity was necessary in order to prove the *absoluteness* of racial differences. He ridiculed Agassiz' indictment of the Brazilian mixed blood by pointing out that Agassiz' anachronistic view of Brazilian geology had already been refuted by a French geologist who, as a professor in the Catholic Institute of Paris, was "as beyond reproach as the deist Agassiz."* Since Agassiz' theory of mulatto degeneracy had been based on the then-discredited polygenist hypothesis, Bomfim found an easy target:

> There is no reason for us to be impressed with the ideas of the learned reactionary. He travelled through these parts with the set purpose of finding proof that it was the Eternal Father who created, quite separately and at different moments, each of the existing species and that today they are just as they were when they emerged from the workman's hands up in the sky. And he even argued that there is no biological affinity among the races.[89]

The latter point must have struck most Brazilian readers as especially absurd, given the reality of the multi-racial society.

---

* He also cited other scientists (Waitz, Martin de Moussy, and Quatrefages) as authorities for the view that mixed bloods were no less intelligent than the separate races that produced them. Interestingly enough, Bomfim was using the most recent trends in anthropology to refute scientific racism when few European and North American opinion-makers had come around to doing so.

Bomfim was equally contemptuous of the historical school of racist thought. He found the Aryanist version most ridiculous, since much of Western science and culture had come from the "swarthy" (*moreno*) Mediterranean peoples who did not qualify as "blond dolychocephalics."[90] Here again Bomfim cited contemporary scientific authority—the anthropologists Zabrowski and Topinard had recently given papers discrediting the "scientific" definition of Aryan.[91]

Finally, as for the Social Darwinists, Bomfim argued that they were applying biological theory to human selection in an inappropriate way. Compared with the differentiations in the theory of physical evolution, the historical period in which the "stronger" human races were supposed to have predominated was simply too short. Bomfim chose as his special target the contemporary Portuguese historian, Oliveira Martins, who had invoked the "cruel fatality of Nature" to rationalize the liquidation of the seventeenth-century runaway slave community of Palmares, after having earlier praised the high degree of social organization displayed by the fugitives whose complex community had survived for almost a century. If it was a "Negro Troy and its history an Illiad," as Martins himself said, then how could the African have represented such a primitive level of civilization?[92]

In fact, argued Bomfim, all these racist theories were little more than rationalizations by the strong for the status quo. "They unhesitatingly translate this present inequality and the historical conditions of the moment into an expression of the absolute value of races and peoples—the proof of their aptitude or inaptitude for progress. The argumentation—the scientific demonstration—fails to reach even the level of deceit because it is so foolish. Yet it suffices to earn the title of 'The Scientific theory of the value of races,' so that the exploiters, the strongmen of the hour, can take over."[93]

Bomfim's special contribution was to make his anti-racism part of a nationalist, anti-imperialist position. Latin Americans had to reject racism not only because it was scientifically false but more importantly because it was an instrument being used by foreigners to demoralize and disarm them. It was the "sociology of greed," which "should only impress us by the threat it carries and not by its scientific merit."[94] Latin Americans had too often accepted racist theories of their own inadequacy, thereby dismissing their native-born populations as inherently inferior because of Indian and/or African blood, and blindly seeking supposedly superior immigrants from Europe. (Here Bomfim was attacking the population policy of Brazil, which he singled out from other Latin American countries for having neglected the ex-slaves after abolition.)[95] Furthermore, he charged, Latin Americans had uncritically copied foreign institutions, especially in politics. They had assumed that mere transplantation of legal structures would suffice to create the constitutional processes that had taken centuries to develop in Europe and North America. (Brazil was again singled out, this time for its new Republican constitution which Bomfim criticized as a naïve attempt to apply the North American federal system to the chaotic regionalism of Brazil.)

Bomfim's rhetoric had the immediate purpose of awakening Latin Americans to the threat of loss of the minimal nationality they had developed through "progressive absorption of our sovereignty by the United States." The European powers had already acknowledged a *de facto* United States "protectorate" in Latin America, as embodied in the Monroe Doctrine. "All this is extremely dangerous because, at certain moments, great nations cannot resist the temptation to expand and absorb, especially these Anglo-Saxon peoples."[96]

Bomfim's prescription was less novel than his diagnosis. He called for massive increases in education, which had been shamefully neglected by the colonial governments and their successors after Independence. Brazil, in particular, should diversify her economy, tied to monoculture because of the "idiotic" dogma that she should remain "purely agricultural." This policy had been promoted by an alliance of planters and foreign economic interests (especially British) who gained mutual profit from Brazil's "manifest inferiority."[97]

Despite centuries of parasitism, Latin Americans could still overcome their backwardness by "correcting, educating, or eliminating the degenerate parts."[98] Latin America's real inferiority lay in its lack of training and education. "But this is curable, easily curable. . . . If Latin America wants to save itself the inescapable necessity is to concentrate on popular education." As for Brazil, the struggle to overcome the colonial heritage implied no "narrow nationalism," but rather "the eternal conflict of the oppressed and exploited against the dominant exploiter—of the parasitized and the parasites."[99]

Alberto Tôrres, our second example of a critic who rejected the frame of reference, came to his criticism with impeccable credentials. He had been an enthusiastic young Republican in the 1880's, later Minister of Justice (1896–97), Governor of the State of Rio de Janeiro (1898–1900) and finally a member of the Brazilian Supreme Court (1901–9).[100]

Like Bomfim, Tôrres was outspoken on the subject of race. In furnishing evidence he showed an impressive knowledge of anthropological and archeological trends in North America and Europe. Essentially, he endorsed the environmentalist school of thought which was then (the decade before World War I) emerging under the leadership of Franz Boas of Columbia University. Like Bomfim he ridiculed the high priests of Aryanism and noted that the views of the Teutonic scientists coincided neatly with the international ambitions of their own countries. He believed that recent scientific writing (citing Boas and Ratzel specifically) had proved that essential characteristics could be inherited, thus establishing environment as the most important factor in social evolution. Nordic "superiority" was now outdated by the archeological discoveries of the great civilizations in the Mediterranean (by Schliemann et al.) built by "dark" peoples.[101]

Closer to home, Tôrres argued that Brazil was a "living museum" which disproved theories of Aryan superiority, since German and other Saxon types were no better off than any other ethnic group in their struggle to adapt to conditions in Brazil. Despite the diversity of ethnic stock Brazil had produced a "brilliant civilization," and had achieved remarkable cultural unity in the face of enormous size and poor communication. Tôrres repeated the familiar observation that Brazil had never lapsed into the kind of cruel treatment handed out to the Negro in the United States.[102]

Having demonstrated to his satisfaction the falsity of racist theory, Tôrres was appalled that the Brazilian elite continued to believe it. Brazil's supposed ethnic inferiority was too often accepted as an explanation for her problems. The causes were elsewhere—lack of education, poor nutrition, faulty hygiene. In short, a failure to adapt intelligently to the environment.[103] Such adaptation was equally challenging for *any* racial type living in Brazil.*

Tôrres took the trouble to refute racist theories, as Bomfim did, because he thought "Brazil's national problem" (as he entitled one of his books) could only be explained *after* racist doctrine had been liquidated. The nature of Brazil's problem could be seen in her exploitation by foreigners whose greed for profits was leading to the exhaustion of the natural resources at an alarming rate, the increasing domination of the dynamic economic sectors by foreign investors and managers, and the systematic neglect of the native-born population while foreign immigrants were given special privileges.[104]

At first glance Tôrres appears to have embraced an economic

---

* Tôrres was so confident in his refutation of the Aryanists that he occasionally asserted that the best ethnic types were those most indigenous to their area. Thus, the Indian was the "best" stock in Brazil, and the Negro the next best, since the latter came from areas in Africa more like Brazil than the homelands of the Europeans who settled in Brazil. This put the Nordics at the bottom of the ethnic ladder. Tôrres succumbed to one dogma of scientific racism: he concluded that miscegenation was possibly harmful and should therefore be avoided (Tôrres, *Organização nacional*, 196; Tôrres, *Problema nacional*, XIX, 66-75). But his Brazilian popularizers gave this far less emphasis than his general attack on doctrines of racial superiority, and, inconsistent as it must seem, he did not allow his doubts about miscegenation in the future to qualify his vigorous refutation of the belief that Brazil's previous ethnic evolution had produced an "inferior" population.

nationalism that was remarkably aggressive for pre-1914 Brazil. Since the demise of the Jacobins in the mid-1890's, no other writer of Tôrres' elite background and political prominence had expressed such strongly anti-imperialist views. He acknowledged the rapid internationalization of the capitalist financial and trade structure, as well as the growth of a world-wide "proletarian movement." He argued (as did Lenin later) that the relatively high living standards of the workers in advanced countries were made possible by their exploitation of poor countries.[105]

Yet Tôrres seemed to see the foreign exploitation as a symptom rather than a cause of "Brazil's national problem." He remained fixed on what Marxist-Leninist analysis later called the "national bourgeois phase." He strongly denied being a "nativist," the contemporary term for an uncompromising opponent of foreign influence. He even suggested that foreign capital had a role to play if it served the interests of Brazil.[106] The root cause of the national problem, in Tôrres' view, was the alienation of the elite from their own national reality. Inheritors of an impractical, rhetorical educational tradition from Portugal, educated Brazilians had lived off theoretical knowledge and superficial phrases. Tôrres ridiculed Rio intellectuals (most of his intended readers were such) as pallid copies of their colleagues in more advanced countries. Their intellectual immaturity had made them "superstitiously" respectful of foreign ideas, especially from France. They were thus easy prey for the theories of degeneracy peddled by European racists. This intellectual immaturity and alienation, in his view, had a historical explanation; they were symptoms of a lack of national consciousness, the absence of an accepted set of values.[107]

The model of historical development to which Tôrres pointed was Europe. The "old" nations there enjoyed an "instinctive" heritage of traditions and habits. There was a natural, historic identification between the government and the society. Not so in the "new" nations. They were "accidental" nations—settled by colonization and maintained for the profit of the metropolitan power.

They could become genuine nations only by stopping their false "progress" and studying their exact situation.[108] Unless the elite saw that they still inhabited a historical accident, they could never hope to become an authentic nation—perforce different from the European model because of Brazil's climate and basic resources.*

The place to begin, he thought, was the mentality of the elite. By recognizing the historical origins of their plight, Brazilians had to transform their national character and assume new habits of work. The patriot's true task was to take up the cause of those peoples whom historical accident had placed in an "inferior" position.[109]

Once the elite had assumed a new mentality and begun the essential task of political reorganization, they would need to find Brazilian solutions to Brazilian problems. This "sociological nationalism" was a constant theme in Tôrres and became one of his most influential ideas. He constantly attacked his countrymen for attempting to apply blindly techniques and ideas developed in older societies. This criticism had obvious relevance to areas such as agriculture, where Tôrres correctly pointed out that a tropical region presented scientific problems unknown in northern Europe.[110] Man's failures in the tropics could be explained by his failure—so often true of the Europeans in Brazil—to study and adapt to his new environment.**

As his analysis progressed to positive prescriptions it became

---

* Tôrres was careful to explain the faster economic growth of the United States as resulting from a better climate and a higher level of statesmanship. He thought the United States was *also* surrendering its character and resources by a similar weakness for imitating European culture (Tôrres, *Problema nacional*, 28-29, 93, 102-3.). Along with pointed comments about America's brutality toward the Negro, this helped protect Tôrres against the charge of unduly praising the United States.

** At one point he even argued the tropics might be better for settlement than the temperate zone—thereby hoping to turn on its head the widely accepted image of the "insalubrious tropics" (Alberto Tôrres, *A Organização Nacional*, Rio de Janiero, 1914).

less impressive and has not stood the test of time well, at least in economic policy. For Tôrres a uniquely Brazilian approach meant a curiously old-fashioned economic formula. Despite his nationalism he opposed industrialization and even urbanization. He had only contempt for industry and commerce, believing that true wealth in Brazil could come only from the land. This led him, ironically in view of his economic nationalism, to support the theory of the international division of labor. He repeated the familiar view of the laissez-faire liberals (many of whom were beholden, indirectly or directly, to the import-export sector), that protection for native industry would only bring higher prices and lower quality for the consumer. Since Brazil had a comparative *dis*advantage in industry Tôrres thought it should stick to agriculture as its "natural" path.[111] Rural life was, furthermore, "healthier" than city life, which he considered corrupting. Cities he saw as entrepôts for the alienating, enervating influences of Europe—especially France. They were the spoilers of men and the conduits of Brazilian wealth. The migrating populace ought to be *returned* to the countryside, he argued repeatedly. Tôrres was so adamant on the need to preserve a stable rural order that he opposed improved transportation (roads, railroads) because it would facilitate the population flight to the cities and promote the exchange of luxury goods for vital natural resources.[112]

In the political sphere Tôrres' recommendations had greater influence. He outlined a detailed revision of the Republican Constitution, urging greater federal powers, to be exercised especially in economic policy (although not to include protective tarrifs). A National Council of life-time appointees would act as part of the "Coordinating Power," a new fourth branch of government alongside the Executive, Legislative, and Judiciary.[113] The spirit of Tôrres' political reforms was later evident in the steady trend toward increased federal power, especially after 1930. Many of these constitutional reformers cited Tôrres, whose influence grew rapidly after his death in 1917.

In his lifetime Tôrres presided over a group of young intellectuals who gathered regularly to debate his socio-economic critiques and formulae for reform. Among their number were Oliveira Vianna, one of the most influential social and political writers of the 1920's and 1930's, Antonio Tôrres (no relation), a widely read Jacobinist writer of 1920's, and Alcides Gentil and Saboia Lima who both became effective popularizers of Tôrres' thought. In the decade after his death Alberto Tôrres emerged as a beacon for nationalist thinkers, more and more of whom praised his pioneering insights.[114]

Why such influence? As always in the history of social and political thought, it was a matter of timing. Tôrres articulated concerns, posed criticisms, and outlined reforms that were on the minds of many around him. But few had gotten to the point of spelling out their worries. He hammered away on themes that were about to capture the attention of the elite—anti-racism, economic nationalism, constitutional reform, and the need for "Brazilian" solutions, not foreign formulae. His most lasting contribution was his outright attack on racist thought. Tôrres had the courage to reject the deterministic frame of reference. By helping lay to rest the specter of racial inferiority, Tôrres opened the way to new questions about the future of Brazilian nationality.

4 The National Image and the Search for Immigrants

Long before the fall of the Empire, the Brazilian elite were concerned about the need to "sell" Brazil abroad—acting on the classical liberal belief that human progress could best be served by the free flow of men, goods, and ideas within and among nations. The English, who had perfected this doctrine, were the leading exporters of capital and technology to the less developed societies. Brazil, in this liberal universe of mobile factors, was destined to be a recipient. And during the Empire it seemed to Brazilians that they ought to get everything they could. They saw the United States as an unambiguous example of how prodigious growth could be achieved by welcoming foreign investment and large-scale immigration.

Throughout the years between the end of the Empire and 1920, almost all educated Brazilians still assumed that Brazil could, indeed should, welcome immigrants, especially from Europe. In order to attract them, Brazilian politicians and writers were concerned to project an image intended to impress western Europeans and North Americans. An examination of this propaganda offers insight into what the Brazilian elite wanted their nation to *become.*

"SELLING" BRAZIL DURING THE EMPIRE

The policy of promoting Brazil's image abroad was at least as old as the reign of monarch Dom João VI (1808–21), who brought in foreign scientific missions to help launch a number of Brazil's educational, scientific, and artistic institutions.[1] Peter II had also been interested in foreign assistance in these areas, although he was less systematic in his efforts.[2] English engineers had been instrumental in helping to build the railroad system in Brazil, as well as the construction of modern mines and factories in light industry.[3] Liberal intellectuals were directly involved in "selling" Brazil to prospective immigrants. Baron Rio Branco, for example, spent much time in Paris attempting to improve public relations for Brazil.[4] And the Paulistas were particularly active and effective. Although their efforts did not bear significant fruit until after abolition, the Paulista provincial authorities had begun during the Empire to create a well-organized network that would bring immigrants to the coffee fields.[5]

The selling efforts also included appeals for capital and merchants. In the last several decades of the Empire there was a rash of propaganda aimed at France. There were invitations to invest in Brazil, often justified on the grounds that Brazilian culture and civilization was profoundly French, thereby giving the French a special incentive to invest in Brazil's future.[6] Among the Brazilian propagandists who contributed to this campaign were Rio Branco, Baron Santana Nery, and Eduardo Prado. Typical of their efforts was Rio Branco's pride in the fact that he had been able to get more space for the entry on Brazil in *La Grande Encyclopédie* (published in 1889) than the editors allotted to England.[7]

But it was an uphill battle. Brazil's image in Europe and North America was often shaped by famous travelers such as Louis Agassiz and Richard Burton, whose racist assumptions led them to emphasize the large African influence which Brazilian propagandists were trying to downplay. And some European audiences even found it difficult to distinguish among the Latin nations of the New World. Plays produced in Paris in 1863 and 1873, for example, showed a total confusion of Brazilians with Spanish Americans.[8] When Emperor Pedro II visited Paris in 1871, his French hosts searched the city for a copy of the Brazilian national anthem. And they were embarrassed to find not a single one.[9]

A few Brazilian intellectuals were already eyeing the United States as promising territory for propaganda aimed at attracting capital. Afonso Celso wanted to improve the shipping and telegraphic service between Brazil and North America in order to "create by every possible means a rival to the English monopoly." As he explained to the Brazilian consul in New York in 1887, "wouldn't it be an extremely fruitful economic policy for the future to attract American capital to our country, thereby profiting from their surplus?"[10]

But the principal effort continued to be directed at Europe, where potential immigrants could often choose from several options in the 1870's and 1880's. Climate was said to be an important consideration for many. The United States, Argentina and Chile (all of whom also wanted immigrants) were in the temperate zone. Brazil, on the other hand, suffered from the image of a tropical country; and the supposed health hazards of the tropics (discussed below) were much discussed in Europe, at least in the circles that showed interest in Latin America. Brazilians were helped somewhat by the fact that the most economically dynamic part of Brazil *was* in the temperate zone—and indeed it was this area (Southern São Paulo and the states to the South) that attracted the majority of immigrants.[11] But the Brazilian elite felt that they were being beaten to the punch, especially by Argentina and the United States.[12]

A major and frequent forum for propaganda by the Brazilians was the great international expositions that followed the Crystal Palace exhibition of 1851 in London. Brazil managed to send exhibits to all of them, and the resulting publicity was generally favorable. The catalogues and official reports of these international events give interesting evidence of the kind of image Brazil sought to project. The Paris Exposition of 1867 was difficult because Brazil's energies were absorbed by the Paraguayan war. A display was sent nonetheless. The official catalogue lamented Brazil's involvement in a war waged "unjustly and unexpectedly" against her. It went on to note defensively that Brazil's "immense natural resources and productive forces" could hardly be described adequately in the brief time the exhibitors had to prepare. But, they said, "all that Brazil needs in order to become one of the greatest nations of the world is population, and the latter will be attracted simply by making the country known."[13] Brazilians were delighted with their impact on the public in Paris. Their special press briefings had even impressed newspapers which had been anti-Brazil over the Paraguayan war. The Brazilian organizers claimed these same papers now had to admit that Brazil was a "liberal, rich, progress-loving country destined for great prosperity."[14]

For the Vienna Exposition of 1873 the Brazilians updated their 1867 catalogue, making a greater effort to dramatize the fertility of Brazil's soil. Pains were also taken to explain that the climate was "generally very healthy." Potential migrants were invited to consider Brazil's land, "for Nature appears to have fated Brazil to become one of the leading agricultural countries of the world."[15] The introduction to the catalogue for the Philadelphia Exposition of 1876 made this role for Brazil even more explicit: "If the international expositions are not yet able, in the case of Brazil, to contribute to her industrial capacity, it is undeniable that they have given the opportunity to become better known and appreciated as an agricultural region of great fertility and as a peaceful, intelligent and hardworking nation."[16]

The next major international occasion was the Paris Exposition of 1889. It almost took place with no Brazilian section at all. Antônio Prado (a member of the cabinet in 1885–87) had pressed hard for Brazilian participation. But he left office in 1887. By the end of that year the imperial government was so preoccupied with the political crises over abolition and military discipline that no one in the cabinet was willing to spend time worrying about Brazilian participation in a foreign fair. In January 1888 the government announced that Brazil would not take part. But the story was not quite over. A new cabinet was formed in May 1888, and Antônio Prado returned as Minister of Agriculture. He succeeded in reversing the decision. The appropriation bill to finance Brazil's effort was introduced into Parliament by Afonso Celso, was strongly supported by Joaquim Nabuco, and passed.[17] (This collaboration of Celso, Nabuco, and Prado typified the range of opinion supporting the "selling" of Brazil during the Empire.) The introduction to a companion volume for the Exposition explained their presence thus:

> Brazil has not come to Paris to seek the empty satisfaction of honorific prizes, but rather to strengthen the ties that bind her to Europe, to open new outlets for her primary products, and especially to encourage all who might be prepared to choose Brazil for their new homeland or to bring their labor or send their capital to multiply there.[18]

PROMOTING THE BRAZILIAN IMAGE, 1890–1914

Efforts to promote Brazil continued after the fall of the Empire. Despite the fact that very few immigrants came from France, much propaganda continued to be aimed at the French-speaking public. Perhaps it was simply a reflection of the elite's strong preference for French culture. One writer published a book in Paris in 1891 (in French) describing Brazil's great need for engineers, machinists, and merchants. He frankly admitted that "although very large, my country has never been able to gain the serious attention of old Europe." Until recently, his "French friends" knew little more than that "in our country there were Negroes and monkeys along with half-a-dozen whites of dubious color." The climate and incidence of disease were other stumbling blocks. He tried to dismiss yellow fever: "How much nonsense had been said and written about it! Certainly people die . . . sometimes. But do you know a country where people live forever . . . ?"[19]

The fact of the matter was that yellow fever was still a deadly killer—not eliminated in Rio de Janeiro until the sanitary campaign of Oswaldo Cruz in the first years of the twentieth century, and not brought under control in the North and Northeast until the following decade (although jungle yellow fever is ineradicable and has continued down to the present day).

Domingos Jaguaribe, another propagandist of the early Republic, also railed against Europeans for indicting the climate "without knowing the least thing about it." Even granting the incidence of yellow fever, which was "on the verge of being forever banished from the country," the mortality rate in Rio de Janeiro was lower than that of Brussels, "considered to be the healthiest city in Europe." (Jaguaribe gave no source for his statistics.) He praised the behavior of the ex-slaves, who had demonstrated "admirable moral conduct everywhere in Brazil." Then he continued: "Fortunately there is no race prejudice in Brazil and one sees colored men marrying white women and vice versa, with the result that the black population is declining extraordinarily. Within fifty years it will have become very rare in Brazil."[20]

Voices of greater scientific authority joined the campaign to refute the "slander" against Brazil's tropical climate. In 1907 Afrânio Peixoto, a prominent public health specialist, published a pamphlet which was his chapter for the Brazilian Yearbook of 1908. It was an attack on "certain facile European minds" who had propagated the "myth" of tropical disease. Health problems were no different in tropical areas than in temperate areas, he argued, since the important thing in all cases was proper hygiene. Brazil, he maintained, had no indigenous diseases—all had been imported. Malaria had been wiped out (the danger of contracting it was greater in Italy!), and other epidemic diseases were on their way to being conquered. Peixoto reproduced a mortality table for major world cities showing São Paulo and Rio de Janeiro to have lower death rates than Madrid, Lisbon, and Rome. Bahia and Curitiba, smaller Brazilian cities, actually had lower mortality rates, according to this table, than Boston and New York. "In sum, Brazil has a pathology equal to that of Europe, with some advantages in particular cases." Because the Brazilian climate "has absolutely no importance for questions of health," men in Brazil can be assured of a "prosperous and happy development."[21]

The Brazilian press between 1889 and 1914 showed a constant concern with the country's image abroad. Gil Vidal (the pen name of Leão Veloso), regular columnist for the *Correio de Manhã* (Rio), wrote repeatedly on the need for more effective propaganda in Europe. In late 1904 he compared Brazil's efforts to those of Argentina and the United States in Italy, and urged a better planned campaign.[22] In 1908 the Japanese began arriving in small numbers, since under the new immigration decree of 1907 they no longer required special Congressional approval.[23] Said Vidal: "We are not very sympathetic to yellow immigration. We prefer that the white races come to settle in our country." In 1911 he praised the attempt of the Agriculture Minister to attract European immigrants to northern Brazil as well as the south.[24]

Similar sentiments could be heard from minor publicists. In a pamphlet published in 1914, Caio de Menezes called for Brazil to welcome the German immigrant

> as an ethnic coefficient of the highest quality [because] the Brazilian people, more than any other, needs the influence of advanced peoples in building a race, especially at the historic moment when the percentage represented by the African race is beginning to decline and must disappear into the whirlpool of the white race. . . . The ethnic preponderance of the foreigner can only bring marvelous results for the formation of our race.[25]

As was common among the elite, Menezes felt quite free to reject North American racial practice. Indeed, it was Brazil's *lack* of prejudice that made possible her ethnic salvation. As Menezes explained, "we enjoy an advantage over the United States—the good fortune to have discarded color prejudice with the result that the Negro himself tends to dissolve in the inexorable whirlpool of the white race"[26]—fed by the intimacy of Brazilian race relations. *

Like every other country courting the capitalist investors, Brazil had to reassure their benefactors on what was then known as the "social question." As the Brazilian catalogue for the Louisiana Purchase Exposition of 1904 put it, there is "no need of labor organizations and there are practically no labor disturbances or disputes . . . [and] the working classes are as a rule well-housed." (A claim belied by the favelas already spreading in Rio.)[27]

Even a nationalist such as Serzedello Correa backed the campaign to attract European immigrants. After a trip to Europe in 1907, he complained bitterly that Brazil's propaganda there was ineffectual compared to the efforts of Canada or Mexico (although Mexico attracted very few European immigrants).[28] Typical of the faith in immigration was the view of Arthur Orlando, a minor product of the Recife School, who argued that "the commercial expansion and industrial growth in the world" could be "largely" attributed to international migration.[29]

In an effort to increase foreign assistance and to become "modern" themselves, Brazilian governments undertook ambitious public works projects. The rebuilding of Rio was a visible exercise in the drive to Europeanize. As João de Barro (a regular contributor to the elegant monthly *Renascença*) explained in 1904, foreigners disembarking in Rio "take away from their brief visit to our neglected city an unhappy impression of the entire country" —unfortunate, he continued, because "this is a vital question for us, in a country that above all needs help from abroad—foreign blood, foreign brawn, and foreign capital."[30]

---

* The whitening theory, as we saw above, allowed its believers to entertain seemingly contradictory ideas—to condemn American treatment of the Negro (segregation and suppression) while at the same time justifying the submergence of the Brazilian non-white.

At the turn of the century Rio was still the crowded city which had grown up during the Empire—"dirty, backward and fetid." The rich fled to the mountain resort of Petropolis from this "miserable town without luxury hotels, sufficient carriages and especially any kind of comfort or *chic*." The same chronicler went on to say that "the city belonged to the illiterate commanders [minor honorific title given by the Portuguese government]. . . . There was no place where an aristocrat could enjoy himself. So he fled the city or retreated into isolation."[31]

In the decade after 1900, Rio de Janeiro not only replanned its streets and laid out a new set of principal buildings (the Biblioteca Nacional, the Palácio Monroe, the Teatro Municipal), it also eradicated yellow fever. For his achievement as the architect of the unpopular campaign to establish sanitary conditions in Rio, Oswaldo Cruz quickly became a hero. Afrânio Peixoto, a leading member of the literary establishment in the late belle époque, delivered the address welcoming Cruz into the Brazilian Academy of Letters in 1913, praising the scientist's work in carrying out President Rodrigues Alves' promises to "clean up the capital city which had taught corruption to Brazilians, while at the same time making the foreigner suspicious of all Brazil." "Before we can lay claim to a place in the world, we must prepare for such a role, exhibiting the decency and confidence of the civilized. Any sacrifice is small in pursuit of such an inspiration."[32]

Confidence in the success of this effort was evident in the National Exposition of 1908, organized to celebrate the centenary of the opening of Brazilian ports a hundred years earlier when the Portuguese Court had arrived in 1808. The exhibits in 1908 emphasized the rapid material progress of Brazil in recent decades—the growth of transportation (railways) and communications (telegraph), the improvement in public services (urban schools; public health programs, such as those that led to the pasteurization of milk and the elimination of yellow fever—although the minor residual problem of jungle yellow fever has never been eliminated). The *Boletim Comemorativo* for the Exposition of 1908 reflected the confident tone—it was printed in three languages (Portuguese, French, and Esperanto). The exhibits, according to the *Boletim*, were to present "in a magnificent panorama the image of Brazilian progress which in a century of accelerated activity has followed the path necessary to achieve the level of culture that earlier peoples took millions of years to attain." The entire purpose of the organizers was "to stimulate progress in Brazil and to raise her reputation in the civilized world."[33]

João do Rio thought the Exposition a marvelous opportunity for the European-centered elite of Rio to discover their own country. "At heart we have the idea that we are phenomenally inferior, because we're not like the others and are completely ignorant of ourselves." The snobs of the capital will be amazed "at the gold, precious stones, wood, and cloth."[34] In a burst of enthusiasm, he even predicted that this "extraordinary apotheosis" would transform the old attitude that it was "chic to pose as unBrazilian," and the feeling that patriotism was "some kind of intermittent attack of Jacobinism." Anyone who remained "impassive" after viewing the Exposition must lack "the simple ability to reflect on what he sees."[35] In fact there is no evidence that the 1908 Exposition affected the cultural alienation of the elite.

The most famous "salesman" of Brazil in this era was Baron Rio Branco, Foreign Minister from 1902 until 1912. Rio Branco worked mightily to present a "civilized" image of Brazil by employing writers in diplomatic posts—especially in Europe—and by inducing distinguished European public figures to visit Brazil.[36] He had promoted Brazil's image abroad long before he became a government Minister. During the Empire he had helped write and edit publications such as the Brazilian catalogue at the Paris Exposition of 1889. Now he was able to use the full resources of the Foreign Office for a sophisticated propaganda campaign. Above all, he wanted to present Brazil as a cultured country. One way to do this (and he did) was to fill the ranks of his diplomatic service with white men whom foreigners would consider civilized and sophisticated—to reinforce the image of a Europeanized country growing whiter and whiter.

This could be seen in his choice of intellectuals for diplomatic assignments. There had been writers in Brazil's diplomatic service since the beginning of the Empire. Given such a small elite, it was natural that men who held diplomatic posts should also have been among the small number of literary figures. Rio Branco, however, was conspicuous for his selection of handsome, imposing (which effectively meant white) men.[37] One intellectual worthy of special mention as an effective propagandist for Brazil abroad was Oliveira Lima. His credentials as a member of the Brazilian intelligentsia were impressive. He was a founding member of the Brazilian Academy of Letters, and produced a series of distinguished works on Brazilian history, including the definitive study of the first Portuguese monarch to rule in Brazil, Dom João VI. He wrote interesting and well-informed volumes about his diplomatic service in Japan, the United States, and Spanish America. He lectured on Brazilian history at major universities in the United States, France, and England.[38]

Another prominent intellectual sent abroad by Rio Branco was the noted jurist-politician Rui Barbosa, who headed the Brazilian delegation to the Second International Peace Conference held at the Hague in 1907. Although the conference ended in a deadlock over the structure and membership of a proposed International Court of Justice, Rui was named *President d'honneur* of the first commission, a distinction gained by no other Latin American delegate. Rui also became the champion of the smaller nations by arguing for complete equality in national representation on the court. His allegedly multi-lingual eloquence, as reported to the Brazilians in their press coverage, thrilled the Brazilian elite who believed their erudite orator had bedazzled world diplomatic circles; they gave Rui a tumultuous welcome when he arrived home from Europe.[39]

Other writers used by Rio Branco were Graça Aranha, Joaquim Nabuco, Rodrigo Octávio, Domício de Gama, and Aluísio Azevedo. Euclides da Cunha, however—a small, physically unimpressive, man—had to implore the Foreign Minister to give him employment in the Foreign Office, and Rio Branco never sent him abroad. He received a domestic assignment: surveying the Purús River in the Amazon Valley. It was not Euclides' first choice of a diplomatic assignment, but it enabled him to discover yet another region of Brazil. Like his journalistic assignment to Canudos, it widened Euclides' knowledge and stimulated him to produce a new analysis of Brazil's failure to integrate her national territory.[40]

Rio Branco's image-building efforts were not limited to Europe, where attention had centered during the Empire. Indeed, balancing European influence with American influence was the basis of his foreign policy. His cultivation of America reached a high point in 1906 when Brazil played host in Rio to the Pan-American Conference. The Conference fitted admirably the drive to "civilize" Rio. In order to house the gathering, a palace was built—an exact replica of the Brazilian pavillion at the Louisiana Purchase Exposition in St. Louis. The new edifice was called "Monroe Palace," possibly indicating the relative absence of nationalist sentiment.[41]

The press gave lavish coverage to the deliberations of the delegates, of which United States Secretary of State Root was one. His presence marked the first time *any* American Secretary of State had attended a diplomatic conference *in* Latin America. Rio de Janeiro had been chosen as the locale for such an "honor" in Latin America because of the strong political and economic alliance with the United States which Rio Branco had successfully promoted.* For enthusiastic Brazilian commentators the choice

---

* The Brazilian ambassador in Washington, Joaquim Nabuco, was an effective agent of Rio Branco's policy to cultivate relations with the United States. A famous abolitionist who had fled politics after abolition, he played an ironical role. The supreme example of the Europeanized Brazilian who revered France "to which we owe our culture, our tastes, our intellectual life," and England as his political model, he faithfully performed the function of a propagandist for Brazilian-American harmony (*Dinner at the Brazilian Embassy at Washington, D.C. on the 18th of May, 1907, in Honor of Rear Admiral Huet de Bacellar and the Captains of the Brazilian Ships on a Visit to the Jamestown Exposition* [pamphlet]), 3.

proved that Rio was "incontestably the center of greatest culture, and atmosphere most appropriate" for such an occasion.[42]

Despite this emphasis on a closer diplomatic link with the United States, however, Rio Branco's cultural preoccupations remained essentially European. The visiting celebrities sponsored by the Foreign Office were Frenchmen such as Clemenceau, Italians such as Ferrero, and Englishmen such as Lord Bryce.[43] It was only after Rio Branco's death in 1912 that the list of lecturers regularly began to include Americans.[44]

Notwithstanding all these activities, Brazilian governments had proved less energetic and effective than their Argentine rivals in promoting their country's image abroad between 1890 and 1914. The public relations effort and immigration promotion by Argentina was vastly superior in the 1890's, as Brazilian critics bitterly noted.[45] It was in the search for immigrants that competition was most obvious.

IMMIGRATION POLICY, 1887–1914

By the late 1880's, the whitening ideal had combined with political and economic liberalism to produce a more sharply defined national self-image. It can be seen clearly in the official attitudes toward immigration and in the propaganda aimed at foreigners by official agencies, as well as by the intellectuals who reflected elite thinking in Brazil.[46]

The popularity of the whitening ideal was no accident. As we saw above, it made possible an ingenious compromise between racist theory and the facts of Brazilian social life. During the late Empire liberal reformers had preached their formulae while sometimes entertaining doubt about the practicality of their doctrine in a tropical, multi-racial setting. Joaquim Nabuco went so far as to express open doubt about Brazil's viability after abolition. The process of whitening, however, seemed to offer reassurance, at least on the racial front. A whiter country would be a land fit for liberalism, and the laissez-faire element in liberal ideology in turn furnished a rationale for the neglect of the masses, which included most of the non-whites.

Even before the new Republican Constitution for the federal government had been approved the Provisional Government issued a decree which revealed the whitening ideal at work in the search for immigrants. The decree, dated June 28, 1890, stated that the country was open to "free entry by persons healthy and able to work," and not subject to any criminal prosecution in their own country. To this liberal provision was added the clause, "except natives of Asia or Africa, who can be admitted only by authorization of the National Congress and in accordance with the stipulated conditions." And the succeeding article underlined its gravity: "The diplomatic and consular agents of the United States of Brazil will prevent by all means at their disposal the dispatch of immigrants from those continents, immediately communicating with the federal government by telegraph when they are not able to do so." Another article provided that "The police of the ports of the Republic will prevent the disembarkation of such individuals, as well as beggars and indigents." A later article provided that any landowner "who wishes to settle European immigrants on his property" could enjoy all the special incentives granted in the law, further proof of the racial references felt by the new government.[47] In fact, there was little likelihood that Asians or Africans would try to emigrate to Brazil. One student of immigration history has noted that the decree "never had any practical application," by which he may have meant it was never tested.[48] In any case, it stood as a law of the land, countersigned by the President and his Minister of Agriculture, Francisco Glicério, who was, ironically enough, a mulatto.*

---

* In 1907 a new decree was issued, setting regulations on immigration and agricultural colonization. Elaborate provisions were made for barring "criminals, hoodlums, beggars, vagabonds, the insane, and the invalids," but there was no mention of continent of origin. Apparently the implicit racial bar had been quietly dropped, perhaps because there seemed little danger of attempted entry by Asians or Africans (Decreto N. 6455 of April 19, 1907).

The Republicans strongly believed in the need to attract immigrants to Brazil. It was part of their commitment to economic development through the use of imported European labor. This commitment came naturally to a movement that was the strongest in São Paulo, the province where economic growth—via coffee —demanded an expanding supply of workers. In the late Empire the coffee planters knew that slavery was doomed and that in its remaining years as a legal institution it could not satisfy the need for plantation labor in the coffee fields (even if the Law of Free Birth was evaded—as often happened in practice). Being practical men who foresaw the great profits still to be made in Brazil's coffee exports, they wanted immigrants primarily as a labor force, whose ethnic contribution to Brazil's population would be a welcome by-product.

Instead of seeking free migrant labor from other regions of the country (especially the economically declining Northeast), the coffee planters tried to replace their slaves after 1870 with European immigrants. The only functions they saw for the native-born Brazilians were hard labor such as the clearing of virgin forest land. For the highly organized labor of cultivating and harvesting coffee the planters saw immigrants as abler and more reliable.[49]

In 1886 a group of leading planters in São Paulo joined to found the Society for the Promotion of Immigration (Sociedade Promotora da Imigração), a well-staffed private organization designed to recruit European immigrants (almost exclusively in Italy), pay their passage to São Paulo, and arrange their work contracts on plantations. The Society, although non-governmental, received heavy subsidy from the treasury of the Province of São Paulo. In effect, the provincial government was using public funds to finance the recruitment of immigrant labor by a consortium of wealthy planters.[50] Their leader was Martinho Prado Junior, who explained in a report in 1887 that the Society had avoided spending money for agents or extensive propaganda in Europe. Instead, they relied upon direct contacts from prospective immigrants who had relatives or friends already living in São Paulo. Prado was supremely confident that discontent in the Old World would solve Brazil's labor problem: "The great European armies and the heavy taxes necessary to maintain them will succeed in a few years in populating South America."[51]

In 1889 the Society's functions began to be taken over by the government of the state of São Paulo (the former provinces were redesignated as states under the Republic). The state gradually resumed responsibility for the massive program of subsidized immigration (again primarily Italian), using its public funds to pay for ship passages to São Paulo, the construction and maintenance of a huge reception center located in the capital, and the administrative costs of placing immigrants in jobs. By 1895 the transition to official state sponsorship was complete, and the Society was dissolved. The program received a set-back in 1902, when because of complaints of mistreatment from disgruntled Italians, the Italian Foreign Ministry prohibited further subsidized emigration to Brazil (meaning São Paulo). But the flow of subsidized immigrants from other countries, along with non-subsidized Italians* and other nationalities, led to a recovery of the flow by 1904, which continued with ups and downs until diminished by World War I. It increased after the war, with the program of subsidy by the São Paulo government continuing until 1928, by which time domestic migrants from other Brazilian states were beginning to meet São Paulo's labor needs.[52]

Thus government-subsidized immigration was aimed at recruiting labor for commercial agriculture, especially in the state of São Paulo. During the Empire there had been repeated efforts to bring immigrants to settle in government-sponsored colonies, where it was hoped they would become self-sufficient farmers on the model of European yeomen, but most of the colonization schemes failed. The cause was also taken up in the late

* Some Italians managed to circumvent the prohibition by collecting a refund on their fare after *arrival* in São Paulo.

TABLE 4-1
FOREIGN-BORN POPULATION, 1870–1920 (in thousands)

YEAR	ARGENTINA			BRAZIL			CANADA			UNITED STATES		
	Total Pop.	Foreign Born Popu-lation	(2) as % of (1)	Total Pop.	Foreign Born Popu-lation	(2) as % of (1)	Total Pop.	Foreign Born Popu-lation	(2) as % of (1)	Total Pop.	Foreign Born Popu-lation	(2) as % of (1)
1870[1]	1,737	210	12.1%	10,112	338	3.8%	3,689	594	16.1%	39,905	5,567	14.0%
1890[2]	3,955	1,005	25.4%	14,334	750	5.2%	4,833	643	13.3%	63,056	9,250	14.7%
1903[3]	–	–	–	17,319	1,070	6.2%	5,371	700	13.0%	76,094	10,341	13.6%
1914	7,885	2,358	29.9%	–	–	–	–	–	–	–	–	–
1920[4]	8,314	1,930	23.2%	30,636	1,566	5.1%	8,788	1,956	22.3%	106,466	13,921	13.1%

NOTES: 1. Argentina (1869); Canada (1871); Brazil (1872)
2. Argentina (1895); Canada (1891)
3. Canada (1901)
4. Canada (1921)

Sources: Argentina: *Tercer censo nacional*, I, 205-6; *Cuarto censo general de la nación*, I, XXVIII, LXII. Although the fourth census of 1947 revised the total population estimate of the previous census, it only provided a gross figure and did not indicate what constituted that gross figure. To preserve consistency between the total population figure and the foreign born population the uncorrected census figures are presented. The following adjustments were made by the fourth census: (1) For the first census of 1869 the population estimate was revised from 1,737,076 to 1,905,973; (2) For the second census of 1895 from 3,954,911 to 4,044,911; and (3) For the third census of 1914 from 7,885,237 to 8,042,244. The estimate given for 1920 is taken from the following source: República Argentina, *La Población y el Movimiento Demográfico de la República Argentina en el Período, 1910-1925* (Buenos Aires, 1926), 12. The population estimate provided by various official documents occasionally differ from one another, but the difference is not significant enough to alter the general trend indicated by the table.

Brazil: *Anuário Estatístico do Brasil*, I (1908-12), 242; *Anuário Estatístico do Brasil*, V (1939/1940), 1302.

Canada: *Historical Statistics of Canada* (Toronto, 1965), 14, 20.

United States: U.S. Bureau of the Census, *Historical Statistics of the United States Colonial Times to 1957* (Washington, D.C., 1960), 7, 66.

Empire by the Central Immigration Society (Sociedade Central de Imigração), which had the sponsorship of Emperor Pedro II. Its leaders were writers and intellectuals in Rio de Janeiro, but they lacked funds and wielded little influence against the powerful Paulista planters who wanted obedient plantation workers, not independent yeomen-farmers.[53] All the pro-immigrationists were agreed on one thing—the absolute necessity of recruiting European agricultural labor. And both groups thought Europeans superior to native-born Brazilians.[54]

As Brazilians realized, they were competing directly with other New World countries for European immigrants.* The United States had already become a favorite destination for millions, whose example constantly led Latin American visionaries to hope that they might somehow duplicate that achievement—all the more since many observers attributed America's phenomenal economic growth, as we observed earlier, to her steady influx of immigrant labor.[55] As can be seen from Table 4–1, a relatively small percentage of Brazil's population was foreign-born (therefore attributable to net immigration) during the years between 1879 and 1920, especially if viewed in comparison to Argentina, or even Canada and the United States. In part this reflected the absolute level of Brazil's population, which was much larger than Argentina (six times larger in 1870, declining to three and a half times larger by 1920). But even the totals of reported immigration show Brazil to have attracted only a little more than half of Argentina's total for the period 1871–1920 (see Table 4–2).**

Taking as an index the increase in foreign-born, rather than

---

* Argentina proved to be the most successful Latin American bidder. They courted immigrants, at least partly, by projecting the image of a white Republic, which they had become by the 1880's. The United States attracted immigrants primarily to the North, where the non-white population was still minimal.

** The obvious discrepancies between the reported immigration and the foreign-born totals in Argentina apparently reflect, in part, the failure of official data to record *net* immigration, especially important in the case of Argentina where many immigrants did not take up permanent residence.

TABLE 4-2

NATIONAL SHARES OF TOTAL REPORTED
IMMIGRATION FOR FOUR COUNTRIES, 1871–1920

	Total Reported Immigration (000's)	ARGENTINA		BRAZIL		CANADA		UNITED STATES	
		(000's)	% of Four Country Total	(000's)	% of Four Country Total	(000's)	% of Four Country Total	(000's)	% of Four Country Total
1871–1880	3,799	451	11.9%	193	5.1%	343	9.0%	2,812	74.0%
1881–1890	7,736	1,090	14.1%	513	6.6%	886	11.5%	5,247	67.8%
1891–1900	6,104	933	15.3%	1,144	18.7%	339	5.6%	3,688	60.4%
1901–1910	13,130	2,103	16.0%	689	5.2%	1,543	11.8%	8,795	67.0%
1911–1920	9,819	1,553	15.8%	818	8.3%	1,712	17.4%	5,736	58.4%
Totals 1871–1920	40,588	6,130	15.1%	3,357	8.3%	4,823	11.9%	26,278	64.7%

NOTE: Reported immigration figures are in all cases gross; comparable net figures (after subtraction of immigrants who do not take up permanent residence) are not available for much of this period.

Sources: Argentina: Vicente Vazquez-Presedo, *Estadísticas Históricas Argentinas, Primera Parte, 1875-1914* (Buenos Aires, 1971), 15-16; República Argentina *La Población y el Movimiento Demográfico de la República Argentina en el Período, 1910-1925* (Buenos Aires, 1926), 82; República Argentina, *Tercer censo nacional,* X, 399.

Brazil: *Revista de Imigração e Colonização,* I, No. 4 (Oct. 1940), 617-22; *Revista de Imigração e Colonização,* I, No. 2 (Apr. 1940), 227-28.

Canada: *Historical Statistics of Canada* (Toronto, 1965), 23. United States: U.S. Bureau of the Census, *Historical Statistics of the United States, Colonial Times to 1957* (Washington, D.C., 1960), 56-57.

TABLE 4–3

INCREASE IN FOREIGN-BORN AS PERCENTAGE
OF TOTAL POPULATION INCREASE, 1870–1900

	Total Pop. Increase (000's)	Reported Immigra- tion (000's)	Foreign- Born Increase (000's)	Foreign- Born Increase as share of total Pop. Increase (%)
Argentina (1869–1895)	2,218	1,912*	795	36.0%
Brazil (1872–1900)	7,207	1,844	732	10.2%
Canada (1871–1901)	1,682	1,624	106	6.3%
United States (1870–1900)	36,189	12,569	4,774	13.2%

* Does not include 1869 and 1870.

Sources: Same as Table 4–2.

reported immigration, Brazil's inferiority to Argentina was less great, at least for the last two decades of the nineteenth century (see Table 4–3).* Although data for exactly comparable periods are not available, Brazil's increase in foreign-born population (732,000) in 1872–1900 was only 8 per cent less than Argentina's increase (795,000) for the years 1869–95. But this absolute number again represented a much smaller share of the total population increase for these periods—only 10.2 per cent in Brazil, while it was 36.0 per cent in Argentina.

Although comparison with Argentina was not encouraging, Brazil's inflow did increase significantly in the late Empire. In 1887 almost 56,000 immigrants arrived in Brazil. The annual

* Unfortunately the official statistics do not explain whether immigration figures and census figures were gathered on different criteria.

figure fell below 50,000 only three times before 1914, by which time 2,700,000 had entered the country. More than half went to the state of São Paulo where coffee continued its expansion westward and southward. The largest national group among the newcomers was the Italians. Next were the Portuguese and Spanish, followed by the Germans, a distant fourth. Paradoxically, the immigrants thus reinforced the "Latin" character of Brazil's white population, despite the hope of many boosters of immigration that northern Europeans could be attracted in large numbers.

5 The New Nationalism

This chapter is concerned with the second decade of the twentieth century—the third decade of the Brazilian Republic and the era which encompassed World War I. Certain common themes in Brazilian social thought during this period had great influence on the debate over race.

First, the political facts led critics to find increasing signs that Brazil was in trouble. Critics pointed, as they had since the founding of the Republic, to political and financial chaos. They lamented the crises in the export market and Brazil's failure to occupy all its territory effectively. Brazil was still lagging behind other countries. Since the turn of the century, Argentina had been attracting many more immigrants than Brazil, and its per capita income had grown much higher—or so most observers believed.[1] The United States had achieved the status of a major industrial power. But the alarm of the critics had a new ring because no one could any longer attribute Brazil's relative lag to its new political system. The Republic was now twenty years old.

The warnings about the predatory ambitions of foreign powers in the American hemisphere, such as had been made by Eduardo Prado and Raul Pompéia in the 1890's and Sílvio Romero in 1906 (in his speech welcoming Euclides da Cunha into the Brazilian Academy of Letters), now became commonplace.[2] Brazil was pictured as vulnerable to the inevitable North American need to find overseas markets for her surplus production and capital—waiting, passive, at a historic crossroads.

This feeling grew more pervasive as the European war continued and Brazilians were forced to think of their country in relation to that war. The influence of the ideas of Manoel Bomfim and Alberto Tôrres—isolated figures in the previous era—became more widely evident. The need for a realistic assessment of Brazil grew in people's minds. The gap between Brazilian reality and the models previous thinkers had so often mistook for it became more widely appreciated. The tone became empirical; suspicion of formulae grew.

This in turn produced a stimulus to nationalist thought. Writers became sensitive to the claim they should study Brazil's situation in its own right. They began to assume more explicitly that Brazil was a country worth protecting and developing; and thought of mobilization as a way of forwarding this development. They began, for the first time on a large scale, to feel that they could change the role in which Social Darwinism and an inherited European culture were casting Brazil. The corollary of this was obvious—and helped along by their reaction to the war in Europe: the Brazilian nation had an identity and a destiny that should and could be controlled by Brazilians. For the first time the mainstream of Brazilian thought learned how to rebel against the framework within which European ideas had straitjacketed it—most important, to reject the determinism of racist thought.

EVENTS BETWEEN 1910 AND 1920

An effective political machine (the "politics of the governors") had produced a relatively calm decade in the Republic's political history after Prudente de Morais was elected President in 1898. But the situation changed in 1909, with a growing quarrel over who would succeed to the presidency in the 1910 election. The machine's first candidate was acceptable to party regulars and new reformers (especially the bright young politicians contemptuously labeled the "Kindergarten" by their opponents among the elder statesmen of national machine), alike—João Pinheiro, an able and idealistic Mineiro politician. His sudden death in 1908 left everyone stunned and reopened the nomination.[3] A long and unedifying struggle ensued—with Rui Barbosa, the famous Constitution writer and parliamentary orator, entering the battle, first competing for the official candidacy, then running as an opposition candidate.[4] When the machine delivered the expected majority for the official candidate, General Hermes da Fonseca, Rui published his own "exposé" of the election talleys, allegedly proving he had lost votes at the hands of dishonest local bosses working in cooperation with the federal regime.[5]

General Hermes was sworn into office on November 22, 1910, and days later a naval mutiny erupted in the Bay of Guanabara.[6] The following year there was another on the Ilha das Cobras. Unfortunately for Baron Rio Branco, the foreign minister who labored day and night to give the "civilized world" a favorable impression of Brazil, Lord Bryce was visiting Rio de Janeiro at the time of the Guanabara mutiny. The incident earned several graphic pages in the book Bryce wrote about his travels in South America. Summing up his impressions of Brazil, Bryce noted "not even the great North American republic has a territory at once so large and so productive." But "what will be its future? Is the people worthy of such an inheritance? The white part of the Brazilian nation—and it is only that part that need be considered—seems altogether too small for the tasks which the possession of this country imposes." At least the English visitor ended on an ambiguous note: "In the long run doubtless the lands, like the tools, will go to those who can use them. But it may be well to wait and see what new conditions another century brings about for the world: and the Latin American peoples may within that time grow into something different from what they now appear to the critical eyes of Europe and North America." It could have been Buckle. Had the last twenty years amounted to nothing?[7]

The most serious political problem during Hermes da Fonseca's presidency was the series of coups against the incumbent political machines in the lesser states. Rio de Janeiro, Bahia, Ceará, Pernambuco, Pará, and Mato Grosso all suffered violent changes of leadership. In each case, the "outs" deposed the incumbent machine with the help of federal forces. In several states, such as Ceará, the federal army intervened directly and seated the rebel faction in the governorship and the state legislature. These government interventions were called "salvations," sometimes carried out for the direct benefit of members of President Hermes da Fonseca's family.

The Brazilians were too absorbed in their own quarrels to give European politics much attention. As the presidency of Hermes da Fonseca drew to a close, the political bosses of the major states managed to agree on Wenceslau Braz, a respectable if lackluster official candidate, for the presidential election held in March 1914. On November 15, the twenty-fifth anniversary of the coup that ushered in the Republic, Wenceslau moved into the presidential quarters at Catete Palace. Meanwhile, Europe had stumbled into war.

The four years of the European conflict, which happened to coincide with Wenceslau's term, saw relative stability in Brazil's internal politics. Most notable was the success in resolving the many simmering power struggles within the states. In Mato Grosso and Rio de Janeiro (state) the President managed to pick a winning faction and make his decision stick. He also resolved a border conflict between Paraná and Santa Catarina. All these successes helped Braz to reassert the power of the presidency against Pinheiro Machado, the Senator from Rio Grande do Sul who had become a political king-maker in national politics.*

But the war in Europe came to dominate the elite's attention during Wenceslau Braz' term of office. The pro-Allied faction was

---

* Pinheiro Machado was defeated on several key issues even before he died in 1915 at the hands of a deranged assassin.

greatly strengthened when German U-boats began sinking Brazilian ships in 1917 and helped force Brazil into declaring war against the Central Powers in October 1917. In the presidential election of 1918, the voters once again turned to Rodrigues Alves, the able Paulista administrator who had already served a term as President from 1902 to 1906. At least on the surface, the political system seemed that it might have become viable again.

BRAZIL AND THE OUTBREAK OF THE EUROPEAN WAR

World War I had a delayed effect on Brazilian intellectuals; insofar as they considered it at all, they approached the issue in the terms Europeans offered them.[8] Their French orientation made sympathizing with the Allies inevitable. Rui Barbosa, the perennial liberal knight, spent much time pleading with Brazilians to enter the war on the Allied side. Among prominent writers and literary critics who supported the Allies were Coelho Neto, Mário de Alencar, José Veríssimo, and Medeiros e Albuquerque. They argued that Brazil must join the struggle to defend Latin civilization against German barbarism. For them the question of war guilt was quickly settled, as in an article that concluded: "Germany not only wanted war, she precipitated it out of fear that a peaceful solution might abort it."[9] In 1914 Coelho Neto wept for Latin civilization: "Poor land of France!" And João do Rio turned his hysteria against Kaiser William II.

By 1915 the pro-Allied intellectuals had founded the League for the Allies (Liga Pelos Aliados), to organize rallies and publish propaganda mobilizing Brazilian sentiment against the Central powers. The moving spirits of the League were José Veríssimo, the distinguished literary critic, and Rui Barbosa. It very much reflected the cultural ethos of the pre-war era. The League sponsored speeches and plays to dramatize the plight of Latin civilization, threatened by the "Huns" and the "Goths." Afrânio Peixoto, for example, consented to write a play to be presented by the League, with proceeds to benefit the "war victims." The script was entirely frivolous, with the warring powers symbolized by young women who giggled over the heartaches produced by the battle of the sexes.[10]

The most widely read newspapers and magazines generally followed the pro-Allied line, presenting the war as a barbarian threat to freedom and culture. English propaganda about the rape of Belgium, along with descriptions of the slaughter of babies, was faithfully repeated by the Brazilian press. Such loyalty to the Allied cause was hardly surprising. The Brazilian elite was steeped in French culture. Few of them had ever been truly conversant with German civilization. Tobias Barreto, the evangelist for German philosophy, had remained an isolated and bizarre rebel against the French (and English, to a lesser extent) cultural straightjacket.

The Central powers, on the other hand, had only an occasional outright defender. Sampaio Ferraz, for example, wrote in 1915: "Their enemies do not find the Germanic evil to lie in their institutions, but in the wealth of their character, the steadfastness of their will, the vigor of their resistance and the heroism of their self-sacrifice. Whether these are evils or worse, they will in the end guarantee the victory of Germany."[11] A few Brazilian officers who had trained with the German Army before the war wrote newspaper commentaries to blunt the predominantly anti-German war dispatches. But they took the precaution of writing under pseudonyms (Gneisenau and Scharnhorst were favorites).[12]

A few writers, such as Dunshee de Abranches, presented their *own*, anti-Allied, explanation of how Europe had come to all-out war. Dunshee gave a speech in September 1914 in which he declared that what was happening was "a commercial war and nothing more." He praised Bismarck and Emperor William II for their remarkable success as demonstrated by the rapid economic, social, and cultural development of the German Empire. The "German Peril" was no more real, he explained, than the "Yankee Peril" which it had recently replaced in the "hypocritical" language of international propaganda. Throughout the war Dunshee remained an indefatigable opponent of the pro-Allied enthusiasts.[13]

Other real opposition to the pro-Allied propagandists came from an outspoken minority arguing that Brazil did not *necessarily* have a common interest with the Allies and therefore ought to remain neutral. They reasoned that Brazil had little to gain from entering the war. Such intervention would be expensive and futile. Among the intellectuals who took this line were Oliveira Lima and Capistrano de Abreu. They were suspicious that entry into the war might make their country too dependent on the United States, since Brazil would be the only major country in Latin America to join the United States on the side of the Allies. They expressed their cynicism about the lurid tales told against Germany.[14] "I don't know if the Germans have been particularly barbarous," wrote Oliveira Lima in the second month of hostilities. "In wartime everyone becomes equally barbarous; war itself is an act of barbarity."[15]

One other group resisted pro-Allied propaganda—the champions of the German colonists in Brazil. Like their fellow countrymen in the United States, German immigrants found their loyalty questioned. Even the German-born members of religious orders were accused of being agents of German imperialism.[16] Their defenders, usually politicians from the southern states where German immigrants were concentrated, argued for separating the German Empire and its role in the war from the German immigrants who had chosen to cast their lot with Brazil. One pamphlet published in Rio Grande do Sul, home of a large German colony, appealed for an end to the "flood of hate and jealousy" heaped on the Germans in Brazil by the "Germanophobic Jacobins." It praised the immigrants as prosperous contributors to Brazilian progress who had every right to defend their former homeland's role in the war.[17]

The German colony also entered the propaganda battle directly. In May 1915 the German-language newspaper of São Paulo published a supplement in Portuguese violently attacking earlier stories of German atrocities printed elsewhere in Brazil. French government money was behind the campaign, the paper alleged.[18]

During the first year of the war, intellectuals for the most part continued to see events largely through the prism of Allied propaganda. At the same time, however, they became more and more aware of their own isolation. The European fighting of these early months had a curious effect. Watching the armies slaughter each other, the Brazilians began to feel left out. A sense of remoteness set in. Paulo Silveira, a newspaper columnist, noted lugubriously in November 1914: "We watch the formidable European struggle, dumbfounded, our existence paralyzed and our activity drugged, complete slaves of Europe."[19] The comparison with Europe was odious: "Any Balkan country has more vitality than Brazil"; what Brazil needed was "new blood in her veins." By June 1915 the same commentator was despairing of his country's younger generation: "Our youth does not dream any more," and the country is consumed by a "devastating skepticism."[20] "The war is beating on our door," wrote another commentator, "while the city [Rio] presents a picture of delirium."[21] Capistrano de Abreu was more concrete in his pessimism. In September 1915 he wrote a friend that "after the war things will be worse because the reconstruction of Europe will be the greatest enterprise ever undertaken and we shall not be able to expect any money or capital from there."[22]

NATIONAL DEFENSE: NATIONALISM
OF THE ESTABLISHMENT

The first phase of Brazil's reaction to the war lasted about a year. During 1915 the air of isolation began to give way to a growing martial spirit. One of the first signs of change was the reception given to Miguel Calmon—a member of a prominent Bahian family, an engineering graduate of the Polytechnic School, and former Minister both of Agriculture and of Trans-

portation and Public Works—when he returned from Europe
where he had witnessed the beginning of the war. He was one of
the first Brazilians to bring back a first-hand report. In July he
gave a speech in Bahia calling for an "awakening." He was not in
fact endorsing a call to arms, although the military immediately
took it as such. He was urging a new attack on Brazil's social
and economic problems. "You have the major lesson of the war
right here. . . . It is the arousing, under adversity, of the underlying but dormant energies of which man is often unaware. Any
misfortune, with or without war, has the same effect: it gives
men the glory of sacrifice and elevates our soul. . . ."[23]

He received a congratulatory telegram from *A Defesa Nacional,* a military magazine edited by "Young Turk" officers, and
was soon repeating his speech before an enthusiastic contingent
of military who felt they were finally getting some civilian
interest.[24]

Calmon's call to action was rapidly overshadowed by a more
famous figure of the cultural establishment. In October 1915
Olavo Bilac addressed the students of the Law Faculty in São
Paulo. It was the graduation address—often a good index of the
prevailing intellectual mood.[25] He began by painting a dreary
picture of Brazil's lack of moral integrity, echoing the tone of
other recent assessments: "A demoralizing wave of apathy is
debilitating everyone's soul" because "indifference is today the
moral law and self-interest the only incentive." While he deplored
the selfishness of the elite, he acknowledged the common man's
"primitive ignorance" showing only "apathy, superstition, and a
total lack of confidence." He pointed to the interior [*sertões*]
where "men are not Brazilians, or even men. They are creatures
without free and creative souls—like wild animals, insects, trees."
To Bilac, Brazil had failed to exploit the potential of its people
through education. "What is being done to build our national
future? Nothing."

"The first step toward convalescence and a cure"—his views
showed the influence of events in Europe—would be an imple-

mentation of the compulsory conscription law that had been
passed in 1907 but remained a dead letter.[26] "The army barracks
is an admirable filter to make men cleaner and purer. It produces
thinking and upright Brazilians out of those unhappy creatures
who lack consciousness, dignity, or even a country, and who
constituted the amorphous and melancholy mass of people." He
appealed to the pride of his young audience: "Join with youth
and students all over Brazil. In a wonderful army you will be the
pioneers of faith!"

Bilac's call to arms, more consciously military than Calmon's,
found a ready response among the elite, as he launched into a
nation-wide speaking tour to promote the new patriotism.[27] Although hardly distinguishable from countless laments of the
previous year or two, his moral indictment came at an oppor-
tune moment. Because of his prominence, his forum, and the
speed with which the military capitalized upon his comments,
Bilac received credit as the catalyzer of national discontent.
Coelho Neto, a fellow member of the Brazilian Academy of Letters, praised his call to arms, and called it an application of
Alberto Tôrres' ideas.[28]

The young lawyers heeded Bilac's challenge. They went forth
to organize—with ample help from the military—the League of
National Defense (Liga da Defesa Nacional). By early 1916 the
League had begun to function under the presidency of Rui Barbosa. Rui was struggling mightily to whip up Brazilian support
for the Allies. The reaction to a speech by him in Buenos Aires in
July 1916 is evidence of the growing intensity of debate over the
war. As the official Brazilian delegate to the celebration of the
centenary of Argentine independence, he chose the occasion to
repudiate neutrality: "the courts, public opinion, and conscience
are never neutral as between the law and crime." Although he
stopped short of advocating a declaration of war, the implication
was clear. He had deliberately attempted to force Brazilian
policy-makers toward intervention, to the delight of the French
and the dismay of the Germans. The speech had not been

cleared with the Brazilian Foreign Minister, who was furious and repudiated it at once.[29] The speech provoked an angry debate in the Brazilian press. Pro-neutralists dismissed Rui's oratory as "the product of vanity and inconsistency, a masterwork of style and eloquence but dangerous for Brazil." Oliveira Lima published a refutation and aroused the charge that he was "more Germanophile than the Germans."[30]

The debate over the war, which had begun on the question of Brazil's neutrality, soon aroused nationalist sentiments from other prominent literary figures. One of the most notable was Afonso Arinos, the aristocratic writer who before the war had begun to promote interest in exploring the rich fund of Brazilian folklore and popular culture. In 1915 Arinos gave a stirring lecture in Belo Horizonte on "The Unity of the Fatherland." He saw an urgent need to consolidate national unity which, although yet to be achieved, was fortunately *not* prejudiced by the existence within the country of "a subordinated race, considered inferior and therefore rejected as is the Negro race in the United States." The "superior classes" needed to lead a "veritable civic campaign for the resurrection of Brazil, a country excoriated in the world press as a swindler and a fraudulent bankrupt." In short, Brazil had territory but it was not a nation. And time was critically short. "National sovereignty itself is at stake and more than a few responsible men think that our crisis will culminate in foreign tutelage."[31]

The war began to affect other writers in a similar manner. João do Rio, for example, turned his attention to Brazil (as he had in his description of the 1908 Exposition)—the neglected, unreflecting, disorganized Brazil that Bilac caricatured in his oration to the law students in São Paulo. The habitué of the shaded haunts of the Avenida Central began to tour Brazil, pouring forth his own patriotic call to arms. He spoke in Belo Horizonte in 1917: "For us the war is awakening, the recognition of our own worth. There are a thousand ideas germinating in the atmosphere. Each one expresses a faith and is being translated into reality."[32] The neglect of the land was his principal explanation for Brazil's backwardness. His indictment was worthy of the best that the critics of the post-war era were later to offer: "Can you not see how completely the people of Brazil are alienated from their land? The people are parasitic, like a customs collector." His view of the cause was "irresponsible hostility toward the cultivation of the soil. The teachers think about Europe. The classical spirit of Europe reigns in what is a new country, suffocating the youth. In this, a new country, men think like French bureaucrats."[33]

He also viewed the war as an occasion for forcing Brazilians to rethink their national identity: "Certainly no other people so distant from the hostilities felt the war as strongly as Brazil." As the war began, Brazil was "denationalized by its reading habits and rendered a foreign imitation by alien customs." Now the opportunity had come: "if we wish to epitomize Brazil at this time of conflict, one must think of those young men—the sons of good families—who are living on the borrowed hopes of a great inheritance in the future." The villain was the educational system: "We are creating the ignorance of lawyers in an ocean of the ignorance of the illiterate."[34]

He repeated his indictment and his call to action in speeches and articles throughout the war period. Here was a literary *raffiné* rushing into the uncharted new territory of Brazilian nationalism. His willingness to discuss the more difficult questions—the educational system, the neglect of agriculture in the interior, the failure to develop authentic national styles in literature and art— made him a notable example of the mobilization mentality at work.[35]

Calmon and Bilac, as we saw above, offered the opening that frustrated Brazilian army officers needed. Ambitious officers had long wanted a more powerful army, but the civilian politicians had failed to vote the funds and the machinery necessary to enforce the conscription law passed in 1907.[36] In any case, Brazil lacked a strong military tradition. The war in Europe seemed to offer an opportunity to remedy that situation. Bilac's speech in particular, which gained far more publicity than Calmon's, signalled the beginning of a new and important tie between mobilization-minded intellectuals and ambitious officers. Bilac was elevated to national-hero status, and he was used effectively as a propagandist. One Congressman accused the government of subsidizing his speaking tours around the country. The denials of his apologists were not convincing.[37]

The Liga da Defesa Nacional retained a semi-official character, receiving heavy support from the Army. The signs of government support were evident here too. Its steady stream of free pamphlets and books were evidence of ample propaganda funds. It is important to note, however, that the Liga was an eminently respectable organization, notwithstanding the possibility of its subsidy from government coffers. Although "nationalist," it faithfully reflected the status quo in politics and economics. It was the elite's attempt to harness the nationalistic awakening for its own purposes. From the outset the Liga interpreted patriotism in the narrow and traditional sense of civic duty. Its moralistic tone was an extension of the middle-class (i.e., urban, professional) element in the liberal ideology. Yet the militaristic overtone, everpresent because of the central role played by military officers, negated the spirit of classical liberalism. Militarism was even more inconsistent with internationalism. So the established politicians and intellectuals were beginning, inadvertently, to move into conflict with the international commitment implied by their previous positions.

The Liga da Defesa Nacional was not the only product of the new martial spirit. The Liga Nacionalista was another such organization. This group was founded in July 1917—a year and a half after the earlier league—and received the support (free use of schoolrooms, etc.) and encouragement of the state government of São Paulo. It appears to have been a largely civilian organization, although it campaigned for the effective application of compulsory military service. The Liga Nacionalista's "Deliberative

Council" comprised a Paulista honor roll: Júlio Mesquita Filho, Nestor Rangel Pestana, Plínio Barreto, Antônio de Sampaio Dória, and many others. Prominent medical figures were also included, such as Luiz Pereira Barretto, the Positivist scientist, and Arnaldo Vieira de Carvalho, founder of the São Paulo Medical Faculty. The President was Frederico Steidel, a professor at the Law Faculty.[38]

The Liga Nacionalista's propaganda had a different ring from its counterpart in Rio. It reflected the juridical liberalism so characteristic of São Paulo's intellectual atmosphere. During his founding address, Antônio Pereira Lima sounded a note similar to Miguel Calmon two years earlier. Brazil, he lamented, was "a country immensely poor in the midst of her riches, unarmed in the face of the armed foreigner, a land unorganized and scattered through her vast backlands [sertões]." Worst of all, Brazil "lacked confidence in herself" and showed the "halting and hesitant steps of the valedictorian whom a dissolute life has brought to the verge of death." Fortunately, however, it now faced an unexpected crossroads—either a "rocky path" toward a "bleak and hostile land" and the "supreme disgrace" of Brazilians confessing themselves "unworthy" of the opulent earth they had been given, or the "other road," which would lead to a "solid plateau where the nation would emerge unified and cohesive." Most interestingly, this Eden "would be the dawn of a splendid rural civilization, benign and lovable in the sober and simple customs of its people."[39]

Lima's speech combined several elements common to both nationalist leagues, but the Paulista league in fact had a different emphasis. Its organizers were among the leading liberal reformers in São Paulo—men who believed that Brazil's greatest need was a stronger dose of political liberalism. So they campaigned for reforms such as a secret and compulsory vote. Steidel spoke bitterly of the "tyrannical will of local bosses," to whom "the electors do not wish to submit themselves." Sampaio Dória, one of Liga Nacionalista's patrons, became a leading popularizer in this campaign to "purify" the vote. The Liga Nacionalista propaganda had a strong moralistic tone which reflected the reaction of the urban professional classes—whose bastion was the city of São Paulo—against the manipulation by back-country bosses. It was middle-class nationalism.[40]

Meanwhile, the military continued their own direct propaganda efforts. One Army captain lectured the Military Club in Rio on the "ridiculously" small size of the Brazilian Army (only 18,000 men) which was supposed to protect a country feeling only "indifference" toward the military and sunk in "confident serenity." The Brazilians had erroneously thought they could remain "mere spectators of the European war, simply gaining advantages for our industries. As a good peace-loving people we never wanted war and so we could never believe that it might rudely awaken us." His moral was Social Darwinist: "The European war is eloquently showing the destiny of weak peoples."[41]

MOBILIZATION AND THE NEW NATIONALISM

In Brazil, as in the United States, the interventionists grew stronger as German submarines sank more ships. It took until April 5, 1917, however, shortly before the United States declared war, for a Brazilian ship (the *Paraná*) to go down. This led to a break in diplomatic relations with Germany (even a previously strong advocate of neutrality such as Oliveira Lima supported that), but nothing more.[42] Then, on June 1, Brazil revoked her neutrality decree and authorized the use by her own navy of German ships that had been seized in Brazilian ports at the outbreak of the war. Another Brazilian vessel, the *Macau*, was sunk on October 23, and President Wenceslau Braz asked Congress to "recognize the state of war imposed upon us by Germany."[43] The Chamber and Senate agreed, and the decree was published on October 26. Brazil had joined the belligerents.

It had taken Brazil six months longer than the United States. Her ships were sunk less often and later in the war; and it was less clear that her national interest required her to become a belligerent. Yet in the end she was the only *major* Latin American country to declare war. The other belligerents were all Caribbean or Central American countries under direct American influence—Cuba, Costa Rica, Guatemala, Haiti, Honduras, Nicaragua, and Panama. The other major countries of Latin America did not even break diplomatic relations with the Central Powers.[44]

By following the example of the United States, the Brazilian government was cultivating U.S. friendship as part of the long-term diplomatic policy launched by Baron Rio Branco soon after he became Foreign Minister in 1902—a gamble that Brazil could maximize her world position by allying with the hemisphere's giant.[45] There were interventionists who made no secret of their view that Brazil's future interests would best be served by close alliance with the United States. One writer, Valente de Andrade, argued frankly that the United States was going to emerge from the war much stronger than Europe, that Brazil badly needed foreign investment, as well as markets for her primary products, and that a close alliance with her biggest customer and largest potential creditor-investor would be highly advantageous. This would guarantee peace in Latin America and protection against Argentina, whom Andrade saw as Brazil's principal foreign threat.[46] Assis Brasil, the Republican reformer and Brazilian diplomat who had served in the United States, included closer ties with America as a central theme in an address sponsored by the Liga da Defesa Nacional in September 1917. Reading from a diplomatic report he had written in 1900, he called for Brazil to "cultivate systematically the friendship of the United States," "a new country, showing more similarities with us than any other," and "learn the thousand things necessary for our progress." "Wisdom and dignity dictate that we use the protection [of the Monroe Doctrine] without subservience to the protector."[47]

This shift from the question of helping to "save" European civilization, as the League for the Allies had argued in its early propaganda, to the context of Brazil's post-war position in the hemisphere could be seen in the speeches of Coelho Neto, who began to produce exuberant praise for the United States.[48] The new rationale was also clearly stated by the writer and Congressman Gilberto Amado, an outspoken admirer of French culture, who told the Chamber of Deputies that Brazil's entry reaffirmed that "we are above all an American power," which "owes its progress to Europe but is uniquely linked to America." To reaffirm the "special tie of solidarity to the great nation of the north" at this moment of entry into the war was logical and natural.[49]

Brazil's final decision to declare war came after a general shift in public opinion. During 1917 the Foreign Minister, Lauro Müller, long a target of suspicion in the pro-Allied press, was subjected to a crescendo of charges that his German ancestry (his parents were German immigrants who settled in the state of Santa Catarina) made him potentially disloyal to Brazil.[50] In January 1917 A Razão charged that he was failing to defend Brazilian interests against the belligerents, and in February a Bahian newspaper columnist accused Müller of being a "paid agent and a scum."[51] On March 10, the literary critic Medeiros e Albuquerque accused Müller of "compromising the interests of Brazil."[52] In early May 1917 Müller resigned. The rapid swing in public opinion was shown by the fact that later in May, a Riograndense Congressman, Pedro Moacyr, gave a speech attacking German submarine warfare, even though he was from the area of Brazil where German settlement was greatest. "From the north to south" the pro-Allied feeling ran high, he noted, leading to "certain immoderate explosions."[53] And explosions there were—crowds smashing shops in Recife, and sporadic harassment of Brazilians of German descent all over the country.[54] So Brazil entered the war. No Brazilian combat forces saw action, although training missions were arranged with France and the United States. Had the war lasted another year, Brazilians might well have joined the trench warfare.[55]

Few Brazilians believed that their country was directly threatened by the war. Although ships were torpedoed and trade interrupted, no invasion was even remotely likely.[56] Talk of "defense" and "mobilization" remained distant from the war theater; having started out as a strictly military concept, however, used by the military to increase its own power, it became a new vocabulary in which intellectuals could discuss the problem of stimulating increased public efforts in health, education, and other basic areas.

For Europeans, the idea of mobilization was hardly new. The French Revolution was probably the first example of large-scale mobilization, and Napoleon had shown the feats an ambitious leader could perform on the basis of a highly organized nation-state. But the century of relative peace in Europe between the Congress of Vienna and the assassination of the Archduke of Sarajevo had blurred the importance of mobilization for many foreign observers of European civilization. In Brazil, for example, the idea of mobilizing national resources to meet a crisis was virtually unknown.

Their entry into the war, however, stimulated just that. After helping to launch the League of National Defense, Olavo Bilac had gone on to urge immediate efforts to reach the "masses of the people who lack food, education and health facilities. . . ." Although the government responded slowly, a Public Food Commission (Comissariado da Alimentação Pública) was finally created in June 1918 to cope with the skyrocketing inflation of food prices, caused in part by the rise in Brazil's food exports to aid the Allies. Here was a first step toward a state-sponsored effort to study hunger and malnutrition in Brazil.[57]

Education was another area. Despite the increased interest in science and technology that marked the late Empire, Brazil had continued to educate many more lawyers than scientists or engineers. Between 1889 and 1910, eight new law faculties were founded, including two in Rio, and only three new schools of engineering.[58] As one critic put it: "There are thousands of savants with a profound knowledge of the *jus scriptum* and the *jus scribendum* as it relates to property or anything else, but there are precious few capable of intelligently exploiting the richly fertile earth."[59] In fact, the political decentralization introduced with the Republic had facilitated the continued stranglehold enjoyed by the liberal professions because the states, now given autonomy in education, simply followed the example set during the Empire of establishing more law faculties than scientific institutes or technical faculties.

Brazil's mania for lawyers had been denounced before, Alberto Tôrres having been one of the more eloquent critics. By the eve of the war, given the mood of mobilization in Brazil, it was an obvious target for attack. One such new indictment in 1916, by Tobias Monteiro, a widely read historian-journalist, attributed Brazil's backwardness to her neglect of agriculture, industry, and commerce. The only solution was to reduce the swollen army of lawyers, poets, novelists, and orators and to increase the meager ranks of the productive. Minas Gerais and Goiás had recently founded law faculties instead of veterinary schools or animal health stations. This "superabundance of functionaries and university graduates [doutores]" was the natural result of "the liberalism of the reforms that began in 1878 with the so-called 'free instruction.'"[60] In São Paulo, he said, "one of the greatest agricultural centers in the world," only one hundred and seventy-eight agronomists had graduated from the agricultural school at Piracicaba in twelve years, while the law faculty was producing some two thousand graduates during the same period. Furthermore, the example of the "more intelligent classes" was being followed by the "uneducated" who aspire to the "lower positions in offices and bureaus" when they "ought to go into trade, crafts and small businesses."[61] As a result, Brazil was governed by men of no practical sense or experience. Of the sixty-three members of the Senate (three seats were vacant), only nine were farmers (agricultores) and two were landlords (proprietários). The rest were all from the liberal professions—lawyers, medical doctors, military officers, engineers, journalists, or government employees. The Chamber of Deputies was equally unbalanced. Out of two hundred and two members, there were only eight farmers, three industrialists, two landlords, and one merchant. More than half the entire number were lawyers, the rest being primarily medical doctors, engineers, and journalists.[62] What Monteiro found most disturbing was the relative absence of entrepreneurs.

Monteiro's specific worry was over Brazil's ability to achieve social regeneration—a preoccupation common to the intellectuals who had picked up the language of mobilization. "There will never be a transformation of our national character" if Brazil "continues to be a country of graduates [doutores] and government workers." Instead, it will continue on the same "path of fatalism and resignation" that had made Brazil "a nation of hangers-on side-by-side with prosperous and dominant foreign colonies."[63] Monteiro was also worried about the native Brazilian, who showed a "complete lack of ambition" and a "moral indolence" stemming from the "fatalism of the race." "God is a Brazilian" really meant "don't worry, everything will work out."[64]

Assis Brasil launched a similar attack on Brazil's impractical and inadequate educational system.[65] He, too, was disturbed by his countrymen's addiction to a set of pernicious values—the prestige of ornamental culture and non-entrepreneurial professions. In fact, the war-time debate had stimulated a wide-ranging reconsideration of the elitist-oriented educational system. A younger generation of educational reformers arose to urge a more practical and democratic approach, much along the lines John Dewey was advocating in the United States.[66] In effect, these reformers, like the public health propagandists, were arguing from environmentalist assumptions. They implicitly assumed that the native-born Brazilian, whatever his racial origins, had been grossly handicapped by the lack of social institutions to prepare him for the modern world.

Re-evaluation of Race. Along with their new language of mobilization, Brazilians' preoccupation with their national identity increased during this period as they questioned the received racist doctrine. Miguel Calmon's speech (quoted above) did not simply call for Brazilian mobilization. He also dealt specifically with race—having seen colored colonial troops fighting in the French Army. "How comforting it is to hear from the mouths of the French descriptions of heroic acts by Negroes and *mestiços*. . . . Fortunately for us, it did not take the war to abolish such prejudices, since we have always honored merit wherever it may be found."[67] Although Calmon's denial of prejudice was clearly unfounded, he was groping toward an explanation of the origins of Brazil's multi-racial social system. He went on to praise Brazil's own "native element" which contributed the "intransigent spirit of independence and of devotion to the soil" that enabled Brazil to "repel repeated invasions" and "permitted us to confront and transform such an unhealthy tropical environment."[68]

A similar defense of the native-born Brazilian was offered by Gilberto Amado, who gave a long parliamentary speech in December 1916 reviewing Brazilian history and urging the need for practical, reform-minded leadership. Significantly, he began by rejecting the "exaggerations of Gobineau, Vacher de Lapouge and Chamberlain, not to speak of . . . Agassiz and Gustave Le Bon. . . ." Amado then analyzed Brazil's legalistic culture, which had led to an excessive reliance on constitutional formulae and the copying of foreign models.[69] The following year Amado ridiculed the Brazilian elite's obsession with proving their "Latinness" and suggested: "Let's just resign ourselves to being *cafusos* [mixture of black and Indian] or *curibocas* [mixture of white and Indian], trying to honor our blood by the dignity of our style of men, instead of boasting about heredity we haven't got."[70] In short, this young intellectual was developing a *historical* analysis of Brazil's problems from an anti-racist position similar to that of Alberto Tôrres and Manoel Bomfim.

Another example of this shift in thinking was a set of lectures given by Basílio de Magalhães in 1915. Magalhães had long been active in writing history and geography schoolbooks for use in São Paulo, but his lectures were unusual in explicitly rejecting both race and climate as explanations of Brazil's being "the great sickman of South America." "It has been proclaimed as an incontrovertible truth that miscegenation, such as predominates in Brazil, saps physical as well as moral energy." Authorities have "all condemned the cross-breeding that produced the majority of the Brazilian population"—Darwin, Agassiz, Spencer, Hellwald, Le-Bon. Magalhães quoted Comte as refutation enough for this view.[71]

Like Calmon, he sought to refute the Aryan thesis by pointing to the historic accomplishments of the *mestiço*. "Was it not this race," he asked, "virtually without foreign help until the end of the nineteenth century, that opened up our vast territory and preserved the integrity of this great country for us?"[72] He even took comfort from Europe's distress: "Our country is undergoing the throes of puberty just when Europe is entering the throes of menopause." Carried away by his medical metaphor, he referred to the "tragic and insane process of senile degeneration inflaming Europe." Brazil, on the other hand, could take heart from her past when she had "always" demonstrated "a prodigious capacity for recuperation."[73] Furthermore, Magalhães saw that the war could have great positive results because the "concomitant" crises of puberty in Brazil and senility in Europe would "help transform the Brazilian organism in the manner predestined by its historic antecedents." Although no friend of "Yankeemania" and eager to preserve the "special character of our nationality, the sacred consciousness of our Latinness," Magalhães was quite sure "Brazil [would] have to fix her personality definitively within the American and world-wide context."[74]

Along with most of the elite, Magalhães still accepted the doctrine that Brazil was "essentially agricultural," but he attacked the failure to mount a significant program of scientific agriculture. While "this paradoxical Brazil" imported corn from the United States, condensed milk from Europe "and even toothpicks from Portugal," the country contained "fewer agricultural schools than law faculties."[75]

What was Magalhães' solution? Education. The challenge was

"to strengthen physically and morally this race through a well oriented and systematic education, both of the aesthetic and civic senses." Only thus could the Brazilian be "valorized": "Our entire future depends upon wisely amalgamating our heterogeneous ethnic elements, developing them into fixed and strong types." It was "education" that could maximize the "good qualities" and, "where possible," suppress "the defects and the original vices."[76]

Magalhães was not original enough to repudiate completely attempts to compromise with racist theory. A second-rate spokesman of the elite, he still felt it necessary to voice the following assumptions: (1) racial differences, although important, were not inherent; (2) theories of absolute and permanent inferiority or superiority were therefore unfounded; and (3) cross-breeding, if properly pursued, would upgrade a population and did not produce "degenerates." The conclusions he drew from history, however, showed him to be well on the way toward a new rationale for Brazil's racial past: (1) the Latin peoples, far from having proved weak, had made a healthy contribution to Brazil's growth; (2) the Brazilian *mestiço* had also contributed mightily by settling and unifying the country; and (3) the war had revealed Europe to be aged, thereby leaving greater opportunities to the young countries such as Brazil. In other words, although not yet willing to discard his belief in racial regeneration entirely, he was willing to place a higher value on the *present* Brazilian population than most previous articulators of elite opinion. And he expressed greater faith that Brazil's ethnic evolution would make make possible her rise to the status of a major nation—if managed *properly*, Brazil could successfully build upon her past, including her ethnic inheritance.[77]

Rethinking Brazilian Nationality: The wider concern over nationality, of which the restatement of the whitening ideal was a part, found significant expression in 1916. In January of that year a new monthly magazine was founded in São Paulo, *Revista do Brasil.* This journal was launched as a rallying point for those writers who wished to re-examine Brazil's national identity. It was significant that the magazine appeared in São Paulo–the center of science and technology in Brazil. The editorial in the first issue (January 1916) was the manifesto for a new era in Brazilian self-analysis: "What lies behind the title of this magazine and those who are sponsoring it is something simple and measureless: the desire, the decision, the commitment to establish a center of nationalistic propaganda. We are a nation that still does not know itself, does not value itself, is not self-sufficient. More accurately, we are a nation which has not yet had the courage to launch out on its own in a dynamic projection of its own personality." This "is not a war cry against the foreigner. It is a call to unite under a common flag, it is an appeal for an alliance of love and glory, directed to the sons of a common land born under the light of a common sky."[78]

Revista do Brasil published contributions on every aspect of the "Brazilian problem." Along with articles on literary subjects by members of the Brazilian Academy of Letters (José Veríssimo contributed an article entitled "O modernismo" just before his death in 1916), there were frequent treatments of such subjects as the application of modern American management techniques to Brazilian factories (Taylorism) and the need to modernize agriculture. There were long debates over how to strike the proper balance between nationalism and the adoption of foreign methods in educational reform. There were regular reports on the press of Rio and São Paulo, the dispatches from overseas, especially London, Paris, Berlin, New York. *Revista* kept its readers in touch both with the centers of North Atlantic civilization and with the new debate over modernizing Brazil.

Revista do Brasil showed clearly the rapid growth in the number of Brazilian writers who had committed themselves to analyzing the problems of Brazil. Criticism, debate, controversy—a chorus of voices now swelled. Monteiro Lobato, whose contribution we shall examine in the next chapter, purchased *Revista do Brasil* in 1918 and made himself the center of a campaign to educate the elite in the economic and social problems of Brazil.[79]

Along with the founding of *Revista do Brasil*, there appeared in 1916 a primer called *My Land and My People* (*Minha terra e minha gente*) by Afrânio Peixoto. This was the first schoolbook to tackle head on, as its title showed, the problems of both race and climate. Peixoto was well equipped to write such a book—a literary figure (his novel *A Esfinge*, published in 1911, justified his earlier election to the Brazilian Academy of Letters) and also a doctor who had campaigned to introduce modern scientific methods in legal medicine and public health. As he explained in the preface to *Minha terra e minha gente*, "Neither whining nor lyricism is productive. It seemed to the author that it would be a useful innovation to write for the children of his country an honest, uninhibited, calm book, in which he would try to put forward the necessary truths about the basic problems of our nationality."[80]

The myth of the unhealthy tropics was easy to refute, as Peixoto had shown in his earlier writings. "These diseases do not exist. Yellow fever, malaria, hookworm and other diseases are not unique to any climate, except those regions whose inhabitants do not know how to, or can't combat them." The matter of race, however, he found less easy to deal with:

> Will the gradual fusion of ill-formed mixed bloods, along with the repeated selection by culture and the discipline imposed by social life, create out of this mass a strong, wholesome, and happy people? Will the protoform of today produce a strong-minded, sensitive, intelligent people worthy of the land and the time in which it lives?

It was Graça Aranha's question being put to Brazilian schoolchildren.[81] Peixoto did not venture an answer. He did, however, exhort his readers to make their best effort to "acquire the combination of self-awareness and knowledge of others that will enable us to create our own destiny and cease living . . . from day to day, because of our inability to plan ahead. Brazil is a giant letter without an address. It will arrive, if at all, where it does not want to be."[82]

Ambiguous though it remained on the question of race, Peixoto's *Minha terra e minha gente* was a step in the direction of
realism. João do Rio thought the book's message was: "We must
become practical, abandon our utopias, our vain contempts, our
poetry, and our parasitism," and that his work was "the manifesto
of the soul of an energetic and glorious generation" and a message "which distills all of our hectically scattered aspirations."[83]
Social questions that had previously remained the concern of isolated reformers or a few far-sighted politicians (usually in São
Paulo) now took center stage. The Pernambucan essayist José
Maria Bello gave one of the most forward-looking diagnoses:

> We have always invoked questions of race and climate . . . to ex-
> plain [*justificar*] our weakness. Fortunately all these pompous phrases
> of a poorly assimilated philosophy have gone out of style. Neither
> race nor climate has a decisive influence in the development of a
> country. Under normal conditions of health and education we are the
> equal of any other people.[84]

THE WAR'S STIMULUS TO BRAZILIAN NATIONALISM

As the war drew to a close in late 1918, Brazilians could begin to
digest their wartime experience and consolidate their new relationship with Europe and the United States. Since the 1880's the
Brazilian elite had been explicitly committed to the integration
of their country into the North Atlantic economy and culture.
Brazil would export agricultural products needed by the North
Atlantic world while at the same time attracting their immigrants
and investments. The occasional nationalist critics were argued
down on the grounds that nationalism had become obsolete in
the internationalist era.

The war, however, was a brutal reminder that nationalism was
far from obsolete. The conflict within Europe had contradicted
the liberal ideology, which in effect prescribed for Brazil a minor
role within a world increasingly dominated by Europe. All the
major European powers were accused of territorial and economic

greed as the debate over "war guilt" grew more bitter. Caricatures of the national character of enemy nations became commonplace, with systematic modern-style propaganda making its
first appearance. The result in Brazil was to give new relevance
to discussions about nationality and national purpose.[85]

The war also dramatized the need for a new kind of national
effort—mobilization. Brazil's most recent effort to mobilize had
been in 1865–70 for the Paraguayan war. Emperor Pedro II and
his Prime Minister, Viscount Rio Branco, used the war emergency to justify reforms long needed. Some intellectuals and
Army officers hoped World War I would offer a similar opportunity. They saw European nations commandeering all economic
resources—men, farms, factories—in order to maximize their war
effort. Brazil never experienced this level of mobilization, but
reformers in public health, agriculture, education, and industrial
policy used the language of mobilization to urge stepped-up efforts in each field. Even more interestingly, they often added a
Social Darwinist tone, saying that the war in Europe "proved"
that the world was still a jungle in which only the strongest could
survive. Would Brazil marshal her resources and become a major
nation, or would she succumb to the domination of foreign powers conquering either by direct invasion, or by indirectly acquir-
ing gradual control over her economy and culture? As Olavo
Bilac proclaimed in November 1917, "At this moment Brazil's
fate is being decided. Shall we live or shall we die? . . ."[86] Such
warnings had been heard since the 1880's, but the bloodshed in
Europe gave them a new immediacy.

Paradoxically, this Social Darwinist preoccupation proved reassuring to some intellectuals who seemed almost pleased at the
prospect of Europe's self-destruction. Long having felt inferior
and often resenting it, these Brazilians were now eager to believe
that Europe had entered its decline. They seemed to be resuming
the dream that European civilization would find a rebirth in the
New World, uncontaminated by the ancient rivalries and class
conflicts that debilitated the Old World. For these Brazilians,

Europe's agony was a purgative. And they were encouraged in this analysis by European intellectuals such as Oswald Spengler, who freely predicted the demise of European culture.

This intellectual nationalism was accompanied by an increase in economic nationalism, although the latter was still a minority position among the elite and policy-makers.[87] Before 1914 Brazil had imported many essential goods which could have been produced at home. Foreign foodstuffs were common in the more expensive shops of the major cities. Trade was interrupted during the war because of upheaval in Europe and submarine warfare in the Atlantic. The Brazilian economy was therefore apparently thrown back upon its own resources. This strengthened the hand of economic nationalists who argued that Brazil should support the development of home industry. In fact, industrialization was hampered by the cut-off of capital equipment imports, although the need for greater "self-sufficiency" was dramatized.[88]

A final symptom of the growing national confidence was the heightening of Brazil's sense of involvement in international politics outside the hemisphere, a logical outgrowth of the satisfaction over Brazil's notably successful border diplomacy under Baron Rio-Branco (Foreign Minister, 1902–12). Brazil was the only major Latin American country to declare war on the Central Powers. As a result of this intervention and of her close alliance with the United States (in both cases contrasting sharply with Argentina's neutralism), the Brazilian elite began to conceive of their country as having a major international responsibility. As a direct result of Brazil's participation in the war she was invited to the Versailles Peace Conference. Brazilian politicians now, more than ever, considered themselves, to be the leading country within the significant power bloc Latin America.[89] One troublesome question remained, however. What was the future ethnic identity of this aspirant to nationhood?

6 The Whitening Ideal after Scientific Racism

The 1920's and 1930's in Brazil saw a consolidation of the whitening ideal, and its implicit acceptance by the idea-makers and social critics. The doubts about race expressed by the elite in earlier years lost any tone of real conviction in this period. Interestingly, most writers did not come out and state unambiguously that race made no difference and therefore the question should be ignored. Rather they said that Brazil was progressively whitening, and therefore the problem was being solved.

This is an important point. Certain scientists during the era were subscribing to the pure environmentalist hypothesis; certain Brazilian writers were turning with enthusiasm to favorable treatments of the African heritage; and it is in this period that Gilberto Freyre made his reputation on optimistic national character interpretations that depended on a positive reinterpretation of the history of miscegenation in Brazil. At the same time (at the other end of the spectrum) German Nazism was reviving pure heredity arguments to downgrade Jews and blacks. The Brazilian elite steered their way between these positions. Political arguments about immigration and social criticism by the elite took place against the backdrop of the shared assumption that Brazilians were getting whiter and would continue to do so.

1920'S: POLITICAL CRISIS AND LITERARY FERMENT

Although the administration of President Wenceslau Braz maintained relative domestic stability from 1914 to 1918, the leaders of the Republican Party in the major states could find no acceptable new face to present for the election of 1918. They turned to Rodrigues Alves, the former *Conselheiro* of the Empire, who had already served a term as President during the Republic (1902–6). Rodrigues Alves won the election but, as if to symbolize the exhaustion of a political generation, became too ill to assume office on inauguration day, November 15, 1918, and died in January of the following year. A new election was held early in 1919, in which Rui Barbosa, in his seventies, ran a campaign essentially the same as his 1910 crusade against Hermes da Fonseca, another reminder of the lack of new blood.[1] He was defeated by the official nominee, Epitácio Pessoa, who became the first Northeasterner to win the highest post in the Republic. Pessoa's term saw an upsurge in nationalist sentiment (usually directed at the Portuguese in Brazil) and a steady repression of working-class organizers.

The choice of his successor in 1922 precipitated a challenge to political authority from within the elite. Arthur Bernardes, the Governor of Minas Gerais, was chosen as the political bosses' nominee for President. His opponents were so embittered, however, that they split off to form a dissident faction (the "Republican Reaction"), which nominated its own slate of candidates. The dissidents included state leaders with important links to the Army, and the ticket it nominated was headed by Nilo Peçanha (another shadow of the past, having been the Vice-President who filled out Afonso Pena's presidential term in 1909–10).

The campaign proved to be the most bitter in the history of the Republic, culminating in the publication by a major Rio newspaper of a series of letters attributed to Bernardes that contained "insulting" references to the military. Bernardes won the election, but the letters (later proved to be forgeries) and the slander campaign surrounding their publication was successful in whipping up mutinous sentiments that wracked his term in office (1922–26). An abortive military revolt in Rio in 1922 was the first of a series (including a three-week rebellion in São Paulo in 1924). The Government responded with repressive measures, including martial law and internment camps.[2]

Although the military challenges themselves were successfully repressed, their occurrence deepened the divisions within the political elite and between those in power and the younger generation; it also facilitated the emergence of a counter-elite which began to question the legitimacy of the established political system.[3] Criticism that had earlier been restricted to a few isolated figures now became widespread, as epitomized in an interesting collective work which appeared in 1924—À Margem da História da República (On the Edge of the History of the Republic).[4]

Although the book per se made only a minor impact, it brought together a group of authors who were rapidly joining the ranks of the leading social critics of the 1920's. All had been born with the Republic, and the Introduction described all of them as disciples—to a greater or lesser degree—of Alberto Tôrres. In their chapters they outlined critical stances that were to become virtual dogma in progressive circles by the end of the decade, when they all published extensively. Oliveira Vianna, for example, contributed an essay entitled "The Idealism of the Constitution" ("O Idealismo da Constituição") which contained the essence of his influential and later often-repeated criticism that the Republic was perniciously imitative, that Brazil could make real progress only by developing institutions tailored to Brazilian realities. A. Carneiro Leão, the propagandist for educational reform, attacked Brazil's archaic educational system. As proof of its failure, he cited the fact that in recent national elections fewer voters turned out in Brazil than in Argentina (both countries had a literacy test for voters), although Argentina had only one-third the population of Brazil. Gilberto Amado reprinted his wartime speech stressing the need to "make the Republic Brazilian." The literary critics Ronald de Carvalho, Tasso da Silveira, and Tristão de Athayde all presented analyses of Brazilian culture which, if they fell short of the aesthetic revolution of the Modernists (discussed below), did represent a far more nationalist attitude than had been typical before the war. Vicente Licínio Cardoso, one of the organizers of the volume, produced a critique of the fading idealism which had accompanied the founding of the Republic, while Pontes de Miranda offered a blueprint for fundamental constitutional reform.[5]

Although these criticisms bore similarities to the 1889–1910 dissatisfaction over the political system (described in detail above in Chapter 3), the context of the debate had changed in a very significant way. In the earlier period the critics spoke from a less confident position, expressing a deep sense of uncertainty. The critics of the 1920's felt free to offer a straightforward *nationalist* critique of the Republican political system. Their view that Brazil should not continue to copy foreign models of government implied a new faith in their own ability to come up with a workable political system reflecting the uniqueness of Brazil. This confidence came, in turn, from a new confidence that the variable of race did not necessarily preclude Brazil's future as a great nation. The long-prevalent assumption that race was the most important issue in historical development was no longer considered self-evident.[6]

A new and robust sense of confidence was also reflected in Brazil's new feeling of its own literary identity, which in turn had important effects on thought about race. This new feeling received expression in a cultural revolution that later became known as "Brazilian Modernism." Ironically, it began with the attempt of some younger poets to introduce the latest European literary fashion into Brazil.[7]

While the Parnassians, the literary school of poets who placed great emphasis on correct form, continued their stranglehold on the Brazilian Academy of Letters, revolutionary esthetic movements were under way in Europe. Before the war the Italian poet-novelist, Marinetti, had helped launch a group of writers on an aggressive attack upon the traditional canons of grammar and literary form as used in Europe and especially in France and Italy. In order to emphasize their break with the past, these artistic rebels called themselves "Futurists." They glorified the dynamic pace of modern life and tried to translate the velocity and fluidity of modern technology into artistic expression.

Obviously this literary movement was antithetical to the staid, formalistic literature still dominant in Brazil.[8] Furthermore, most of Brazil remained untouched by the urban industrial change that produced the atmosphere European Futurists were concerned to glorify. The major exception was the city of São Paulo. Less internationalist than Rio de Janeiro, it was nevertheless Brazil's most dynamic economic center. The profits of a booming coffee economy had helped to finance a growing modernization of commercial agriculture and the beginnings of a modern industrial park. Not surprisingly, therefore, it was primarily young artists from the city of São Paulo who first got to know the esthetic revolution in Europe and attempted to spread it in Brazil.[9]

Oswaldo de Andrade, for example, became a convert to Futurism after his return from Europe in 1912, and during the war a few young Brazilian poets began writing Futurist verse. But it was not until an exhibition of painting by Anita Malfatti in São Paulo in 1917 that the antagonism between old and new artistic styles was significantly dramatized within Brazil. Malfatti's paintings, which showed much Futurist influence, were given a vicious review by Monteiro Lobato, the Paulista essayist. Malfatti's supporters counterattacked, led by Oswaldo de Andrade, and gained great publicity for the rebel cause. Victor Brecheret, a sculptor from São Paulo also much influenced by European anti-traditional ideas, gained further prestige for the innovative movement in 1921 by winning an important international prize for sculpture in Paris against four thousand other contestants. By the end of 1921 the esthetic rebels had become revolutionary in their attacks on the cultural establishment headed by Olavo

Bilac, Coelho Neto, and Rui Barbosa. They declared total war-fare against the careful grammatical phraseology of literature blessed by the Academy of Letters; they praised a new esthetic based on impulse and simultaneity. Authors such as Menotti del Picchia and Candido Mota Filho issued broad-scale manifestoes calling for a repudiation of the prevailing artistic forms and spirit, one of their favorite targets being the traditionally senti-mentalist regionalist literature.

This growing artistic movement reached a climax in the Mod-ern Art Week—a series of three "festivals" (Painting and Sculp-ture, Literature and Poetry, and Music) held in the Municipal Theater of São Paulo in February 1922. Although the festivals did not arouse the violent opposition later claimed by the prop-agandists of the movement, they did give new prestige to what was soon known as "Modernism," a term which grew out of the title for the festival. By 1922 the artistic rebels represented tend-encies much broader than Futurism, which had in any case al-ready faded after 1915 as an organized movement in Italy. Graça Aranha, the literary lion who had produced little since *Canaan* in 1902, became an enthusiastic convert to Modernism. In 1922 he publicly attacked the Academy of Letters, where he himself held a chair. Two years later he arose in the Academy itself, first to denounce the backwardness of his fellow academicians, and then to resign his seat amid Modernist cheers in the galleries.[10]

The Modern Art Week in fact marked a transition from a de-structive to a constructive phase, as the prestige of the establish-ment writers began to fade under the Modernist onslaught. The younger generation of writers became totally caught up in the new movement, of which the most prominent figure for the re-mainder of the decade was the poet-musician-painter Mário de Andrade.[11] The Modernists sought to consolidate their esthetic revolution by incorporating Brazilian themes into their innova-tive artistic forms. Some returned, ironically, to regionalist themes, as in Mário de Andrade's *Macunaíma* (1928), an epic story based on a blending of folklore—told in regional variations on the Brazilian vernacular, in contrast to the previous heavy literary sentimentalism.[12]

The cultural revolution led by the São Paulo rebels (and their Rio allies) was not restricted to that state. There were innovative currents in all the major states, linked in varying degrees to those in São Paulo and Rio de Janeiro. The Regionalist Movement in the Northeast, in which Gilberto Freyre played a leading role, had strong roots of its own and owed least to the São Paulo-Rio axis.[13] By the end of the 1920's the younger generation of Brazilian writers could feel that they were on their way to creating a truly national literature, however much they may have exaggerated the profundity of their break with Brazilian literary traditions.[14] Inevitably, they had had to spend much time attacking their literary elders—the leaders and symbols of an anachronistic culture. But at least they had begun to know what they did *not* want to be. And in the process of attempting to apply the latest European artistic fashions, they ended up looking for new, more originally Brazilian subject matter on which to practice their up-to-date literary techniques.[15] As in the case of the political reaction, what counted most was the mood of increased confidence—confidence in their ability to articulate their *own* vision of Brazil's identity and future.[16]

RESCUING THE CABOCLO

We have seen above that the war years changed the context of the Brazilian debate over national development from a discussion of race to a discussion of mobilization. In the latter the elite spokesmen went through a period of judging their progress as a nation by their country's ability to create and mobilize a national sense of purpose (a standard so obvious among the belligerents in Europe and North America). Not surprisingly, very few of those urging mobilization were encouraged by examining the population they would have to mobilize—thus being led back to questions about the racial material they had to work with.

They found, especially in the interior, people who were miserably poor, illiterate, undernourished, and disease-ridden. In the words of Miguel Pereira, a noted pioneer in public health, Brazil was "one immense hospital."[17] In 1914 most of the elite would have given, explicitly or implicitly, a racist explanation for this. The Paulista writer-publisher Monteiro Lobato provides a good example.[18] Back in 1903, as a law student, Monteiro Lobato had described Brazil as "the son of inferior parents . . . producing a useless type, incapable of continuous development without the invigorating inflow of some original race. . . ."[19] In 1908 he was even more explicit when he described (in a letter to a friend) his disgust at watching the population of Rio de Janeiro going home from work:

> In the afternoon parade . . . every kind of degenerate passes by, every human type . . . except the normal. . . . How will we put these people right? . . . What terrible problems the poor African Negro created for us by his unintentional revenge [i.e., miscegenation]! . . . Perhaps our salvation will come from São Paulo and other areas which have had a heavy influx of European blood. The Americans preserved themselves from miscegenation by the barrier of racial prejudice. We have that barrier here also, but only among certain classes and in certain areas. In Rio it doesn't exist.[20]

In 1914 he began publishing newspaper articles about the backward state of Brazilian agriculture—in particular an article about the native-born subsistence farmer from the Paraíba valley of São Paulo.[21] Lobato knew the area first-hand, having owned and managed a run-down coffee plantation there for three years.

This essay focused on the laziness and ignorance of the *caboclo* (a catch-all term for the native-born Paulista—with a suspicion of Indian blood—found in the interior), to whom he gave the fictional name of "Jéca Tatú."[22] Lobato charged that a new school of writers (unspecified) was dressing up the *caboclo* in the old Indianist virtues of fierce pride, loyalty, courage, and heroic virility, whereas in fact he "exists merely to hunker; he is incapable of evolution and is immune to progress."

Lobato pictured the lethargic, superstitious, ignorant *caboclo* who thought it not worthwhile (*"Não paga a pena"*) to build a decent house, cultivate his manioc, or store his harvest. Forever hunkering, he vegetated, bestirring himself only to vote for whomever the local boss named. In the midst of the luxurious excesses of nature (Lobato's lyric description was ironical) the *caboclo* was a "dark fungus on a rotten tree dozing silently in a valley alcove—the only one not to talk, not to sing, not to laugh, not to love. The only one not to live. . . ."

The obvious assumptions about the *caboclo's* inherent character went uncontested when the article first appeared in 1914. Four years later, however, it was reprinted in a collection of Lobato's essays and short stories bearing the title *Urupês*. It now (1918) created an uproar—evidence of the changes in attitude during the war. Some critics charged him with libeling the Brazilian, others with generalizing from a local (Paulista?) problem to the national level. One prominent politician from the state of Ceará published a counter-essay describing the man of the Northeastern interior (whom he dubbed "Mané Chique-Chique") as a model farmer, intrepid cattle-breeder, skillful fisherman, and efficient rubber-gatherer. In short, he was the "anonymous motor" and the "anonymous pillar of the nation" who had built an independent Brazil—just the stereotype Lobato was trying to expunge from the record.[23] Rui Barbosa, the liberal knight who had decided to run for President again in 1918, entered the fray by seizing upon Lobato's portrait, calling Jéca untypical of the Brazilian, but using his plight as an excuse to attack the government's failure to improve the appalling social and economic conditions.[24] Rui's citation gave increased publicity to the relatively unknown Lobato, who was delighted with the unexpected boost to sales: "The book has stirred up the natives and now, with the speech by the Big Chief, it'll go off like a rocket."[25] Lobato was right, and Jéca Tatú (already gaining fame) became a household name among the reading public.[26]

The re-publication of Lobato's portrait of Jéca came, then, just when Brazil was caught up in a debate over the true causes of the backwardness of the interior. Advocates of public health measures and education were arguing that disease and illiteracy, not racial origins or inherent character (as in the case of the *caboclo*), were the explanation.[27] And they were being listened to.

During the Empire public health had been a realistic concern of government only in a few major cities. During the early Republic efforts increased, but were still limited primarily to the major cities, especially on the coast. A full-scale attack on yellow fever, for example, became an urgent matter in Rio de Janeiro and the Northeast in order to improve Brazil's image and attract more immigrants, but was never broadened into a nation-wide public health effort before the war, despite the efforts of Oswaldo Cruz, who organized scientific expeditions to survey health conditions in the interior.

As the war progressed, however, interest in public health became much broader. In part this growing interest was stimulated by the publication (in 1916) of a health survey commissioned by Oswaldo Cruz in 1912. Two doctors, Belisário Pena and Artur Neiva, traveled through the interior of the states of Bahia, Pernambuco, Piauí, and Goiás compiling a detailed (and illustrated) inventory of health conditions. Their findings were a definitive refutation of those patriots who had argued that major health problems were restricted to a few localized areas (known only to Monteiro Lobato?). The forgotten man of the interior, Euclides da Cunha's *sertanejo*, was a walking (or hunkering) specimen of every imaginable disease. If he escaped malaria, smallpox, Chagas disease, and venereal disease, he was racked by intestinal parasites and weakened by malnutrition.

Although first published in a technical scientific journal in 1916, the Pena-Neiva report was reprinted in 1918 (the year of Lobato's book version of *Urupês*) and gained wide publicity.[28] Politicians and editorial writers denounced the supposed "exaggerations" in the alarming health statistics, just as they had reacted to the portrait of Jéca Tatú, but they merely served to arouse more interest in the health question.[29]

Before this, Belisário Pena had done much to expand the debate by publishing a series of articles in *Correio da Manhã* (Rio) in late 1916 and early 1917 on the urgent need to clean up the backlands (*saneamento dos sertões*). One could hardly be surprised, he argued, at the "proverbial and much discussed indolence of the Brazilian or at his incapacity for any work requiring energy and health. . . . His condition is not the result of race or climate. He is simply a defenseless victim of disease, ignorance and malnutrition."[30] What Brazil needed was a massive campaign to finish the battle against epidemic and endemic disease, and educate the population on how to preserve good health. And these campaigns could turn for support to such authorities as Afrânio Peixoto, who assumed the professorship of hygiene in the Rio medical faculty in 1916, and who had long been arguing against the theory of the "unhealthful tropics."[31]

Reform-minded Congressmen took up the cause. President Wenceslau Braz responded to the growing pressure by creating the Rural Preventive Health Service (Serviço de Profilaxia Rural) in 1918, but the reformers wanted a cabinet level ministry and founded the Liga Pro-Saneamento do Brasil to press their campaign. Public health projects were also launched in provincial centers such as Recife and Pôrto Alegre.[32]

Given the fact that the figure of Jéca Tatú played a significant role in the debate over the causes of backwardness in Brazil's interior, it was inevitable that Monteiro Lobato would be challenged on his assumption that Jéca was the *cause* of the misery in which he vegetated, since the argument of the public health advocates was just the opposite. Lobato not only saw their point; he actually reversed his position the same year his article was reprinted and enthusiastically leaped into the public health campaign.[33]

In 1918 he published a series of articles pleading for a vast public attack on disease and for the educational effort needed to keep the *sertanejo* healthy once he was cured.[34] He mocked the romantic boosters of Brazil (*ufanistas*), lavishly praised Oswaldo Cruz and his successors such as Pena and Neiva, repeated the astounding statistics on the incidence of debilitating illnesses (10 million malaria victims out of a population of 25 million!). Lobato also ridiculed those critics who worried over the possible foreign reaction ("Cretins! This eternal mania about European opinion!"), and warned that time was short ("if we want to survive as a sovereign people there is only one path: clean up Brazil"). The essence of Lobato's conversion was contained in the sentence: "Jéca wasn't born that way, he became so" (*"O Jéca não é assim: está assim."*) Science had come to the rescue: "Today we can breathe with relief. The laboratory has given us the argument we hoped for. With the confidence it gives us we shall offer the highest voice of Biology against the sociological sentence of LeBon."

Lobato, seldom a man of moderate opinions, was now a vociferous convert to the cause of public health. His articles were collected in book form (entitled *Problema Vital*) and published in 1918 by the Eugenics Society of São Paulo and the Public Health League of Brazil (Liga Pro-Saneamento do Brasil). Included was a fable called "The Resurrection of Jéca Tatú," which told the story of a Jéca who, after he was cured by a traveling doctor, transformed his farm by hard work and became happy, wealthy, and a world traveler. Millions of copies of this fable (popularly labeled "Jéca Tatuzinho") were distributed in the interior where Lobato's words admonished whoever could read or find someone to read to them: "Children, never forget this story, and when you grow up try to imitate Jéca." Lobato also used his own São Paulo publishing firm (the first in Brazil to have a national, albeit very limited, network of distribution) to help print and distribute great quantities of educational flyers and booklets explaining the principles of hygiene, nutrition, and scientific agriculture.[35]

THE AFRICAN HERITAGE

The public health campaign to rescue the maligned man of the interior had not brought with it a comprehensive revision in the debate over Brazil's "ethnic problem." As noted above, Jéca Tatú did not have, at least in the general conception, any African blood. Rather, he was thought to be (whatever the reality) a retrograde white, with perhaps some Indian blood. Nonetheless, the pejorative portrait of him (as in *Urupês*) made him irredeemable, a victim of *inherent* defects. In short, Jéca was caught in a determinist trap that was described in language very similar to the racist determinism of pre-1914. Insofar as Jéca was thought to be part Indian, the revisionist campaign was attacking one element in prevailing racist theory—the assumption that Indians were inferior to whites. It was ignoring, however, the whole issue of blackness.

As we have seen, only a few curious writers before 1930 had devoted serious attention to the ethnography and sociology of the African and his Brazilian descendants.[36] Sílvio Romero had made an impressive collection of Afro-Brazilian folklore for his pioneering history of Brazilian literature (first edition: 1888), although his example was not followed by any other major literary historian or critic.[37] Nina Rodrigues, the Bahian medical professor of racist views, had begun an ambitious project of documenting Afro-Brazilian survivals in Bahia when death cut short his research in 1906.[38] In that same year the journalist João do Rio published a study of Afro-Brazilian religious customs in Rio de Janeiro.[39] Finally, a doctor from Bahia, Manoel Querino, published a series of studies on Afro-Brazilian customs.[40] Aside from these pioneers, all relatively isolated in their labors and gaining little discussion of their findings, there was no serious interest in investigating or analyzing the African or Afro-Brazilian presence. Even these few investigators had no successors who published significantly until the 1930's.

The one other effective scientific exception to this pattern was the anthropologist Edgar Roquette-Pinto,[41] whose work contributed to the development in Brazil of the rival theory of "culture," which was becoming by the 1920's in Europe and North America a keystone of environmentalist social science.[42] An avid field researcher, he followed in the scientific tradition of his predecessors at the Museu Nacional, where attention was concentrated on the Indian.* He had served as a minor Brazilian delegate to the Universal Congress of Races in 1911 in London, where Batista de Lacerda gave his much-discussed paper on miscegenation. In 1912 he accompanied General Rondon on his famous exploration of the interior state of Mato Grosso, later (1917) publishing a highly regarded and widely cited ethnographic survey of the Indian population.[43] Roquette-Pinto will be dealt with in some detail here, because his career can be seen as a continuous dialogue with Euclides da Cunha, whose work he admired more than any other Brazilian writer's, and who profoundly influenced him from the moment, as a student, he read Os Sertões, and decided to become an anthropologist.[44]

Like Euclides, Roquette-Pinto was deeply troubled by the miserable condition of the man of the interior. Unlike Euclides, he soon came to question the racist assumptions of the anthropogeography (Ratzel et al.) which da Cunha never escaped. Although he never ceased to admire Euclides' courage as a pioneer amateur ethnographer who transformed his science into a literary work of universal appeal, by 1914 he had progressed far enough from Euclides' position to argue that, although much of the black population had been abandoned to "the kind of total ignorance which in the modern world makes man into a helpless biped," thus accelerating their disappearance,[45] blacks (mulat-

---

* The efforts of scientists like Roquette-Pinto were impressive in the light of the rudimentary conditions of academic life then prevailing (Fernando de Azevedo, As Ciências no Brasil, 368-77). Neither Anthropology nor Sociology had become established disciplines in Brazil before 1930. Even if they had, there were no universities to house them. The disparate faculties that had grown up did not begin to coalesce into organized universities until 1934 with the establishment of the first one in São Paulo. Roquette-Pinto's principal scientific institutional affiliation was the Museu Nacional, of which he became Director in 1926. But the museum continued to suffer from very limited financial resources, and to concentrate its major effort on physical anthropological studies of the Indian.

toes were evidently excluded from this discussion) had, with proper education, shown themselves capable of great progress in the United States. Presumably this could also happen in Brazil, although Roquette-Pinto ventured no prediction (significantly, he still cited Nina Rodrigues' research without any critical comment).

Back in 1911 Roquette-Pinto had furnished the population estimates (showing Brazil to be already 50 per cent white) which Batista de Lacerda used in refuting critics who charged him with understanding the degree of Brazil's relative whiteness. Nonetheless, he differed significantly from Batista de Lacerda. Although he assumed the black population would continue to diminish, thus automatically whitening the total population, and that the process would be aided by the probable lightening of the mulattoes, his policy prescription was to play down the whitening process, at least in writing aimed at a Brazilian audience, and to study and work to improve the Brazilian population *as it was* throughout the country.[46] "Our national problem is not transforming *mestiços* into whites. Our problem is the education of those who are here, whether light or dark."[47]

That injunction became his principal message. In later writings Roquette-Pinto continued his emphasis on the importance of environment, but he also argued that the Brazilian population had already shown great vigor simply by virtue of having adapted successfully to their environment, as in the case of the *sertanejo* whose "self-sacrifice, talent and strength had conquered Rondonia" (the Indian region of Mato Grosso explored by the Rondon mission of 1912).[48]

In 1917 he produced a fully developed refutation of the three "erroneous" racist theories to which Euclides had subscribed: the degeneracy of mixed bloods, the inevitability of a struggle among the races, and the view that Indians could be indigenous only to the Western Hemisphere.[49] He noted that Euclides' profoundly pessimistic view of the mixed blood (as reflected in Part I of *Os Sertões*) had come from Agassiz, who, although born in Switzerland, "was a professor in the United States where they lynch a Negro as easily as they kill a mosquito." He ridiculed Agassiz' (already a straw man) views of the geological and biological isolation of Brazil which had been the scientific basis for his polygenist theory of mulatto degeneracy. Euclides had tried "too hard" to learn from such foreign scientists. The neo-Darwinist doctrine of the triumph of the "strong races," as well as the theory of degeneracy of mixed bloods, were products of a "scientific dilettantism" that had been replaced by an understanding that races, though different, were never "inferior" or "superior." "Here was Euclides' great mistake: he considered people to be inferior who were only backward; and men who were merely ignorant he thought incompetent."

Ironically enough, Roquette-Pinto noted, Euclides had *described* the valor of the mixed blood defenders (in Part II of *Os Sertões*) in such a way as to contradict his own endorsement (in Part I) of Social Darwinist theory. And subsequent history had furnished further evidence to refute racist dogma, most recently in the courageous and effective combat of black troops fighting in Europe (the homeland of racist theory) during World War I: "The Negro, who had always been thrown up to us as humiliating proof of our ethnic inferiority, disproved those theories on European soil. . . ." Finally, Roquette-Pinto dismissed as a false issue Euclides' worry that Brazil would never achieve "racial unity," pointing out that no nation really enjoyed it, and that in any case national unity (as Alberto Tôrres had shown) was sociological not racial.

Roquette-Pinto was following squarely in the footsteps of Manoel Bomfim and Alberto Tôrres in repudiating the racist frame of reference and stressing man's response to his environment as the key variable.[50] He was a prime example of the ideal they had urged—a careful, objective student of Brazil's current social conditions. By unequivocally rejecting the theory of mixed blood degeneracy he lent impressive scientific credentials to the growing campaign to rescue the native Brazilian from the determinist trap.* Like Sílvio Romero, he thought that Brazil's greatest need was a realistic sense of confidence, thus avoiding both that "cruel defeatism that threatens to undermine the nation" and the "lazy optimism of those who hide to ward off danger."

His autobiographical retrospect serves as fitting summary of how far some Brazilians had gone in their thinking by the end of the war:

> I come from the last years of the Monarchy. I was five years old when the Republic was born. I think the country owes a great debt to my generation, which began to disbelieve in the "fabulous riches" of Brazil in order to begin believing in the "decisive possibilities of work." We had been given the idea that a well-born and well-bred young man didn't have to work. . . . We had also heard that our sky had more stars than any other. . . . My generation began to count the stars. . . . And we went to see if it was true that our woods had more wildlife. . . . And we began to speak frankly to our fellow citizens. With my generation Brazil ceased to be merely a lyrical theme.[51]

And by 1928 he felt able to give the select members of the Academia Brasileira de Letras, who had just elected him a member, a reassuring prediction:

---

* Scientific evidence against theories of inherent racial differences was offered also by Juliano Moreira, a mulatto psychiatrist who was an important figure in establishing psychiatry as a field in Brazil. In a paper delivered in 1929 at the Faculty of Medicine of the University of Hamburg, Moreira noted that the application of psychological tests (such as Binet-Simon and Terman) in Brazil had shown that the differences among persons of diverse races "depend more on the level of instruction and education of each individual being examined than on his ethnic group." He opted unequivocally for an environmentalist explanation by concluding that when individuals of "groups considered inferior" were born and educated in a large city, they exhibited a "better psychological profile than individuals of Nordic extraction who were raised in a backward area of the interior (1929 paper reprinted in "Juliano Moreira e o Problema do Negro e do Mestiço no Brasil," a chapter by Moreira's widow in Gilberto Freyre, ed., Novos estudos afro-brasileiros, Rio de Janeiro, 1937, 146-50). A tribute to Moreira's efforts to establish psychiatry as a field was given by Antonio Austregesilo in Jornal do Comércio, July 27, 1943. I am indebted to Professor Donald Cooper for this reference.

Brazil's most interesting feature at this historical moment is the effort of its people to unify themselves, coming together in blood and
cooperation to make the ultimate leap that will accomplish simul-
taneously its own consolidation and the final conquest of its territory.
This drama . . . will inevitably become . . . the surprise and the
wonder of the world.[52]

As if to prove that this prediction was not in vain, in the 1930's
attention finally turned in a major way to the African. A leader in
the change was Artur Ramos, a physician from Bahia. Ramos
published a series of influential books and articles on Afro-Brazilian culture, drawing on materials collected by Nina Rodrigues,
whose pioneering work Ramos greatly admired. Ramos added or-
ganizational ability to his research and teaching, and was instrumental in founding the Brazilian Society of Anthropology and
Ethnology in 1941.[53] He was also active in the Afro-Brazilian
Congresses held in Recife in 1934 and in Bahia in 1937. These
large-scale scholarly meetings centered upon papers discussing
the most diverse aspects of Afro-Brasiliana: cuisine, music, folklore, linguistics, religion, drama, and the history of the African
presence, especially under slavery and in runaway slave communities.[54]

Another figure who contributed greatly to the study of the
Afro-Brazilian was Gilberto Freyre, who became a leading figure
in the redefinition of Brazil's racial identity. He was a principal
organizer of the first Afro-Brazilian Congress (1934) in Recife,
his home city, where he had already established himself as the
leader of a varied regionalist intellectual movement. Freyre's
greatest impact came with the publication of *Casa Grande e
Senzala* in 1933 (later translated into English as *The Masters and
the Slaves*)[55]—a social history of the slave plantation world of
Northeastern Brazil in the sixteenth and seventeenth centuries
when the sugar economy furnished the focus for Brazil's multi-
racial society. Freyre's portrait, often impressionistic and idiosyncratic in its structure and documentation, provided a sympathetic
insight into the intimate personal relations among the planter

families and their slaves. In furnishing his detailed picture of this intensely patriarchical ethos, Freyre dwelt on the manifold ways in which the African and mulatto deeply influenced the life style of the planter class, in food, clothing, and sex. His first book was followed in 1936 by *Sobrados e Mucambos* (translated as *The Mansions and the Shanties*)—a study of the urban-rural social conflux of the eighteenth and early nineteenth centuries that followed the same methodology and style.[56]

Casa-Grande e Senzala turned on its head the question of whether generations of miscegenation had done irreparable damage.[57] Brazil's ethnic potpourri, Freyre argued, was an immense asset. He showed how research in nutrition, anthropology, medicine, psychology, sociology, and agronomy had rendered the racial theories obsolete and had pointed up new villains—insufficient diet, impractical clothing, and disease too often undiagnosed and untreated (especially syphilis). He quoted studies by Brazilian scientists, the product of a new and profound concern on the part of Brazilian intellectuals about the long-ignored social problems of their own country,[58] to show that the Indian and the Negro had made important contributions to a healthier diet and a more practical style of dress for Brazilians. Thus Freyre dramatized for a wider public the country's new knowledge of the racial dimensions of its own past.[59]

Equally important for the book's popular success was the author's detailed description of the intimate social history of patriarchal society. While this approach incurred the criticism of a few academic critics abroad, it appealed to Brazilians because it helped explain the origin of their personalities.[60] At the same time, his readers were being given the first scholarly examination of Brazilian national character with an unabashedly optimistic message: Brazilians could be proud of their unique, ethnically mixed tropical civilization, whose social vices—which Freyre did not minimize—could be attributed primarily to the atmosphere of the slave-holding monoculture that dominated the country until the second half of the nineteenth century. The evil conse-

quences of miscegenation stemmed not from race-mixing itself,
but from the unhealthy relationship of master and slave under
which it occurred.[61]

Freyre's writings also did much to focus attention on the inherent value of the African as the representative of a high civilization in his own right. Freyre was thus furnishing, for those Brazilians who might want to take it that way, a rationale for a
multi-racial society in which the component "races"—European,
African, and Indian—could be seen as *equally* valuable. The
practical effect of his analysis was not, however, to promote such
a racial egalitarianism. Rather, it served to reinforce the whitening ideal by showing graphically that the (primarily white) elite
had gained valuable cultural traits from their intimate contact
with the African (and Indian, to a lesser extent).

Other scholars also contributed, during the 1930's, to the exploration of the African and Afro-Brazilian contribution. Mário
de Andrade, acknowledged leader of the Modernist Movement,
studied the samba in São Paulo and folk festival images in Recife.[62] Edison Carneiro published extensively on the influence of
African religion in Brazil.[63] Although many Brazilian readers
must have read this kind of writing for its folkloric appeal, it nonetheless revealed a move away from the racist assumptions that
dismissed the African as a barbarian of inferior stock destined to
be obliterated in the "racial whirlpool" of ethnic evolution (the
phrase of Caio de Menezes back in 1914).[64]

IMMIGRATION POLICY

Although the public health campaigners, the scientific anti-
racists, and later the enthusiasts of Afro-Braziliana gave a new
dimension to the debate over Brazil's ethnic future, the whitening ideal remained firmly entrenched among the elite. It was
clearly illustrated in the concern over immigration. In 1921 the
western state of Mato Grosso made a land concession to developers. According to the press these developers were linked to

organizers in the United States who were recruiting black North Americans to emigrate to Brazil. The President of Mato Grosso (a Catholic Bishop) immediately canceled the concession and so informed the Brazilian Foreign Minister; but the press continued to spread the alarm. As the eminent public health specialist Arthur Neiva wrote, "Why should Brazil, which has resolved its race problem so well, raise a question among us which has never even crossed our minds? Within a century the nation will be white."[65]

Two Congressional deputies, Andrade Bezerra (from the Northeastern state of Pernambuco) and Cincinnato Braga (São Paulo), thought strong action was needed and introduced a bill to prohibit entry into Brazil of "human beings of the black race." Its introduction provoked a heated debate in the lower house of the National Congress.[66] Several deputies branded it unconstitutional and therefore inadmissible for debate. The most vocal, Joaquim Osório, argued that the bill would amount to a "new black code, a policy of race prejudice which fortunately has never existed in our country." Bezerra, who introduced the bill and bore the brunt of its defense in the first reading, replied that it was time to drop "this purely sentimental attitude we have adopted toward our country's vital issues." That sentimentality was promptly revealed. João Cabral observed poignantly that if this bill were passed blacks would be able to enter the Kingdom of Heaven but not Brazil. Alvaro Baptista observed that it was the blacks who had "guarded all of us during our infancy, the race whose women were wet-nurses for most of the honorable deputies." Bezerra reminded his colleagues of the recent immigration in the United States, Canada, and Australia, "especially concerning those of Asian descent," and called for a "policy that will guard our national interests." Having been challenged as a measure not even worthy (on constitutional grounds) of formal consideration, the first vote was procedural. By a count of 94 to 19 the Chamber of Deputies voted to admit the bill for debate and thereby sent it to the committee.

It evidently died there, but the idea did not. In 1923 Fidelis Reis, a federal deputy from Minas Gerais, introduced a slightly different version.[67] The color bar was now included in a larger proposal to expand the colonization service, which had been set up by the immigration law of 1907 but never effectively funded. Article five of the bill prohibited the entry of any colonists "of the black race" and limited orientals ("the yellow race") to an annual rate of no more than 3 per cent of the orientals already resident in Brazil. (Quotas for immigrants had been incorporated in the National Origins Act passed in the United States in 1921.) Fidelis Reis made specific reference to the U.S. law but noted that Brazil still had much greater need of European stock than its powerful northern neighbor. (It is interesting to note that even a spokesman who condemned black immigration stopped short of following in Brazil the implicit U.S. ethnic policy of discriminating *among* European immigrants.)

Reis argued for stepping up the recruitment and systematic settlement of immigrants to meet "the constant complaint of landowners over the lack of labor." Argentina had done far more to attract Europeans and with great benefit to her growth—here he was reiterating the immigrationist arguments so familiar before 1914. Significantly, he felt it necessary at the same time to refute nationalist critics who "feared the foreigner because he might dominate our country." "Only he," argued Reis, "can ensure that our great continental destiny will be realized."

What kind of immigrants should be admitted? There must be no endangering of "the racial type being formed" by introducing "masses of unassimilable ethnic groups." The African? Although he had "worked, suffered and with dedication helped us build this Brazil, it would have been better if we had never had him." The oriental was almost as great a menace because his alleged failure to assimilate would guarantee the presence of "yellow cysts in the national organism" which would be as great a danger to Brazil as the concentration of orientals in California was to the United States.

Fidelis Reis was attacked by other deputies for his racism, as Bezerra and Braga had been. But his critics' comments showed how fully they shared his basic desire to see the population grow whiter. Several explained away the allegedly weak state of the population in the interior on the ground that they lacked proper health facilities, thereby showing the influence of the public health campaigns on their thinking. But even the apologists for the native-born Brazilians endorsed the idea that Brazil's ethnic problem was solving itself. Eurico Valle, who opposed the bill, noted that the *mestiço* is "an intermediary type who will perforce have to disappear." Carvalho Neto, another opponent, said that "in Brazil the Negro will disappear in seventy years, while in the United States he constitutes a permanent danger." Even the defenders of the native-born worker (Napoleão Gomes: "I can guarantee you that the *mestiço* from the backlands [*sertanejo*] is the most energetic type in Brazil") never contested the assumptions of the whitening ideal. On the contrary, the only way the bill's opponents really differed from Reis was in their assessment that the process was going well, while Reis thought the steady ascent toward whiteness seemed by no means assured (evidenced by his reference to the black as "an ever-present threat weighing down our destiny"). He saw the *mestiço* as an unreliable instrument for racial improvement and quoted Euclides da Cunha's famous passage on the instability of mixed bloods as proof. When other deputies expressed faith in the *mestiço* as the intermediary in the whitening process, he cited Agassiz and LeBon as contradicting authorities.

In addition to his Congressional speeches, Fidelis Reis attempted to generate support from intellectuals, producing some interesting results. Clóvis Bevilàqua, the famous jurist and product of the Recife School, opposed his bill, pointing to the fact that Batista de Lacerda in his 1911 paper had demonstrated the great contribution of the *mestiço*. Even more relevant was Bevilàqua's observation that "as Oliveira Lima has noted, there is no danger that colored immigrants will come in numbers great enough to make them difficult to assimilate or to upset the normal development of our ethnic type." (In other words, black immigrants were no threat only because so few were likely to come.)[68] Afrânio Peixoto, the novelist-medical professor whose works were cited earlier, gave the following noteworthy answer. Miscegenation, he said, was "unfortunate." "It will take us perhaps three hundred years to change spiritually and to bleach our skin so that we become, if not white, at least disguised and thus lose our *mestiço* character." The slowness of the process made him worry about any massive black immigration. "It is at this moment that America [the U.S.A.] intends to rid itself of her body of fifteen million Negroes and send them to Brazil. How many centuries will it take to cleanse this human impurity? Will we have enough albumin to refine all this dross? . . . God help us—if He is a Brazilian!"[69]

The strength of the whitening ideology was shown again in the responses to a survey on immigration conducted in 1926 by the National Agricultural Society (Sociedade Nacional de Agricultura).[70] One hundred and sixty-six prominent Brazilians from all major regions replied. As might be expected, most were rural landowners or linked to agriculture. When asked, "do you favor continued immigration?" all but five said yes. But in response to the question, "do you favor Negro immigration?" one hundred and twenty-four said no, while only thirty said yes (seven registered no opinion). The minority in favor thought the Negro would make good rural labor, but the heavy majority against was concerned that the entry of more blacks would delay or set back the whitening process. Their responses showed a familiar pattern of race-thinking. The African had contributed much to building Brazil but was an inferior ethnic element. In their written comments, most respondents expressed faith that the emerging population would overcome the defects of the separate racial strains. The black, as one physician from Rio Grande do Sul explained, "is being absorbed by the white race." Why disturb that process? A judge from São Paulo wrote, "in these days when everyone is striving to purify the race . . . it is not advisable to admit more Negroes to our country."

Opinion was much more divided on the question "do you favor oriental immigration?" Seventy-nine said no and seventy-five said yes (seven had no opinion). Racist criticisms of orientals (this in practice meant Japanese) were made by some respondents, but with less frequency than on the Negro. Many who considered the Japanese inferior thought them ethnically better than the Negro. Unlike the case of black immigration, Japanese immigrants were a reality. Since 1908 about 30,000 Japanese had entered Brazil and were highly regarded in many Brazilian circles for their efficiency as agricultural workers.[71] This survey showed that there was a strong body of opinion favoring continued Japanese immigration, which Fidelis Reis had acknowledged by allowing orientals a small quota in his bill.

A roughly similar division of opinion on the general question of color bars against immigrants occurred among the ranks of delegates to the First Brazilian Congress of Eugenics in 1929. Azevedo Amaral, a prominent newspaper editor and strong advocate of the now increasingly anachronistic scientific racist position, presented a ten-point program which included a proposal to bar all non-white immigrants. The meeting took several votes, first defeating (by twenty to seventeen) a proposal to forbid all non-European immigrants, and then voting down the proposed barring of black immigrants by twenty-five to seventeen. The opposition to Amaral was led by Roquette-Pinto.[72]

What did these debates over immigration signify? First, it was still possible for respected politicians and intellectuals to propose color bars for immigrants. Such a prohibition had, after all, been included in the immigration decree of 1891, although it did not appear in the law of 1907. On the other hand, these bills were not passed, perhaps in part because there seemed so little real prospect of black immigrants coming from anywhere (including the United States). More important, most deputies, like most members of the elite, shied away from such overtly racist gestures as an absolute color bar. They believed in a whiter Brazil and thought they were getting there by a natural (almost miraculous?) process. An overt color bar smacked of the United States, which remained a constant reminder of what almost all Brazilians considered an inhumane (and eventually self-defeating) solution to the ethnic problem.[73] Why miscegenation should have operated so benignly in Brazil and not in the United States (Brazilians often seemed to ignore the fact of extensive racial cross-breeding in the United States) was seldom explained.

In 1934 a nationally elected Constituent Assembly gathered to frame a new constitution. After the Revolution of 1930 the provisional government of Getúlio Vargas had swept aside the Constitution of 1891 and ruled by decree. The Provisional Government had promised to call a Constituent Assembly, which finally met and drafted what became the Constitution of 1934. Article 121, Section 6 incorporated the principle of national quotas which had been urged by Deputies Andrade Bezerra and Cincinnato Braga in the 1920's. The article read: "The entry of immigrants into the national territory will be subject to the restrictions necessary to guarantee the ethnic integration and the physical and legal capacity of the immigrant; the immigrant arrivals from any country cannot, however, exceed an annual rate of two percent of the total number of that nationality resident in Brazil during the preceding fifty years."[74] While debating this article, which was approved and included in the Constitution of 1934, Congressmen said much about the need to avoid endangering the steady process of assimilation of all residents into a unified society. In fact, the restriction was aimed at the Japanese, against whose alleged clannishness and resistance to assimilation a major campaign had been waged for over a decade.[75]

A Paulista deputy, Teotonio Monteiro de Barros, spoke at length in favor of the quota restriction. He disclaimed any racial prejudice, but urged attention to the need to guide Brazil's ethnic evolution. He cited Euclides da Cunha, Licínio Cardoso, and

Oliveira Vianna (whose racial views are discussed below) on the problems of achieving a truly authentic Brazilian ethnic type. He was interrupted by other deputies who suggested he should also consult Gilberto Freyre and Roquette-Pinto. When one deputy objected that despite this supposed contribution of recent European immigrants it was the African who "achieved all the material progress in the country," Monteiro de Barros replied: "thank God the Negro problem has lost the seriousness it might have," owing to the "facility of absorption and assimilation which our physical environment contains." He added the comparison with the United States that Brazilians found irresistible: "On this point, Gentlemen, we are the ones who were on the right path; the United States went astray. While the Negro is growing in numbers and power within the United States, the Negro is disappearing in Brazil, absorbed by the white race's superior capacity for stability and assimilation." Although previously the Negro's role in ethnic evolution had been a cause for concern, now "the disappearance of this Negro stain in the white blood is already clearly underway and unmistakably headed for a favorable conclusion." Although his critics contested his worries about the dangers of unassimilated Japanese immigrants in São Paulo, none thought it worth disputing his faith in the whitening process. He had merely restated the elite's vision of Brazil's racial future.[76]

The same nationality quotas for immigrants were specified in the authoritarian Constitution of 1937 (Article 151) which Getúlio Vargas proclaimed after his coup in November of that year. Just before Vargas was subsequently deposed by the military in October 1945 his government issued an important decree-law (No. 7967 of September 18, 1945) stipulating that immigrants should be admitted in conformance with "the necessity to preserve and develop, in the ethnic composition of the population, the more desirable characteristics of its European ancestry." The framers of the Constitution of 1946, committed to the redemocratization of Brazil, conspicuously avoided putting any specifics on immigration into article 162, specifying instead that it would be regulated by law. Since no new body of immigration law has ever been passed, Brazil has continued to live under the regulations—with all their racist assumptions—laid down before 1946.[77]

THE WHITENING IDEAL

During the 1920's the whitening thesis received its most systematic statement from Oliveira Vianna, a lawyer-historian who became one of the most widely read interpreters of Brazilian reality between the wars. He had studied for the traditional law degree in Rio de Janeiro but soon became one of the fiercest critics of the imitative culture in which he was educated. Born in the state of Rio de Janeiro, he was described by contemporaries as mulatto, which may in part explain his interest in the ethnic question. He was a key member of the circle around Alberto Tôrres and wrote newspaper articles praising Tôrres' plea for a greater national consciousness. Beginning in 1910 Oliveira Vianna published a stream of newspaper articles and books, gaining steadily in influence. In 1916 he became a professor at the Law Faculty in Rio de Janeiro, but preferred to spend most of his time in Niteroi, the provincial capital (across the bay from the city of Rio) of his native state of Rio de Janeiro.[78]

At first glance Oliveira Vianna's ideas on race might have seemed a throw-back. He made no effort to conceal his admiration for the masters of European racist thought. He praised "the great Ratzel" and described Gobineau, Lapouge and Ammon as "mighty geniuses."[79] In 1920 he published the first volume of a historico-psychological study on the southern peoples of Brazil (*Populações Meridionais do Brasil*) in which he sought to apply the doctrines of anthropogeography and anthroposociology. Shortly thereafter he wrote a long chapter for the introductory volume of the official 1920 census (later published separately in book form under the title *Evolução do Povo Brasileiro*), where he offered empirical proof of Brazil's ascent toward whiteness, which he described by the anachronistic term of "Aryaniza-tion."[80]

Although he praised European racist thinkers and constantly referred to "inferior" and "superior" races, he did *not* regard such differences as absolute. This was, in fact, the compromise Brazilians had been making in order to reconcile racist theory and their multi-racial reality. Inconsistent as it must have seemed to doctrinaire racists from Europe or North America, Vianna made *degrees* of inferiority the central concept in his interpreta-tion of Brazil's racial evolution.

The Indian and Negro were inexorably declining as a propor-tion of the population, he said. He quoted several travelers' re-ports (in the late eighteenth and early nineteenth century, such as W. L. von Eschwege in Minas Gerais) on the allegedly low fecundity of the African. He offered tables showing wide per-centage variations in fertility and mortality that revealed the black and Indian to have a much lower rate of net natural in-crease than the whites and mulattoes. (One table showed a nega-tive rate for blacks.)

For final evidence Vianna compared the racial proportions of the population in the 1872 and 1890 censuses. In that period, the white proportion increased from 38 to 44 per cent, while the Negro (black) fell from nearly 20 per cent to under 15 per cent and the mixed (*mestiço*) fell from 38 to 32 per cent (the Indian climbed from 4 per cent to 9 per cent).[81] Vianna's citing of these figures was all the more interesting in view of the fact that the 1920 census (for which his analysis was an introductory chapter) did not include any breakdown by race—an omission officially justified on the grounds that "the responses [on racial categories] largely hide the truth," although it may also have resulted from a desire (obviously shared by Vianna) to gloss over the degree to which Brazil was still non-white.[82] And he had a reassuring conclusion for the elite. Immigration *was* playing the role Joa-quim Nabuco had hoped. "This admirable flow of immigration not only helps to raise quickly the coefficient of the pure Aryan group in our country but also by mixing and re-mixing with the mixed-blood (*mestiço*) population it helps, with equal speed, to raise the Aryan content of our blood."[83]

Oliveira Vianna had given a very optimistic statement of the whitening ideal. It was all the more significant for having been spelled out in the introduction to the officially published census of 1920. Although not carrying any government endorsement, Vianna's theoretical exposition did sum up the elite view expressed in the continuing public debate over Brazil's ethnic future.

Vianna's position as a theoretician of "whitening"—one of the principal elements in the elite's racial philosophy—has been blurred in historical interpretations by too exclusive an emphasis on his display of phrases from the unfashionable theories of scientific racism. "Aryan," "inferior-superior," "primitive races," and comparative cranial measurements—these were not the terms in which enlightened Brazilians wrote as the 1920's continued. Yet Vianna used such language to reach a conclusion incompatible with the assumptions of scientific racism: that Brazil was achieving ethnic purity by miscegenation. Much of Vianna's favorable impact among the public must have come from those Brazilians who concentrated on the conclusion and either were not bothered by the archaic terminology or chose to discount it as not undermining the validity of the conclusion.[84] In one sense the contradiction between assumptions and conclusion was enormously reassuring: if an erudite scholar who knew and believed so much of the (increasingly less) prestigious scientific racist theory from Europe and North America could conclude that Brazil's ethnic future was safe, then Brazilians could feel truly confident.[85]

Some readers were angered by Vianna's assertion that "the two primitive races only became civilizing agents [i.e., contributed eugenically to the formation of superior classes] when they lost their purity and mated with the white."[86] Such an arrogant denial of any cultural role for pure-blooded (or at least without any European blood) Indians or Africans ran directly counter to the pro-African and pro-Indian movement which was then developing a theory of cultural syncretism giving great weight to the non-white ingredients. Gilberto Freyre, a leader in that movement, became one of Oliveira Vianna's most persistent critics, attacking his scientific racist language.[87]

Since such language was soon to lose all respectability, history was on Freyre's side.[88] Yet this should not distract us from seeing that Vianna was an important transitional figure—bridging the gap between the scientific racism prevailing before 1914 and the environmentalist social philosophy predominant after 1930. In both eras whitening was the elite's de facto racial goal. It was Vianna's explanation of the historical origins of that process which made his work so comprehensible to his readers.

Another widely discussed statement of the whitening thesis appeared in 1928, when the Paulista aristocrat, Paulo Prado, published *Retrato do Brasil: Ensaio Sôbre a Tristeza Brasileira* (Portrait of Brazil: An Essay on Brazilian Sadness).[89] Although the purpose of this tract was to analyze Brazilian character in terms of its three vices (lust, greed, and melancholy) and although Prado's contemporaries read and commented on it in those terms, it contained a postscript which was composed, in fact, of a succinct statement as to where Brazil stood on the racial issue, especially "the role of the Negro in our racial formation . . . the most agonizing problem in that process."[90] "All races appear essentially equal in their mental capacity and adaptability to civilization," he said, citing an "American sociologist" (unnamed) to the effect that environment mattered far more than racial origins. Thus the question of racial inequality—"which was the battle-horse of Gobineau and is today the favorite argument of Madison Grant"—was being refuted by "science."[91]

This sounded like interesting evidence of the extent to which a cultivated member of the elite had assimilated the anti-racist message being advanced by Brazilians such as Roquette-Pinto. But in Prado's thought, the issues were not as clear as that:

The so-called Aryanization of the Brazilian is a fact of everyday observation. Even with one-eighth Negro blood the African appearance completely fades away—it is the phenomenon of "passing" in the United States. Thus in the continuous mixture of our life since the colonial era the Negro is slowly disappearing, being transformed into the deceptive appearance of a pure Aryan.[92]

Given that there were no inherent differences among the races, it is interesting that Prado had to add that (in any case!) the Brazilian population was whitening. In effect, he was trying to dismiss the race issue. Race inequality was scientifically disproved, miscegenation (especially involving the Negro) had uncertain results, but in any case the process was irreversible. He saw Brazil as very different from the United States, which Brazilians thought had an insoluble problem because of race hatred, segregation, and the ability of the U.S. Negro population to increase (presumably unlike the Brazilian black who was thought to be disappearing through net natural decrease). Brazil's ethnic future was out of her hands. For Prado, the libidinous Portuguese settlers had decided Brazil's future and only time would reveal what it would be.

He repeated the familiar lamentations about Brazil's failure to develop her enormous resources (even citing Bryce's caustic observation after his South American tour in 1910 that if the Anglo-Saxons controlled Brazil they could really make something of the country). He listed the vital areas that were neglected—public hygiene, transportation, education, virtually every sphere of government—while the economy languished. He also commented on the vice of imitation: "In this country which has practically everything, we import everything: from Paris fashions—ideas and clothes—to broom handles and toothpicks."[93] He sounded like Alberto Tôrres.

Prado in fact set out to produce a national character study—a psychological profile that ended in a call for drastic action—"surgery" in Prado's words.[94] But in painting the portrait he had downgraded the ethnic question by saying, in effect: Brazilians were

naturally getting whiter, they had no control over further miscegenation, and therefore they should concentrate on reorganiz-
ing their country. He saw Brazil's salvation as coming from
within—from a transformation of national character. Although
some readers denounced this as a new kind of determinism, Prado's de facto belief in whitening was combined with an implicitly optimistic and fundamentally nationalistic appeal—for the
construction of a "new order."[95]

In 1930 yet another prominent Brazilian, the historian-politi-
cian João Pandiá Calogeras, described the whitening phenomenon in a set of lectures delivered to a summer school in Rio de
Janeiro for foreigners (especially North Americans). After describing the significant contribution of the African to the building of Brazil, he concluded that

> the black stain is destined to disappear in a relatively short space of
> time because of the influx of white immigration in which the heritage
> of Ham is dissolving. Roosevelt rightly pointed out that the future
> has reserved for us a great boon: the happy solution of a problem
> fraught with tremendous, even mortal dangers—the problems of a
> possible conflict between the two races.[96]

BRAZILIAN REACTION TO
NAZISM: A DIGRESSION

The 1930's also brought news of a new source of racist thought—
Hitler Germany—that could be expected to suggest to Brazilians
that racist ideas were not as dead as recent intellectual trends in
their country might indicate. Brazil actually had its own rightist
political movement which bore some disturbing resemblances to
European fascist parties. The Integralists (Ação Integralista Brasileira) became the fastest growing Brazilian party after its
founding in 1932.[97] Although their official documents never made
racism a central theme, one prominent Integralist, Gustavo Barroso, advocated a virulently anti-Semitic line in numerous books

and articles,[98] and the Integralist press reprinted Nazi propaganda against Jews. Brazilian authorities worried that the sizable German and Italian speaking minorities in Brazil might listen receptively to the propaganda directed at them by the Mussolini and Hitler regimes. In 1938 the Vargas government suppressed Nazi activities in Brazil, which had been extensive in the southern states where German settlement was heavy.[99] In fact, however, the great majority of foreign-born Brazilians and their children maintained their loyalty to their adopted country. Although some German-born showed interest in the Nazi movement, no significant number wanted to apply political racism in Brazil.[100]

A group of twelve well-known intellectuals including Roquette-Pinto, Arthur Ramos, and Gilberto Freyre was worried enough by October 1935 to issue the "Manifesto Against Racial Prejudice," which warned that the "transplanting of racist ideas and especially of their social and political correlates" was an especially grave danger for a country like Brazil "whose ethnic formation is extremely heterogeneous." They announced that such "perversions of scientific ideas" based on "phantasies and pseudo-scientific myths," would create in Brazil "unforeseeable dangers compromising national unity and threatening the future of our country." They called upon Brazilian intellectuals to resist "the corrosive action of these currents which can lead to the dissolution of the Brazilian family."[101]

An even stronger manifesto was issued by the Brazilian Society of Anthropology and Ethnology in 1942.[102] It explicitly endorsed environmentalism (the 1935 manifesto was more cautious on that point), arguing that "Anthropology furnishes no scientific basis for discriminatory acts against any people on the basis of supposed racial inferiority." It also cited other recent anti-racist manifestoes, such as those of the Biologists at the Seventh International Genetics Conference in Edinburgh in 1939 and of the American Anthropological Association in 1938, and included this claim for their country's unique success in the field of race relations:

Brazil is a nation formed from the most heterogeneous ethnic elements. People of Indian, European and African origins have mixed in an atmosphere of such liberality and such a complete absence of legal restrictions on miscegenation that Brazil has become the ideal land for a true community of people representing very diverse ethnic origins. This great "laboratory of civilization," as our country has been called, offers the most scientific and human solution to the problem of mixing races and cultures—a problem so acute among other peoples. . . . This Brazilian philosophy on the treatment of races is the best weapon we can offer against the monstrous Nazi philosophy which is murdering and pillaging in the name of race. . . .

As events proved during the 1930's and 1940's, scientific racism was dead in Brazil. The persecution of Jews by the German government served only to discredit further any lingering prestige such theories might have continued to enjoy among the elite. Brazilian revulsion at German racist policies also showed Brazil's continuing rejection of institutionalized racial discrimination. However worried Brazilian anthropologists may have felt, scientific or political racism offered little danger of changing the patterns of thought and behavior established by 1930.

EPILOGUE: WHITENING—AN ANACHRONISTIC RACIAL IDEAL?

We have traced the varying manner in which articulate members of the elite explained their racial hopes in terms of prevailing racial theories. When scientific racism penetrated Brazil, intellectuals responded by trying to produce a rationale for their social system within the framework of scientific racist thought. Even when those theories fell into scientific disrepute, the Brazilian elite maintained its explicit faith in the whitening process. Since that faith could no longer be couched in the language of racial superiority and inferiority, it was described as a process of "ethnic integration" which was (as had been said since the 1890's) miraculously resolving Brazil's racial problems. As the hope for whitening remained constant, confidence in its inevitability grew.[103]

A typical expression of this faith could be found in the prose of Fernando de Azevedo, a widely honored educational reformer who occupied the chair of educational sociology at the University of São Paulo and had earlier directed that state's public school system. Azevedo was asked to prepare an introduction to the census of 1940. His product, A Cultura Brasileira (first published in Brazil in 1943 and issued in an English translation in 1950), gained immediate acceptance as a standard interpretation of Brazilian civilization. The first chapter, on the role of land and race in Brazil, concluded with these words about the future:

> If we admit that Negroes and Indians are continuing to disappear, both in the successive dilutions of white blood and in the constant process of biological and social selection, and that immigration, especially that of a Mediterranean origin, is not at a standstill, the white man will not only have in Brazil his major field of life and culture in the tropics, but be able to take from old Europe—citadel of the white race—before it passes to other hands, the torch of western civilization to which the Brazilians will give a new and intense light —that of the atmosphere of their own civilization.[104]

It was significant that Azevedo discussed Brazil's racial future on the occasion of a national census. Oliveira Vianna had given the first systematic exposition of his "Aryanization" theory in a chapter accompanying the census of 1920, although that document was conspicuous for not breaking down data by racial category. The census of 1940, which did include breakdown by race, provided evidence that Brazil's population was growing whiter, thereby furnishing support for the elite consensus that the African and Indian component would inexorably decline.[105]

While still believing that white was best and that Brazil was getting whiter, elite spokesmen after 1930 gained further satisfaction and confidence from the new scientific consensus that black was not inherently worse and thus that the racist claim that miscegenation must result in degeneration was nonsense. For approximately two decades after 1930, this Brazilian satisfaction at the discrediting of scientific racism led to the argument that Brazilians' alleged lack of discrimination made them morally superior to the technologically more advanced countries where systematic repression of racial minorities was still practiced. The United States was the favorite example; Nazi Germany became another. Comparisons with the United States had long been frequent in Brazilian writing about race, but they seemed even more striking after 1930, when the Jim Crow system had lost the cultural sanction once given it by racist theory. Brazilians, who had always found themselves on the defensive in discussing their country's racial past and future, began to take the offensive. It was not the facts of Brazilian race relations that had changed, but the assumptions on which Brazilians argued.

This attitude reached a climax in 1951 when the Brazilian government published a pamphlet extolling the virtues of Brazilian race relations in comparison to the racist system in the United States.[106] Since the publication was issued in English by the Ministry of Foreign Relations, and included a Foreword by Gilberto Freyre, there could be little doubt that it was intended to promote a favorable Brazilian image abroad. In fact, however, the pamphlet was a voice from the past. The early 1950's marked the end of the era when the Brazilian opinion-makers were able to use the whitening ideal both to reassure themselves about their racial future and to establish claim to a morally superior solution to the race problem.

What the Brazilian elite did not realize was the close link between its ethnic self-image and events abroad. Back in the 1930's Brazilians reacted strongly against the racist doctrines of Nazism, which had been a regression to an extreme version of pre-1920 scientific racism. The United States was, at the same time, continuing to practice racial segregation. For obvious reasons, both cases were comforting to the Brazilians, who could continue to define their racial reality as preferable to the extremist situations in the industrialized world—"extremist" as defined by respectable social scientists or the defenders of equal rights for racial minorities.

These foreign points of reference remained unchanged until the end of World War II. In 1942 Brazil entered hostilities on the Allied side, as she had done in 1917. Fighting the racist regime of Hitler did not seem to give Brazilian elite any immediate occasion to rethink their racial ideas. Nor was this surprising, since even the United States, Brazil's powerful ally and the self-proclaimed "arsenal of democracy," fought the entire war with an officially segregated military.

After the war, however, those foreign points of reference changed dramatically. The racist doctrines and concentration camps of the Hitler government were swept away by military defeat in 1945. Within a few years, the United States, after so many decades of brutal repression of the free black, began to move toward official repudiation of legal color bars. In 1948 President Truman issued a presidential decree ending segregation in the Armed Forces and the federal civil service. In 1952 a brief was filed with the Supreme Court leading to the Court's 1954 decision requiring an end to segregation in public schools. By the end of the 1950's blacks in the United States had launched their campaign of "civil disobedience," sit-ins, and protest marches. The legal reality of North American race relations was shifting profoundly, despite bitter resistance.

This change was fateful for Brazil because Brazilians had long defined their race relations and their racial identity by explaining how it *differed* from the United States. Now legalized segregation—the last formal institutional expression of racial discrimination—was gone. It was this institutional structure that Brazilians had long seen as the antithesis of their own, more "humane" system of race relations.

Furthermore, the United States was moving in new directions that made comparisons unexpectedly awkward. Even before the United States Supreme Court decision of 1954, President Truman had proposed the enactment of a fair employment practices law, aimed at prohibiting racial discrimination in jobs. In 1957 the United States Congress passed its first act of civil rights legislation since 1875. Later laws authorized elaborate mechanisms for hearing and investigating complaints of racial discrimination; the federal government was even authorized to punish citizens found guilty of denying services or products on account of race, creed, or color. In the late 1960's and early 1970's the federal government pressed employers to hire and promote minority employees. In two and a half decades since the end of war, the United States had turned the system of racial segregation on its head. Once the law had been used to enforce separation of the races; now it became an instrument of enforced integration. In practice, this meant requiring employers, landlords, and public service institutions (such as universities) to demonstrate their good faith by actively seeking black employees, tenants, students, or customers.

The most recent feature of the transformation in U.S. race relations has been the emergence of a "black is beautiful" movement. This reassertion of blackness was a logical outgrowth of the U.S. white community's long enforcement of a strictly biracial definition of racial identity: white or Negro. Any mulatto not light enough to "pass" had always been subject to the same legal disabilities and physical danger as his darkest brother. The "mulatto escape hatch" of Brazil had never opened in the United States.[107] Ironically, the recent reassertion of blackness may even have aided the upward climb of North American mulattoes, able to benefit from the de facto quota system that government pressures have created.

The contrast with Brazil was striking. Not only could Brazilians no longer point to the odious institution of segregation, or to the horrors of lynching in the United States. They were now witnessing a process of enforced integration. Brazil took one step which might at first seem comparable. In 1951, the same year the Foreign Minister published its pamphlet praising Brazil's race relations in contrast to those of the United States, the Brazilian Congress found itself in the unaccustomed position of passing a law prohibiting racial discrimination in public accommodations.* Significantly, it came after a touring North American black dancer, Katherine Dunham, complained of being refused accommodation in a São Paulo hotel. But the law has remained a symbolic gesture, with no government effort to investigate possible discrimination in such facilities. Although most experienced observers agree that post-war Brazil has experienced little overt discrimination of the kind banned by the Afonso Arinos law, Brazilian politicians have shown a notable lack of interest in actively promoting the social and economic ascension of non-whites per se. The majority of the elite have continued to believe that the striking failure of dark-skinned Brazilians to rise on the socio-economic scale can be attributed to barriers of class, not of race. Since these barriers also exist for millions of "white" Brazilians, policy-makers can easily reject the idea (although the issue is virtually never raised) of offering special aid to a racial minority.

The implications of this contrast are still sinking in for Brazilians. The United States has remained a bi-racial society but has moved from legally barring non-white participation in the power structure to forcing non-white entry into that structure, even if only in token numbers. Meanwhile the Brazilians are left with the legacy of their belief in whitening. Now, as before, the surest means for a Brazilian of African heritage to gain upward mobility is to possess a whiter skin than his parents. The North Americans have embarked on a social experiment the Brazilians never contemplated: the active promotion—with government funds, laws, and personnel—of equal opportunity. All this in the name of social justice—a realm in which the Brazilians, as we have seen in numerous writings and speeches, long considered themselves superior. This is not to deny that Brazilians could

---

* It is known as the Afonso Arinos Law, after its principal legislative author.

still point to great advantages Brazil enjoyed over the United States—as in Brazil's having avoided America's recurrent urban riots with their violent racial confrontations and having escaped the Negrophobia that distorted U.S. white thinking.

The U.S. approach depended on continuing to view its society as made up of easily identifiable ethnic groups. The entire apparatus of civil rights legislation and "affirmative action" is based on this assumption. Whereas being non-white previously subjected a North American to legal disabilities, now it has become grounds for gaining government aid in securing employment, housing, and educational advancement.* Brazil, on the other hand, continues to believe officially that its citizens are entirely equal, in racial terms, in their access to the channels of social mobility. No special provisions have been made or even considered for giving non-whites the benefit of "affirmative action" programs that would require employers to prove that they have honestly tried to locate and consider non-white applicants for jobs. And the overwhelming majority of Brazilian opinion-makers would undoubtedly consider such an idea as "racist" and unworthy even of consideration. Furthermore, the variability with which racial labels are applied in Brazil would make such a program impossible to carry out. The racial question is thus submerged in the larger question of social justice for the millions of poor at the bottom of the scale in Brazil's very unequal pattern of income distribution.

Another development abroad has altered the context of the Brazilian elite's race-thinking—the post-World War II decolonization of Asia and Africa. The newly emergent Third World is

---

* The degree to which non-whites, as a whole, have *succeeded* in gaining improved conditions in education, housing, income, jobs is another matter. An official U.S. government study published in 1972 revealed the continuing gap (which has recently increased by some indicators) between whites and non-whites in areas such as education, occupational status and income. The data was obtained from the 1970 census and from a subsequent survey of families and is analyzed in *The Social and Economic Status of the Black Population in the United States*, Washington, D.C., 1972.

made up largely of "colored" nations which have often asserted their non-white identity, especially in Africa. African black nationalism has been paralleled by powerful nationalist movements (seldom couched in racial terms) in Southeast Asia, where non-white rebels have overthrown European rule in virtually every country. The postwar wave of political liberation in Africa and Asia was a tardy sequel to the earlier demise of the racist doctrines which had been used to justify European control between 1870 and 1920. By the mid-1950's the idea of "whitening" had ceased to be a respectable goal for a Third World country such as Brazil to proclaim, if for no other reason than the embarrassment it would obviously cause in relations with the nationalist non-white governments in Africa and Asia. By the 1960's it would even have been embarrassing vis-à-vis the United States, where blackness was becoming a new source of pride for many non-whites. In short, the achieving of political independence in Afro-Asia and the civil rights revolution in the United States dramatically underlined the loss in prestige for the archaic European-centered culture whose racist assumptions had first led Brazilians to formulate their "whitening" rationale. Brazilians had produced that vision of their racial future because it seemed to reconcile the reality of their multi-racial society with the European-North American model of development they sought to imitate. Now that Europe and North America had politically (as well as scientifically) repudiated racism, and now that non-whiteness had become a source of cultural pride and political power both in Afro-Asia and the United States, Brazilians were left with a badly outdated ideal of their racial future.

In fairness it must be added that explicit discussions of ethnic futures have generally gone out of intellectual fashion since 1950, certainly as explanations for a nation's development prospects. In large part this resulted from the discrediting of scientific racism. Where race had once been an essential factor to discuss in any nation's future (especially in the era between 1870 and 1920), it was quickly replaced by explanations emphasizing economic factors, especially the economic determinism of the Marxians. For those who still wished to stress the human factor, national character became popular—a natural outgrowth of the previous preoccupation with race.[108] But the national character approach to analyzing Brazil's future prospects also fell into disfavor by the end of the 1950's. The last major attempt was Vianna Moog's *Bandeirantes and Pioneers* (first Brazilian edition: 1955).[109] It was a comparative analysis of U.S. and Brazilian national development, in which Moog sought to explain why the United States had so greatly exceeded Brazil in economic growth despite the obvious similarities in size and natural resources. Moog rejected deterministic historical explanations based on unilateral factors such as race or religion, yet he ended by turning to the inherited national personality type in each country as the (suspiciously deterministic) explanation for the national differences in development. Since Moog's book there have been few attempts even to use national character to sketch out a vision of the future of the Brazilian people.

A change in the Brazilian elite spokesmen's thinking about their country's ethnic identity was further necessitated by new knowledge about the reality of Brazilian race relations. As we have seen, there was relatively little serious investigation on this subject before 1930, and only a few pioneers were active before 1945. By that date they had still not made any significant impact on the elite's understanding of their country's racial dynamics. After World War II, however, a growing interest among Brazilian social scientists was reinforced by the greatly increased attention of foreign scholars. In 1950 Columbia University and the state of Bahia began a jointly sponsored research project on social change in Bahia. The Bahia program was expanded later that year when UNESCO granted funds to finance detailed research especially on race relations. This was part of a large-scale study of Brazilian race relations authorized by UNESCO, on the assumption that Brazil's experience might offer the rest of the world a unique lession in "harmonious" relations among races.[110]

Among the foreign scholars who undertook extensive field research in Brazil were Charles Wagley (Columbia University) and Roger Bastide (École Pratique des Hautes Études, Paris). Wagley and his students worked closely in Bahia with Thales de Azevedo (University of Bahia) while Bastide worked with Florestan Fernandes in São Paulo, also with benefit of UNESCO funds. Other UNESCO-sponsored research was conducted in Recife by René Ribeiro (Joaquim Nabuco Institute), and in Rio de Janeiro by Luís Costa Pinto (University of Brazil). Fernandes went on to found an influential school of research at the University of São Paulo, accompanied by his students and fellow researchers, Fernando Henrique Cardoso and Octavio Ianni.[111] Interestingly, this significant expansion in research began in the early 1950's—just when legal segregation came under attack in the United States.

By the early 1960's a new picture of Brazilian race relations had emerged, which did not quite conform to what the UNESCO sponsors had expected.[112] Social scientists, both foreign and Brazilian, used the latest research techniques to depict a complex web of correlations between color and social status. Although comprehensive data were lacking, and although some important regional variations existed, and although researchers' opinions varied on how color might affect future social mobility, it seemed clear that the darker a Brazilian the more likely he was to be found at the bottom of the socio-economic scale by every indicator—income, occupation, education. The journalists soon followed, furnishing anecdotal evidence of a pattern of subtle but unmistakable discrimination in social relations.[113] It was no longer possible to argue that Brazil had escaped racial discrimination, although it had never been codified since the colonial era. The growing weight of evidence demonstrated the contrary, even if the lines of discrimination were far more complex than in the bi-racial society of North America.

Their new findings led some social scientists to launch an attack on the "mythology" of the Brazilian elite's belief about race relations in their society. Florestan Fernandes accused his fellow countrymen of having the "prejudice of having no prejudice" and of clinging to "the myth of racial democracy." By believing that color had been no barrier to social and economic mobility, Fernandes argued, the elite was able to avoid even considering the possibility that the socio-economic condition of the non-white could be due to anything other than the society's relative under-development or the lack of individual initiative.[114]

The attack upon the "myth of racial democracy" in modern Brazil was paralleled by an attack on the long-standing view that Brazil's allegedly more humane race relations could be traced back to a more humane slave system. As we have seen, Brazilian social commentators had often assumed that slaves in their country had received far better treatment than in the United States. Some U.S. historians had even conceded as much, although without offering any primary research to document their conclusions.[115] The revisionist scholar Marvin Harris, one of Wagley's students in the Columbia-Bahia project, labeled this the "myth of the friendly master." Documentation has now been provided showing the treatment of Brazil's slaves often to have equalled the level of dehumanization recorded anywhere else.[116] In fact, the comparison of slave systems in terms of their relative "mildness" or "harshness" has proved a false lead in the understanding of the dynamics of social change, yet by documenting the facts about the Brazilian slave system, scholars have served to erode the Brazilian elite's belief in the uniqueness of their slave history.

Thus the 1950's brought a series of startling developments that combined to make members of the Brazilian elite cautious in discussing their society's current race relations, much less their ethnic future. There was the growing body of evidence produced by social science research and historical inquiry, along with the loss of such an important point of reference as segregation in the United States. In view of forced integration and "black is beautiful" in the United States, and the emergence of nationalism in

Africa and Asia, "whitening" was no longer an appropriate goal to proclaim. Furthermore, white immigration had faded as a likely source of ethnic purification. The great wave of European immigration was over, and any future numbers were bound to be small in proportion to the fast-growing native-born population.

What have Brazilians been able to say about their ethnic identity since the early 1950's? On the one hand, there has been a tendency to believe that no "problem" exists. In the last national census (1970), for example, no data was collected according to race. A principal reason given for the decision was that previous data had been notoriously unreliable, since definitions of racial category (and even more their application in individual cases) lacked uniformity.[117] However true that may be, the result is that researchers (and therefore the public and politicians) have been deprived of nationwide figures on how non-whites have fared in health, education, income, and jobs. In effect, those who control the federal government have declared that color is not a meaningful category in Brazil, at least for statistical purposes. This attitude is paralleled by the relative lack of public discussion of race (despite the work of the social scientists), as compared to the years between 1870 and 1930.

On the other hand, there is a sense of unease which occasionally breaks through to the surface. The black playwright, Abdias do Nascimento, for example, has complained bitterly that the Brazilian cult of whitening has suffocated any attempt to articulate a black consciousness.[118] Even these discussions are often terminated by the charge from other Brazilians that any attempt to heighten racial self-consciousness would be "racist."[119] In effect, Brazilian opinion-makers are still living with the intellectual legacy of the compromise their parents and grandparents struck with racist theory. They are still implicit believers in a whiter Brazil, even though it may no longer be respectable to say so. They have inherited a richly complex multi-racial society but have not yet found a new rationale to describe or justify its future.

Note on Sources and Methodology

The illiteracy rate in Brazil remained well above 50 per cent throughout the period covered in this book.[1] I have therefore been concerned with studying the views on race expressed by the spokesmen of the Brazilian elite—almost all of whom were members of the tiny minority that enjoyed the privilege of higher education within this largely illiterate society.[2] Spokesmen for the elite were considered to be the intellectuals (defined below), politicians, and government public relations men. I have not examined systematically the works of fiction writers or the *technical* works of scientists.

My selection of authors is based on an initial reading of the major secondary works on Brazilian social thought for the period.[3] Most helpful were Gilberto Freyre, *Ordem e progresso,* 2 vols. (Rio de Janeiro, 1959), Dante Moreira Leite, *O Caráter nacional brasileiro: História de uma ideologia,* 2nd edition. (São Paulo, 1969), Brito Broca, *A Vida literária no Brasil: 1900,* 2nd edition. (Rio de Janeiro, 1960), Fernando Azevedo, *Brazilian Culture* (New York, 1950), João Cruz Costa, *A History of Ideas in Brazil* (Berkeley, Calif., 1964), and Roque Spencer Maciel de Barros, *A Ilustração brasileira e a idéia de universidade* (São Paulo, 1959). I also found useful the judgments expressed by the editors of anthologies such as Djacir Menezes, ed., *O Brasil no pensamento brasileiro* (Rio de Janeiro, 1957), and Luís Washington Vita, ed., *Antologia do pensamento social e político no Brasil* (São Paulo, 1968).

Among the best guides to intellectual trends are the literary histories. I profited much from Lucia Miguel-Pereira, *Prosa de ficção de 1870 a 1920* [História da Literatura Brasileira, vol. XII, ed. by Alvaro Lins] (Rio de Janeiro, 1957); Afrânio Coutinho, *An Introduction to Literature in Brazil* (New York, 1969), which is a translation of the general editor's introductions to the volumes in *A Literatura no Brasil*, 4 vols. (Rio de Janeiro, 1955-59); Alfredo Bosi, *História concisa da literatura brasileira* (São Paulo, 1970); and Nelson Werneck Sodré, *História da literatura brasileira*, 3rd ed. (Rio de Janeiro, 1960). The specialized volumes published by the Cultrix publishing firm were also helpful: João Pacheco, *O Realismo: 1870–1900* (São Paulo, 1963); Massaud Moisés, *O Simbolismo: 1893–1902* (São Paulo, 1966); Alfredo Bosi, *O Pré-Modernismo* (São Paulo, 1966); and Wilson Martins, *O Modernismo: 1916–1945* (São Paulo, 1965). The introductory sections in Antônio Cândido and José Aderaldo Castello, *Presença da literatura brasileira: História e antologia*, 3 vols. (São Paulo, 1964), contain much valuable information. After preliminary reading in publications of the era, I then gave added emphasis to writers (such as Batista de Lacerda and Roquette-Pinto) who seemed more important to contemporaries than had been indicated in secondary studies.

To test my assumption that the elite controlling Brazil in this era was relatively well integrated, I first studied the intellectuals and then tested the consensus I found in their views by looking for opinions on race as expressed by politicians in the debates of the federal Chamber of Deputies for several periods: (1) selected abolitionist debates of the nineteenth century; (2) debates over diplomacy and social problems (health, education, etc.) during World War I; and (3) debates on immigration legislation in the 1920's and 1930's.

I also read the exhibition catalogues prepared by the Brazilian government for the international expositions between 1867 and

1904, as well as the official publications for the expositions of 1900, 1908 and 1922 within Brazil. I checked a number of other government publications issued in connection with the census, foreign propaganda, and education. Taken together, these sources helped to furnish a broadly documented picture of the elite consensus on Brazil's racial future.*

For my purposes, the tangled debate among sociologists as to what constitutes an intellectual was not very helpful.[4] I have included anyone who wrote or spoke nationally on the racial issue. In Brazil, as in other developing societies, spokesmen for the elite did not fit into the categories of specialization familiar in industrialized societies.[5] Brazil was just beginning to emerge from an overwhelmingly agrarian economy which neither required nor could afford the elaborate network of specialized intellectual professions supported by developed countries. Without inherited wealth, intellectuals could earn a decent income only by combining their positions in the poorly paid fields of teaching (including secondary schools) and journalism with the professions of law and medicine, and occasionally government employment (preferably a sinecure). Furthermore, Brazil in this era was still a Latin culture that valued the "universal man," rather than the narrow specialist. Real prestige was reserved for the polymath who approximated the ideal cultural type rising above professional specialization while retaining his literary elegance.[6]

Journalism was the focus of activity for most intellectuals interested in social questions and dictated the format in which they published. They produced short essays because the most ready outlet (and most widely read) was the daily newspaper, which could seldom run an article of more than two thousand

---

* My assumption that a predominant attitude would emerge proved justified. But this also assumes that the important thinkers were published in the newspaper, periodical and book outlets which gained national attention. It should be noted that this approach excludes the strictly provincial thinkers who failed to break into the establishment media—and therefore failed to influence the national reading public.

words. Relatively few magazines printed essays of greater length. The market for books was extremely limited and no dependable system of large-scale national distribution appeared until Monteiro Lobato's pioneering ventures of the early 1920's.[7]

Given the limitations of the newspaper format, arguments had to be stated epigrammatically. Although articles could be expanded and refined when collected and published as books or pamphlets, they seldom were: The result was a predominantly journalistic style which often reflected haste in writing and failure, before re-publication, to consult references or to revise for more systematic and coherent exposition on complex subjects. Alberto Tôrres is a clear case in point. His two major books—both influential among the intellectuals—were collections of newspaper articles, often unedited, which seem repetitious and ill-organized in book format.

Before judging these authors too harshly, we should remember that they had to fit their writing into the leisure moments of overcommitted lives. We should also note that they had been educated and lived in a country where the higher education faculties and research institutions—especially in the fields relevant to racial theories such as anthropology, sociology, and genetics—were relatively undeveloped before 1930. They had to train themselves on subjects where the elementary scientific works were not available in Portuguese and foreign-language materials were expensive and difficult to obtain.

Those who had to earn their living from journalism were driven to produce large quantities of prose. Chroniclers such as Coelho Neto and João do Rio frequently resorted to trivia in order to maintain their productivity.[8] Other writers managed to preserve their commitment to serious study, despite their heavy production for the daily press. Among the more prominent examples were Gilberto Amado and José Veríssimo. Brazilian writers were acutely conscious of the incompatibility between their commitment to serious thought and the need of many to maximize their journalistic income. João do Rio published (in 1908) the results of a questionnaire in which he asked the leading Brazilian literary figures whether they thought journalism had a beneficial or negative influence on Brazilian literature. Their careful answers—notably mixed in their final judgments—showed their acute awareness of the problem.[9]

In order to find evidence of Brazilian elite opinion about race I looked widely in the writings of the essayists—primarily public but sometimes also private—since the essay was the chief unit of thought on social questions.[10] The interests of these authors ranged from literature to natural science. Although their views were easiest to find when the writer was forced to discuss race, I found important statements when browsing through writings in which there was no obvious reason to focus on race.

During my search for the main currents of race-thinking, I consulted the complete run of the Rio de Janeiro newspaper *Correio da manhã* for the years 1902–18, Rio magazines such as *Kosmos* (1904–9) and *Renasçenca* (1904–8), and the collected book reviews of literary critics such as Sílvio Romero, José Maria Bello, Sousa Bandeira, Araripe Júnior, José Veríssimo, Alceu Amoroso Lima, and Agrippino Grieco. In the case of figures whom Brazilians of their own day considered to be of major importance, such as Sílvio Romero, Euclides da Cunha, Alberto Tôrres, and Oliveira Vianna, I read not only their published works, but also evaluations by their contemporaries.

Finally, I was fortunate enough to discover an excellent collection of newspaper and magazine clippings gathered by the diplomat-historian Manoel Oliveira Lima (1865–1928) and his wife during his career, which spanned the era from the late 1880's until his death in 1928. This collection of more than thirty scrapbooks proved valuable because Oliveira Lima, who published regularly in the Brazilian press, maintained a vast correspondence with most of the leading literary figures of his day. Despite his constant travel and residence abroad, he kept his domestic clipping file up to date with articles and book reviews from the Brazilian (and North American and European) newspapers.

By the end of my research I felt confident that I had sampled a range of elite opinion wide enough to explain their prevailing assumptions about race. It should be noted, however, that this was done by the old-fashioned method of the intellectual historian—a wide reading of writers and publications which I thought representative. The opportunities for research remain inviting for historians who might wish to apply newer techniques, such as content analysis, to the study of Brazilian thought, whether of the elite or of those millions of other Brazilians who appear in these pages merely as objects of debate for the few who enjoyed the power of the printed word. Although the last decade has produced a number of highly useful secondary works on specific areas of thought, much research remains to be done in such fields as medicine and anthropology.[11] Much also remains to be written about the history of cultural and educational institutions—the faculties, institutes, and academies.[12] A careful analysis of the social history of these institutions will help put Brazilian intellectual history into the wider context of social and economic history which is only touched upon in this study.[13]

Notes

INTRODUCTION

1. I have not discussed the many parallels between race-thinking in Brazil and the rest of Latin America. In general, Spanish America (especially Argentina and Mexico) has received more attention from North American students of intellectual history than Brazil. Martin Stabb includes race as one of the central themes in his excellent analysis of the writings of the Spanish American essayists who diagnosed the "sick continent" in the late nineteenth and early twentieth century. Martin S. Stabb, *In Quest of Identity: Patterns in the Spanish American Essay of Ideas, 1890–1960* (Chapel Hill, N.C., 1967). For discussion of the attitudes of Mexican intellectuals toward race before the Revolution of 1910, see T. G. Powell, "Mexican Intellectuals and the Indian Question, 1876–1911," *Hispanic American Historical Review*, XLVIII (No. 1, Feb. 1968), 19–36; and William D. Raat, "Los intelectuales, el positivismo y la questión indígena," *Historia Mexicana*, XX (Jan.–Mar. 1971) 412–27. For the cases of Argentina and Chile there is much valuable information on elite attitudes toward race in Carl Solberg, *Immigration and Nationalism: Argentina and Chile, 1890–1914* (Austin, 1970).

2. The manifesto is reprinted in Osvaldo Melo Braga, *Bibliografia de Joaquim Nabuco* [Instituto Nacional do Livro: Coleção B 1: Bibliografia, VIII] (Rio de Janeiro, 1952). The quotation is on page 17.

CHAPTER 1

1. Sources on Brazilian church history are few. The most authoritative secondary source for this period is George C. A. Boehrer, "The Church in the Second Reign, 1840–1889," in Henry H. Keith and S. F. Edwards, eds., *Conflict and Continuity in Brazilian Society* (Columbia, S.C., 1969), 113–40. A considerable amount of information may be

found in Nilo Pereîra, *Conflitos entre a Igreja e o Estado no Brasil* (Recife, 1970). Unfortunately Professor Boehrer's death deprived us of the larger study of the nineteenth-century Brazilian church on which he had embarked. A useful general treatment is found in chapter XII of J. Lloyd Mecham, *Church and State in Latin America*, rev. ed. (Chapel Hill, N.C., 1966).

2. My analysis of nineteenth-century Brazilian thought owes much to Roque Spencer Maciel de Barros, *A Ilustração brasileira e a idéia da universidade* (São Paulo, 1959), which is the leading exposition and critique of Brazilian Liberalism. A valuable survey is João Cruz Costa, *A History of Ideas in Brazil* (Berkeley, Calif., 1964). The influence of English ideas on Brazilian liberalism is well treated in Richard Graham, *Britain and the Onset of Modernization in Brazil, 1850–1914* (Cambridge, Eng., 1968).

3. Cruz Costa, *A History of Ideas in Brazil*, 53–57. An excellent analysis of Eclecticism in Brazil may be found in Antônio Paim, *História das idéias filosóficas no Brasil* (São Paulo, 1967), chapter II.

4. Sílvio Romero sarcastically underlined the lack of originality in nineteenth-century Brazilian thought when he referred to his countrymen as "smugglers of ideas." Sílvio Romero, *A Literatura brasileira e a crítica moderna* (Rio de Janeiro, 1880), 6.

5. Paim, *História das idéias*, 104.

6. The party platforms are found in America Brasiliense, *Os Programas dos partidos e o 2° Império* (São Paulo, 1878). Parties and political thought during the Empire are surveyed in Nelson Nogueira Saldanha, *História das idéias políticas no Brasil* (Recife, 1968), 127–216. For an authoritative analysis of the breakdown in the imperial political system, see Sérgio Buarque de Holanda, ed., *História geral da civilização brasileira*, Tomo II: *O Brasil monárquico*, vol. 5 (São Paulo, 1972). This entire volume was written by the general editor, Sérgio Buarque de Holanda.

7. Gilberto Freyre has described the psychological aspects of this social system. See especially his *The Mansions and the Shanties* (New York, 1963). One author has gone so far as to interpret the antimonarchical movement of the late Empire as a patricidal impulse by the younger generation: Luís Martins, *O Patriarca e o bacharel* (São Paulo, 1953).

8. The standard biography of the Emperor is Heitor Lyra, *História de Dom Pedro II*, 3 vols. (São Paulo, 1938–40), which is very sympathetic to its subject, as is Mary Wilhelmine Williams, *Dom Pedro the Magnanimous* (Chapel Hill, N.C., 1937).

9. These works are given detailed analysis in João Camillo de Oliveira Tôrres, *A Democracia coroada: Teoria política do Império do Brasil*, 2nd ed. (Petrópolis, 1964). In his ambitious study Tôrres offers a sympathetic account of the monarchical system.

10. Brazilian Romanticism has produced a large body of literary criticism and literary history. The outstanding work is Antônio Cândido [Mello e Souza], *Formação da literatura brasileira*, 2nd ed. (São Paulo, 1964), vol. II. See also Afrânio Coutinho, *An Introduction to Literature in Brazil* (New York, 1969), 119–51. These pages are a translation of Coutinho's introduction to the section on Romanticism in the survey which he edited: *A Literatura no Brasil*, 4 vols. (Rio de Janeiro, 1955–58).

11. David Miller Driver, *The Indian in Brazilian Literature* (New York, 1942), 41–42.

12. *Ibid.* 106–7.

13. *Ibid., passim;* Raymond S. Sayers, *O Negro na literatura brasileira* (Rio de Janeiro, 1958), 205–21. For an excellent analysis of the stereotypes of Negroes and slaves in the literary works associated with abolitionism, see David T. Haberly, "Abolitionism in Brazil: Anti-Slavery and Anti-Slave," *Luso-Brazilian Review*, IX (No. 2, Dec. 1972), 30–46.

14. Antônio Cândido, *O Método crítico de Sílvio Romero*, 2nd ed. (São Paulo, 1963), 134–35.

15. In 1907 Euclides da Cunha called the decade of the 1860's "the most decisive for our destiny," Euclides da Cunha, "Castro Alves e seu tempo," in *Obra completa*, 2 vols. (Rio de Janeiro, 1966), vol. I, 428.

16. Slaves serving in the Army were granted their freedom by Decree #3725 of November 6, 1866.

17. Richard Graham, *Britain and the Onset of Modernization in Brazil, 1850–1914*, 28–29. The cabinet of Viscount Rio Branco (1871–75) carried out a number of reforms whose necessity had been dramatized by the Paraguayan war. For an admiring brief biography of the Prime Minister, see Visconde de Taunay [Alfredo de E. Taunay], *O Visconde do Rio Branco* (São Paulo, n.d. [1930?]).

18. Sérgio Buarque do Holanda, ed., *História geral da civilização brasileira*, Tomo II: *O Brasil monárquico*, vol. III (São Paulo, 1967), 85–112; The best documented history of the Republican party during the Empire is George C. A. Boehrer, *Da Monarquia à república: História do Partido Republicano do Brasil, 1870–1889* (Rio de Janeiro, 1954).

19. My analysis of the intellectual history of the late Empire owes much to Maciel de Barros, *A Illustração brasileira.*

20. The best secondary source on the Recife School is Antônio Paim, *A Filosofia da Escola do Recife* (Rio de Janeiro, 1966). Sílvio Romero, the most famous product of the School, later made sweeping but extravagant claims for the national impact of the Recife group. See, for example, his Preface ("Explicações Indispensáveis") to Tobias Barreto, *Vários escritos* (Rio de Janeiro, 1900). For further detail on

the Recife School including previously unpublished correspondence, see Vamireh Chacon, *Da Escola do Recife ao código civil: Artur Orlando e sua geração* (Rio de Janeiro, 1969).

21. The standard biography is Hermes Lima, *Tobias Barreto*, 2nd ed. (São Paulo, 1957). See also Paulo Mercadante and Antônio Paim, *Tobias Barreto na cultura brasileira: Uma Revaliação* (São Paulo, 1972).

22. Romero's attacks occurred in a series of articles published in 1879 and cited in Sílvio Romero, *História da literatura brasileira*, 2nd ed., 2 vols. (Rio de Janeiro, 1903), vol. II, 465.

23. José Ramos Tinhorão, *A Província e o naturalismo* (Rio de Janeiro, 1966).

24. The earlier standard studies of Brazilian Positivism tended to concentrate on the "orthodox" Positivists: João Camillo de Oliveira Tôrres, *O Positivismo no Brasil*, 2nd ed. (Petrópolis, 1957), and João Cruz Costa, *O Positivismo na república* (São Paulo, 1956). Later studies, such as Ivan Lins, *História do positivismo no Brasil* (São Paulo, 1964), and Tocary Assis Bastos, *O Positivismo e a realidade brasileira* (Belo Horizonte, 1965), have broadened the focus, although the wider influence of non-orthodox Positivism still awaits an in-depth analysis. The best account written during that era is Clóvis Beviláqua, *Esboços e fragmentos* (Rio de Janeiro, 1899), 70–137.

25. The "official" Positivist biography is Raimundo Teixeira Mendes, *Benjamin Constant*, 2nd ed. (Rio de Janeiro, 1913).

26. Fernando de Azevedo, *Brazilian Culture* (New York, 1950), 413–14.

27. A survey of the origins and growth of Brazilian Positivism is given in João Cruz Costa, *A History of Ideas in Brazil*, chapter 5.

28. The "Positivist Apostolate" began publishing its circulars, pamphlets and books in 1881, and has continued up to the present. These publications are a valuable source on orthodox Positivist opinion.

29. Luís Pereira Barreto, *As Três filosofias* (Rio de Janeiro, 1874). For details of this important Positivist's life and thought, see Roque Spencer Maciel de Barros, *A Evolução do pensamento de Pereira Barreto* (São Paulo, 1967). Maciel de Barros is also editing a new edition of Pereira Barreto's philosophical works, of which the first volume includes *As Três filosofias*: Luís Pereira Barreto, *Obras filosóficas*, vol. I (São Paulo, 1967).

30. Beviláqua, *Esboços*, 96.

31. Engineering education began as a part of military education in Brazil, and was not separated from the *Escola Militar* until 1874, when the Escola Politécnica was established as an independent institution. Both schools remained in Rio. Azevedo, *Brazilian Culture*, 175; Umberto Peregrino, *Historia e projeção das instituições culturais do exército* (Rio de Janeiro, 1967), 11–13.

32. I am indebted to Joseph Love and John Wirth for their ideas on this point.

33. *Província de São Paulo*, July 26, 1878, as quoted in Maciel de Barros, *A Evolução do pensamento*, 132. Pereira Barreto was born in 1840 and José Bonifácio (moço) was born in 1827.

34. The most comprehensive studies of the abolitionist movement are Robert Conrad, *The Destruction of Brazilian Slavery, 1850–1888* (Berkeley, Calif., 1972), and Robert Brent Toplin, *The Abolition of Slavery in Brazil* (New York, 1972), both of which draw heavily on contemporary newspaper sources, especially the active abolitionist press. An outstanding analysis of the decline of slavery and the introduction of free labor is Emília Viotti da Costa, *Da Senzala à Colônia* (São Paulo, 1966), which contains a wealth of information on economic structure and abolitionist thought. The close connection between abolition and the issue of land ownership is stressed in Nilo Odalia, "A Abolição da Escravatura" *Anais do Museu Paulista*, XVIII (São Paulo, 1964), 121–45.

35. His abolitionist manifesto is reprinted in *Obras científicas, politicas e sociais de José Bonifácio de Andrada e Silva*, ed. by Edgard de Cerqueira Falcão, 3 vols. (São Paulo, 1965), vol. II, 115–218.

36. For a detailed and well-documented study, see Leslie Bethell, *The Abolition of the Brazilian Slave Trade* (Cambridge, Eng., 1970).

37. The letter is reprinted in Revista do Instituto Histórico e Geográfico Brasileiro, *Contribuições para a biografia de D. Pedro II*, Part I, Tomo Especial (Rio de Janeiro, 1925), 419. An abridged translation was published in Thomas E. Skidmore, "The Death of Brazilian Slavery, 1866–68," in Frederick Pike, ed., *Select Problems in Latin American History* (New York, 1968), 143–44.

38. Edmar Morel, *Vendaval da liberdade* (Rio de Janeiro, 1967), 89.

39. São Paulo was an area where the equivocal Republican stand on abolition caused much tension between party leaders and members of abolitionist convictions. The topic is subtly treated in José Maria dos Santos, *Os Republicanos paulistas e a abolição* (São Paulo, 1942). The manifesto of 1870 is reprinted in Brasiliense, *Os Programas*. There is a very useful analysis of the Republican manifesto and propaganda in Evaristo de Moraes, *Da Monarquia para a república, 1870–1889* (Rio de Janeiro, n.d.).

40. *Anais do Parlamento brasileiro: Câmara dos Deputados*, Primeiro Ano da Décima-sétima Legislatura, Sessão de 1878 (Rio de Janeiro, 1879), 3, 194–96.

41. The standard biography is Luiz Viana Filho, *A Vida de Joaquim Nabuco* (São Paulo, 1952).

42. In the last two years before final abolition there was significant mobilization in São Paulo against the slave system—including mass

escapes, revolts, and abolitionist infiltration of plantations. Robert Brent Toplin, "Upheaval, Violence, and the Abolition of Slavery in Brazil: The Case of São Paulo," *Hispanic American Historical Review*, XLIX (No. 4, Nov. 1969), 639–55; Toplin, *The Abolition of Slavery*, 194–224; and Conrad, *The Destruction of Brazilian Slavery*, 239–56.

43. Richard Graham, "Landowners and the Overthrow of the Empire," *Luso-Brazilian Review*, vol. VII (No. 2, Dec. 1970), 44–56; Toplin, *The Abolition of Slavery*, 225–46; and Conrad, *The Destruction of Brazilian Slavery*, 257–73.

44. André Rebouças, *Diário e notas autobiográficas*, ed. by Ana Flora and Inacio José Verissimo (Rio de Janeiro, 1938), 135. Joaquim Nabuco, *Minha formação* (Rio de Janeiro, 1957), chapter II. On José de Patrocínio, see Osvaldo Orico, *O Tigre da abolição* (São Paulo, 1931); and Ciro Vieira da Cunha, *No Tempo de Patrocínio*, 2 vols. (São Paulo, 1960).

45. Sud Mennucci, *O Precursor do abolicionismo no Brasil* (São Paulo, 1938).

46. Carolina Nabuco, *The Life of Joaquim Nabuco* (Stanford, Calif., 1950), 109.

47. Nabuco, *Minha formação*, 196–98.

48. The manifesto is reprinted in Osvaldo Melo Braga, *Bibliografia de Joaquim Nabuco* [Instituto Nacional do Livro: Coleção B 1: Bibliografia, VIII] (Rio de Janeiro, 1952), 14–22.

49. Joaquim Nabuco, *O Abolicionismo* (London, 1883), 114–15, 252–53.

50. Odival Cassiano Gomes, *Manoel Vitorino Pereira: Médico e cirurgião* (Rio de Janeiro, 1953), 161.

51. Sociedade Brasileira Contra a Escravidão, *Banquete oferecido ao Exm. Sr. Ministro Americano Henry Washington Hilliard* (Rio de Janeiro, 1880).

52. Osório Duque-Estrada, *A Abolição: Esboço histórico, 1831–1888* (Rio de Janeiro, 1918), 119–20. Patrocínio did get a statement from Hugo and it was used as Abolitionist propaganda, apparently on the assumption that Hugo's great prestige among the elite would help the cause. For the details on the admiration for Hugo, see A. Carneiro Leão, *Victor Hugo no Brasil* (Rio de Janeiro, 1960). Joaquim Nabuco exhibited the same longing for foreign intervention on the abolitionist side when he made a personal appeal to Pope Leo XIII in February 1888, asking that "Your Holiness speak in time for your message to reach Brazil before the opening of Parliament. . . ." Nabuco, *The Life of Joaquim Nabuco*, 160–61.

53. *Anais do Parlamento Brasileiro, Câmara dos Deputados*, Terceiro Ano da Décima-quarta Legislatura, Sessão de 1871 (Rio de Janeiro, 1871), 1, 134–35.

54. [A. Coelho Rodrigues], *Manual do subdito fiel ou cartas de*

um lavrador a Sua Majestade o Imperador sôbre a questão do elemento servil (Rio de Janeiro, 1884), 73.

55. Carolina Nabuco, *Life of Joaquim Nabuco*, 76; Sociedade Brasileira Contra a Escravidão, *Banquete*.

56. Joaquim Nabuco, *Obras completas*, vol. XI: *Discursos parlamentares, 1879–1889* (São Paulo, 1949), 66–67.

57. Braga, *Bibliografia de Joaquim Nabuco*, 17.

58. *Anais do Parlamento Brasileiro, Câmara dos Deputados,* Terceiro Ano da Décima-quarta Legislatura, Sessão de 1871 (Rio de Janeiro, 1871), 295–96.

59. Nabuco, *Abolicionismo*, 22–23.

60. *Ibid.*, 252.

61. *Gazeta da Tarde*, May 5, 1887. Reprinted in Afonso Celso Júnior, *Oito anos de parlamento* (São Paulo, n.d.), 131–32.

62. Quoted in J. Fernando Carneiro, "Interpretação da política imigratória brasileira," *Digesto econômico*, no. 46 (Sept. 1948), 123.

63. João Cardoso Menezes e Souza [Barão de Paranapiacaba], *Theses sôbre a colonização do Brasil: Projecto de solução a's questões sociaes que se prendem a este difficil problema: Relatório apresentado ao Ministério da Agricultura, Commercio e Obras Públicas em 1873* (Rio de Janeiro, 1875), 419–20.

64. The group published a manifesto in 1877: *Demonstração das conveniencias e vantagens á lavoura no Brasil pela introducção dos trabalhadores asiáticos (da China)* (Rio de Janeiro, 1877). It was signed by Antônio Martins Lage, Roberto Clinton Wright, Manoel José da Costa Lima Vianna, João Antônio de Miranda e Silva, and Jorge Nathan.

65. The memorandum is reprinted in José Afonso Mendonça Azevedo, *Vida e obra de Salvador de Mendonça* (Rio de Janeiro, 1971), 361–79. The later book-length version of the memorandum appeared as Salvador de Mendonça, *Trabalhadores asiáticos* (New York, 1879).

66. Süssekind de Mendonca, *Salvador de Mendonça*, 118.

67. Nabuco, *Abolicionismo*, 252.

68. Nabuco, *Obras completas*, vol. XI: *Discursos parlamentares, 1879–1889*, 24.

69. *Ibid.*, 63.

70. *Ibid.*, 60.

71. *Ibid.*, 22–23. For a similar debate in the legislature of the province of Rio de Janeiro, see Odalia, "A Abolição," 129–32.

72. Fernando Carneiro, "Interpretação," 124; Toplin, *The Abolition of Slavery*, 157–60; and Conrad, *The Destruction of Brazilian Slavery*, 33–34.

73. The best analysis of social structure during the late Empire is Graham, *Britain and the Onset of Modernization in Brazil*, 1–49. Due

to the high degree of illiteracy, the literate elite was very small in nineteenth-century Brazil. As of 1867 only 10 per cent of school-age children were enrolled in school. Despite the "modernizing" efforts of the late Empire, the figure had increased to only 14 per cent by 1889. Azevedo, *Brazilian Culture*, 383, 406.

74. A succinct survey of the rise of racist thought is given in Michael Banton, *Race Relations* (London, 1967), 28–54; see also Marvin Harris, *The Rise of Anthropological Theory* (New York, 1968), 80–141. The complex story of changes in scientific thinking about race is examined with great subtlety in George W. Stocking, Jr., *Race, Culture, and Evolution: Essays in the History of Anthropology* (New York, 1968). The influence of racist thought is examined in greater detail below in Chapter 2.

75. Henry Thomas Buckle, *History of Civilization in England* (London, 1857–61).

76. Citations are to the edition of 1872: Henry Thomas Buckle, *History of Civilization in England*, 2 vols. (London, 1872), vol. I, 104–6. Typical of the continuing influence of Buckle on Brazilians was the autobiographical essay of a Pernambucan essayist-politician (born in 1885) who concluded his description of the miserably poor rural workers near his family sugar plantation in the Northeast thus: "Rather than being a Canaan, the fields of Brazil will be the country of Buckle, where the brutal splendor of Nature diminishes and crushes man, who is unarmed for the formidable struggle against the adverse elements." José Maria Bello, *Ensaios políticos e literários* (Rio de Janeiro, 1918), 78. Elsewhere in this volume Bello revealed greater optimism about the ability of the Brazilian to control his surroundings.

77. Georges Readers, *Le Comte de Gobineau au Brésil* (Paris, 1934). Gobineau maintained an extensive correspondence during his fifteen-month stay in Brazil. For several revealing letters, as well as a listing of where other published letters of Gobineau's Brazilian sojourn may be found, see Jean Gaulmier, "Au Brésil, Il y a un Siècle . . . Quelques Images d'Arthur Gobineau," *Bulletin de la Faculté des Lettres de Strasbourg* (May–June 1964), 483–98.

78. Letter to Keller, cited in Ludwig Schemann, *Gobineau: eine biographie*, 2 vols. (Strassburg, 1916), vol. II, 127.

79. Raeders, *Gobineau au Brésil*, 73.

80. J. A. Comte de Gobineau, "L'emigration au Brésil," *Le Correspondant*, vol. 96 [Nouvelle Serie, vol. 60] (July–Sept. 1874), 369; Gaulmier, "Au Brésil, Il y a un Siècle," 497.

81. Gaulmier, *op. cit.*, 493.

82. A letter to Keller cited in Schemann, *Gobineau*, vol. II, 127.

83. Raeders, *Gobineau au Brésil*, 100–103.

84. For a brief analysis of the views of Ingenieros, see Martin S. Stabb, *In Quest of Identity: Patterns in the Spanish American Essay of Ideas, 1890–1960* (Chapel Hill, N.C., 1967), 30–31.

85. Louis Couty, *Ebauches Sociologiques: Le Brésil en 1884* (Rio de Janeiro, 1884), iv. Similar sentiments were expressed by the French journalist Max Leclerc, who wrote in the early 1890's: "The Portuguese, ancestor of the Brazilian, was never averse to the colored races, nor repulsed by mating with black women. In Brazil the promiscuity of races . . . has long been total, so that the institution of slavery . . . was that much more pernicious for . . . the purity of the race. . . ." Max Leclerc, *Cartas do Brasil* (São Paulo, 1942), 157–58.

86. Louis J. R. Agassiz and Elizabeth Cary Agassiz, *A Journey in Brazil* (Boston, 1868), 293.

87. The French edition was published in Paris in 1869. The translator was Felix Vogeli, a professor at the Military School in Rio and a member of Agassiz' expedition to the Amazon.

88. Agassiz, *Journey in Brazil*, 517.

89. The best biography of Romero is Sylvio Rabello, *Itinerário de Sílvio Romero* (Rio de Janeiro, 1944). It has since been reprinted but without changes in the text of the original edition. I learned much from the penetrating analysis in Antônio Candido, *O Método crítico de Sílvio Romero*. For the sources of Romero's thought, see Carlos Süssekind de Mendonça, *Sílvio Romero: Sua formação intelectual* (São Paulo, 1938). The same author has written an invaluable reference work which includes a listing of all of Romero's works in order of publication: *Sílvio Romero de corpo inteiro* (Rio de Janeiro, 1963). For a thoughtful analysis of the historiographical assumptions in Romero, see Elaine Eleanor Derso, "The Historical Method of Sílvio Romero," in Andrew W. Cordier, ed., *Columbia Essays in International Affairs*, vol. IV: *The Dean's Papers*, 1968 (New York, 1969), 49–81. The chapter on Romero in Nelson Werneck Sodré, *A Ideologia do colonialismo: Seus reflexos no pensamento brasileiro* (Rio de Janeiro, 1961), is essentially sympathetic, as its title indicates: "Sílvio Romero: Um Guerrilheiro Desarmado."

90. Sílvio Romero, *História da literatura brasileira*, 2 vols., (Rio de Janeiro, 1888). The second edition was published in 1902, and included revisions and changes. All subsequent citations in this section are to the first edition.

91. Romero, *História da literatura brasileira*, vol. I, 26.

92. At the end of his career Romero published a defiant volume ridiculing his critics, asking the public to "forgive the impetuosity of language, the justified cry of a man constantly harassed by the petty attacks of perverse or impertinent would-be critics." Sílvio Romero, *Minhas contradições* (Bahia, 1914), 7.

93. Romero, "A Poesia Popular no Brasil," *Revista Brasileira* (2ª fase), vol. I (1879), 343.

94. Romero, "A Poesia Popular no Brasil," *Revista Brasileira* (2ª fase), vols. I–VII (1879–80). *História da literatura brasileira*, vol. I, chapter III.

95. Romero, *História da literatura*, 26.
96. *Ibid.*, 38.
97. *Ibid.*, 44–48.
98. *Ibid.*, 48.
99. Romero, *A Literatura brasileira e a crítica moderna* (Rio de Janeiro, 1880), 171.
100. Romero, *História da literatura*, chapter IV.
101. *Ibid.*, 64.
102. *Ibid.*, 130.
103. Romero, *A Literatura brasileira e a crítica moderna*, 98.
104. Romero, "A Questão do Dia: A Emancipação dos Escravos," *Revista Brasileira* (2ª fase), vol. 7 (1881), 191–203.
105. Romero, *História da literatura*, 65, 92.
106. *Ibid.*, 100.
107. *Ibid.*, 67.
108. *Ibid.*, 108.
109. Romero, "A Poesia Popular no Brasil," *Revista Brasileira* (2ª fase), vol. 7 (1881), 30.
110. Romero, *Literatura brasileira e a crítica moderna*, 72.
111. *Ibid.*, 155.
112. *Ibid.*, 53.
113. Romero, *História da literatura*, 67.
114. *Ibid.*
115. Romero, *Literatura brasileira e a crítica moderna*, 168.
116. Romero, "A Poesia Popular no Brasil," *Revista Brasileira* (2ª fase), vol. 7 (1881), 31.
117. Romero, *História da literatura*, 66.

CHAPTER 2

1. Some of the analysis presented here was included in my "Toward a Comparative Analysis of Race Relations Since Abolition in Brazil and the United States," *Journal of Latin American Studies*, IV (No. 1, May 1972), 1–28. The path-breaking research on Brazilian race relations by Florestan Fernandes includes much historical material. See especially his collaborative study with Roger Bastide, *Relações raciais entre negros e brancos em São Paulo* (São Paulo, 1955). Two of Fernandes' students have done important historical monographs: Fernando Henrique Cardoso, *Capitalismo e escravidão no Brasil meridional* (São Paulo, 1962), and Octávio Ianni, *As Metamorfoses do escravo* (São Paulo, 1962). The joint study by Cardoso and Ianni also includes a historical section: *Côr e mobilidade social em Florianopolis* (São Paulo, 1960). There are many interesting ideas and bibliographical leads in José Honório Rodrigues, *Brazil and Africa* (Berkeley, Calif., 1965), chapter 4.

2. Roger Bastide, "The Development of Race Relations in Brazil," in Guy Hunter, ed., *Industrialisation and Race Relations* (London, 1965), 9-29.

3. This discussion treats race relations as far as they concern the African and European and the mixtures of the two. The Indian is not considered here. A consideration of some contemporary attitudes toward the Indian—as reflected in government policy—may be found in Darcy Ribeiro, *A Política indigenista brasileira* (Rio de Janeiro, 1962).

4. One of the best general discussions of comparative race relations is Pierre L. van den Berghe, *Race and Racism: A Comparative Perspective* (New York, 1967). I have drawn also upon H. Hoetink, *The Two Variants in Caribbean Race Relations* (New York, 1967), and Michael Banton, *Race Relations* (London, 1967). All three place Brazil in comparative context. The most comprehensive comparison of race relations in Brazil and the U.S. is Carl Degler, *Neither Black Nor White* (New York, 1971), chapters III and IV.

5. Marvin Harris, *Patterns of Race in the Americas* (New York, 1964). The contrast is described as "race prejudice of mark" versus "race prejudice of origin" in Oracy Nogueira, "Skin Color and Social Class" in *Plantation Systems of the New World* [Pan American Union: Social Science Monographs: VII] (Washington, D.C., 1959), 164–79.

6. See, for example, the description in Florestan Fernandes, *The Negro in Brazilian Society* (New York, 1969), 360–79. Degler finds the essential difference between the two societies to be the "mulatto escape hatch," a graphic characterization of bi-racial versus multi-racial. *Neither Black Nor White*, 223–25.

7. The practical difficulties of describing this system in its modern form are discussed in Marvin Harris and Conrad Kotak, "The Structural Significance of Brazilian Racial Categories," *Sociologia*, XXV (No. 3, Sept. 1963), 203–8. There is an excellent analysis of the present-day multi-racial society (and a critique of some of the erroneous interpretations of it) in John Saunders, "Class, Color, and Prejudice: A Brazilian Counterpoint," in Ernest Q. Campbell, ed., *Racial Tensions and National Identity* (Nashville, Tenn., 1972), 141–65.

8. His neuroses in the nineteenth century have been poetically pictured in Gilberto Freyre, *The Mansions and the Shanties* (New York, 1963). The longing for whiteness could drive sensitive blacks toward contempt for their own color. Such was the case with João da Cruz e Sousa (1861–98), the posthumously famous Symbolist poet, whose desire to be an Aryan came through dramatically in his verse. Roger Bastide, *A Poesia afro-brasileira* (São Paulo, 1943), 87–95. For an analysis of the manner in which most mulatto and black writers embraced an ideal of "whitening" during the nineteenth century, see Richard A. Preto-Rodas, *Negritude as a Theme in the Poetry of the Portuguese-Speaking World* [University of Florida Humanities Monograph, No. 31] (Gainesville, Fla., 1970), 14–22. The persistence of

that ideal can be seen in the self-images which occurred in the black press of São Paulo in the twentieth century. Roger Bastide, "A Imprensa Negra do Estado de São Paulo," reprinted in Bastide, *Estudos Afro-Brasileiros* (São Paulo, 1973), 129–56.

9. The rapid growth of the free colored in Brazil has not yet been adequately explained nor even documented, and it offers a challenge to social historians. A pioneering effort has been made by Herbert S. Klein, "The Colored Freedom in Brazilian Slave Society," *Journal of Social History*, III (No. 1, Fall 1969), 30–52. The socioeconomic ethos facing all freemen before 1888 in the area of coffee culture is carefully examined in Maria Sylvia de Carvalho Franco, *Homens livres na ordem escravocrata* (São Paulo, 1969). For a searching discussion of the historical factors which might explain the emergence of a "mulatto escape hatch" in Brazil and not in the United States, see Degler, *Neither Black Nor White*, chapter V, which emphasizes three factors: the relative number of Africans present in the early years of settlement, the sex ratio among the Europeans when large numbers of Africans arrived, and the relative position of white women (as affecting their ability to prevent their husbands' acknowledgment of mulatto offspring).

10. Evidence of such mobility before 1850 may be found in Jeanne Berrance de Castro, "O Negro na Guarda Nacional Brasileira," *Anais do Museu Paulista*, vol. XXIII (1969), 151–72. The high degree of self-consciousness which mulattoes had achieved was reflected in their active press: Castro, "A Imprensa Mulata," *O Estado de São Paulo, Suplemento Literário*, Nov. 2, 1968.

11. As has been argued in Harris, *Patterns of Race.*

12. Admittedly, this subject is fraught with difficulties because the measurements of racially differential fertility can be easily distorted by untraceable shifts in the racial classification of the offspring. Nonetheless, the apparent findings are so striking as to warrant examination.

13. Kenneth M. Stampp, *The Peculiar Institution* (New York, 1956), 320.

14. Although one Brazilian writer had alleged that there was an excess of deaths over births among slaves after 1850, Toplin demonstrates that between 1873 and 1885 (dates for which abolitionist legislation had produced data) there was a substantial net natural increase among the remaining slave population. Maurício Goulart, *Escravidão Africana no Brasil* (São Paulo, 1949), 155–57; Toplin, The *Abolition of Slavery*, 19–21.

15. Philip Curtin notes that "as a general tendency the higher proportion of African-born in any slave population, the lower its rate of natural increase—or, as was more often the case, the higher its rate of natural decrease." Thus the large stock of Brazilian slaves began to shrink rapidly when the slave trade ended in 1850. Philip D. Curtin, *The Atlantic Slave Trade: A Census* (Madison, Wisc., 1969), 28.

16. Evidence on these points may be found in Curtin, *The Atlantic Slave Trade*, 41; Curtin, "Epidemiology and the Slave Trade," *Political Science Quarterly*, LXXXIII (No. 2, June 1968), 190–216; and Stanley J. Stein, *Vassouras: A Brazilian Coffee County, 1850–1900* (Cambridge, Mass., 1957), 76–77.

17. T. Lynn Smith, *Brazil: People and Institutions* (Baton Rouge, La., 1963), 101–6; J. V. D. Saunders, *Differential Fertility in Brazil* (Gainesville, Fla., 1958), 51; Klein, "The Colored Freedmen."

18. Saunders, *Differential Fertility*, 59–62.

19. René Ribeiro, *Religião e relações raciais* (Rio de Janeiro, n.d.), 159.

20. Klein, "The Colored Freedmen."

21. Hoetink, *The Two Variants*, 120–26.

22. An earlier version of this analysis was presented in Thomas E. Skidmore, "Brazilian Intellectuals and the Problem of Race, 1870–1930," Occasional Paper No. 6: Graduate Center for Latin American Studies, Vanderbilt University (Mar. 1969). The phenomenon of "whitening" and the Brazilian faith in its inexorability has been noted by several scholars (with extensive experience of field research in Brazil) on whose analyses I have drawn: T. Lynn Smith, *Brazil: People and Institutions*, 73–74; Donald Pierson, *Negroes in Brazil*, 2nd ed. (Chicago, 1967), 125, 218; and Charles Wagley, ed., *Race and Class in Rural Brazil* (Paris, 1952), 153. It is noted also in Degler, *Neither Black Nor White*, 191–95.

23. In the 1940 census racial classification was supposed to be made by the census enumerator, whereas in 1950 the respondent was asked to declare his own racial category. Saunders, *Differential Fertility*, 42.

24. Saunders, *Differential Fertility*, 51; Smith, *Brazil: People and Institutions*, 101–6; Fernandes, *The Negro in Brazilian Society*, 57–71.

25. Smith, *Brazil*, 73–74; Saunders, *Differential Fertility*, 58–62.

26. Anor Butler Maciel, *Expulsão de estrangeiros* (Rio de Janeiro, 1953), 30–32. There has been relatively little systematic study of the fate of the ex-slaves, including those freed before 1888. A useful starting point is Toplin, *The Abolition of Slavery*, 256–66. See also Peter L. Eisenberg, "Abolishing Slavery: The Process on Pernambuco's Sugar Plantations," *Hispanic American Historical Review*, 52 (No. 4, Nov. 1972), 580–97; and Florestan Fernandes, *The Negro in Brazilian Society* (New York, 1969), chapter 1.

27. *Correio da Manhã*, Aug. 9, 1904; Feb. 4, 1906.

28. *Correio da Manhã*, Feb. 8, 1907.

29. *Correio da Manhã*, May 8, 1907.

30. *Correio da Manhã*, June 27, 1905.

31. George Frederickson, *The Black Image in the White Mind: The Debate on Afro-American Character and Destiny, 1817–1914* (New York, 1971), xi.

32. One of the clearest analyses of the emergence of racist theory is Harris, *The Rise of Anthropological Theory*, 80–141. Harris defines scientific racism thus: "According to the doctrine of scientific racism, the significant sociocultural differences and similarities among human populations are the dependent variables of group-restricted hereditary drives and attitudes," 81. My analysis of racist theory is based on Frederickson, *The Black Image in the White Mind;* Philip Curtin, *The Image of Africa* (Madison, Wisc., 1964); Harris, *The Rise of Anthropological Theory;* and Thomas F. Gossett, *Race: The History of an Idea in America* (Dallas, 1963).

33. Detailed analyses of scientific race-thinking in the United States during the nineteenth century may be found in William Stanton, *The Leopard's Spots: Scientific Attitudes toward Race in America, 1815–59* (Chicago, 1960), and John S. Haller, Jr., *Outcasts from Evolution: Scientific Attitudes of Racial Inferiority, 1859–1900* (Urbana, Ill., 1971).

34. Frederickson, *The Black Image*, chapter III.

35. *Ibid.*, 232.

36. Freyre, *Ordem e progresso*, I, clx–clxi. For an example of a Brazilian essayist explaining the racist ideas of Gobineau and Lapouge without adding any critical comments, see Arthur Orlando, *Brasil: A Terra e o homem* (Recife, 1913), 12.

37. The Germanic challenge to the declining Latins was spelled out, for example, in Candido Jucá, "O crepúsculo dos povos: as conferências de Ferrero," *Correio da Manhã*, Nov. 2, 1907.

38. An anonymous newspaper columnist in 1908, for example, explained in detail how the Anglo-Saxons were industrious and disciplined, while the Latins, especially the Brazilians, were sentimental and undisciplined. Diogenes, "Outros Factores," *Correio da Manhã*, Mar. 6, 1908; the claim was sometimes repeated that the early Portuguese settlers had been criminals, thus compounding the weakness of Brazil's European ancestry. Frota Pessôa, *Crítica e polémica* (Rio de Janeiro, 1902), 5.

39. Lapouge, a French disciple of Gobineau who was widely read in Brazil, declared that "the simple operation of the laws of heredity will be sufficient to bring about the decadence of the mixed peoples." Citing the experience of specialists in Horticulture and Zoology, where strict selection was necessary in order to cross-breed successfully, Lapouge concluded that the lack of such selection in human societies of mixed races would "eliminate the race of the conquerors and soon even the mixed breeds." There was no way to avoid Gresham's Law of Biology: "when classes and races conflict, the inferior drives out the other." For evidence he pointed to the Caribbean: "Among well-known examples are the Antilles, where the white element has almost disappeared, and Haiti, where even the mulattoes have succumbed, giving

way to African barbarism." Georges Vacher de Lapouge, *Les sélections sociales: Cours libre de science politique* (Paris, 1896), 66–67. Elsewhere the Latin American Republics were described as having "arrived on the world scene too late, with a race which is too inferior. The only two nations of numerical importance are Mexico, where the Indian element has taken over, and Brazil, an immense Negro state returning to barbarism." Lapouge, *L'Aryen: Son rôle social* (Paris, 1899), 500.

40. A very useful survey of racial thought in the early Republic is given in Robert Conrad, "The Negro in Brazilian Thought in Colony, Empire and Republic" (M.A. thesis, Columbia University, 1964). Conrad argues that "prior to the legal emancipation of Brazilian Negroes, racism was generally alien to the Brazilian mind." Although the early Republic saw an upsurge of racist thought, this seems an overstatement, in view of the pre-abolitionist attitudes of liberal reformers such as Joaquim Nabuco and Tavares Bastos. Conrad, "The Negro in Brazilian Thought," 127.

41. The origins of this pattern have been explored in detail in Winthrop D. Jordan, *White Over Black: American Attitudes Toward the Negro, 1550–1812* (Chapel Hill, N.C., 1968).

42. *Ibid.*

43. The origin of the word "mulatto" illustrates the preoccupation with possible sterility. The English word "mulatto" comes from the Spanish and Portuguese word *"mulato,"* meaning "young mule," an animal unable (except in rare cases of the female) to procreate.

44. Curtin, *The Image of Africa*, 368; Frederickson, *The Black Image*, 233–35.

45. Sílvio Romero, *Passe recibo: Réplica a Teófilo Braga* (Belo Horizonte, 1904), 54–55.

46. Sílvio Romero, *A América latina* (Pôrto, 1906), 229, 262–347.

47. Sílvio Romero, "Carlos Frederico F. de Martius e Suas Idéias Acerca da História do Brasil," *Revista da Academia Brasileira de Letras,* III, No. 8 (1912), 245, 264–65, 269-71.

48. Fernando de Azevedo, ed., *As Ciências no Brasil,* 2 vols. (São Paulo, 1955), vol. II, 365–69. For a very critical survey of the views of Brazilian sociologists and anthropologists in this era, see Guerreiro Ramos, *Inrodução crítica à sociologia brasileira* (Rio de Janeiro, 1957).

49. Azevedo, *Brazilian Culture,* 255. Von Ihering was also an unequivocal supporter of European immigration and a pessimist about the possibility of the survival of primitive Indians in Brazil. See, for example, his article "Extermínio dos indígenas ou dos sertanejos?" *Jornal do Comércio,* Dec. 5, 1908.

50. Afrânio Peixoto, "Prefácio" to Raimundo Nina Rodrigues, *As Raças humanas e a responsibilidade penal no Brasil,* 3rd ed. (São Paulo, 1938), 11–26. There is no modern critical study of Nina Rodrigues. For biographical and bibliographical data, see Augusto Lins e Silva,

Atualidade de Nina Rodrigues (Rio de Janeiro, 1945); Henrique L. Alves, *Nina Rodrigues e o negro do Brasil* (São Paulo, 1962); Azevedo, *Brazilian Culture*, 257–58; Antônio Caldas Coni, *A Escola tropicalista bahiana* (Bahia, 1952), 62–75; and Edison Carneiro, *Ladinos e crioulos* (Rio de Janeiro, 1964), 209–17. Evidence of his influence and prestige may be found, for example, in the lavish banquet held in his honor (with major public figures attending) in 1903, as described in *O Estado de São Paulo*, Oct. 25, 1903; and the obituary (full of tributes to Nina Rodrigues' scientific leadership) in *Brazil-Médico*, XX (No. 28, July 22, 1906), 285–87. Nina Rodrigues comes in for a very heavy-handed caricature in Jorge Amado's novel, *Tent of Miracles* (New York, 1971). Titles of Rodrigues' publications are given as the work of the fictional character Professor Nilo Argolo de Araújo, but Amado liberally exercises the novelist's right to make up passages from these publications along much more exaggeratedly racist lines than Rodrigues ever wrote.

51. Raimundo Nina Rodrigues, *Os Africanos no Brasil*, 3rd ed. (São Paulo, 1945), 19.

52. As one of his most distinguished students was later (1939) to explain, "the supposed evil of miscegenation is generally an evil of inadequate hygienic conditions." Acknowledging his teacher's erroneous racial view, Arthur Ramos noted that these "ideas acquire complete and total contemporary relevance" if the reader simply "substitutes the term culture for race and acculturation for miscegenation." Such a formula was unfortunately not available in Rodrigues' day. Arthur Ramos, Preface to Raimundo Nina Rodrigues, *As Coletividades anormais* (Rio de Janeiro, 1939), 12–13. Elsewhere Ramos noted that Rodrigues was greatly influenced by the "distorted scientific vision of the era which was saturated in Gobineau, Lapouge, and the other theoreticians of racial inequality," Arthur Ramos, *O Negro brasileiro*, 2nd ed. (São Paulo, 1940), 19–20. The more idiosyncratic and extreme racist views of Padre Ignace Etienne Brazil apparently had little impact when he published articles in the *Revista do Instituto Histórico e Geográfico Brasileiro* in 1909 and 1911. They are discussed in Conrad, "The Negro in Brazilian Thought," 145–47.

53. Nina Rodrigues, *As Raças humanas*, 44.

54. Nina Rodrigues, *Os Africanos no Brasil*, 414–17.

55. *Ibid.*, 25.

56. Nina Rodrigues, *As Raças humanas*, 161, 169, 215–17.

57. *Ibid.*, 219.

58. Nina Rodrigues, *Os Africanos no Brasil*, 28.

59. Nina Rodrigues, *As Raças humanas*, 126.

60. Nina Rodrigues, *Os Africanos no Brasil*, 29–30.

61. *Ibid.*, 28.

62. Nina Rodrigues, *As Raças humanas*, 203–4.

63. "Introdução ao Relatório Apresentado ao Sr. Presidente da

República pelo Ministro da Indústria, Viação e Obras Públicas, Doutor Joaquim Murtinho 1897," reprinted in *Revista do Instituto Histórico e Geográfico Brasileiro*, vol. 219 (Apr.–June 1953), 243.

64. Herrmann Byron de Araújo Soares, *O Caráter nacional* (Pôrto, 1916), xxix, 10.

65. João Grave, article in *O Estado de São Paulo*, Aug. 9, 1914.

66. Alcides Bezerra, *Ensaios de crítica e filosofia* (Paraíba, 1919), 243, 245.

67. Soares, *O Caráter nacional*, 21–22.

68. *Ibid.*, 22, 27.

69. *Ibid.*, xlii–xliii.

70. A useful survey of the opinions of major Brazilian writers on the subject of miscegenation may be found in Arthur Ramos, *Le Métissage au Brésil* (Paris, 1952), chapter IX. Essentially the same material is to be found in Ramos, *Introdução à antropologia brasileira*, 3rd ed., 3 vols., (Rio de Janeiro, 1962), vol. III, *passim*.

71. João Batista de Lacerda, "The *Métis*, or Half breeds, of Brazil" in G. Spiller, ed., *Papers on Inter-racial Problems Communicated to the First Universal Races Congress held at the University of London, July 26–29, 1911* (London, 1911), 377–82. For an analysis of the Congress, see Michael Biddiss, "The Universal Races Congress of 1911," *Race*, vol. XIII (No. 1, July 1971), 37–46. Gilberto Freyre argues, without giving evidence, that Lacerda's paper had considerable international influence: Freyre, "Euclides da Cunha: Revelador da Realidade Brasileira," in Euclides da Cunha, *Obra completa*, 2 vols. (Rio de Janeiro, 1966), vol. I, 30. Lacerda had also been a researcher on beri-beri and had been one of the many scientists who unsuccessfully tried to track down the cause of yellow fever.

72. Martim Francisco [Ribeiro de Andrada], *Viajando*, 2 vols. (São Paulo, 1929–30), vol. I, 12. Clóvis Beviláqua, a prominent lawyer and essayist, thought even the psychological remnants of the non-white elements were rapidly disappearing. Clóvis Beviláqua, *Esboços e fragmentos* (Rio de Janeiro, 1899), 288.

73. João Batista de Lacerda, *O Congresso universal das raças reunido em Londres (1911): Apreciação e comentários pelo Dr. J. B. de Lacerda, delegado do Brasil nesse congresso* (Rio de Janeiro, 1912), 85–101.

74. Pierre Denis, *Le Brésil au XXᵉ Siècle* (Paris, 1909), 259–66.

75. Tobias Monteiro, article in *Jornal do Comércio*, Mar. 29, 1909. Earlier another Rio newspaper had attacked Monteiro for allegedly arranging to omit dark-skinned Brazilian sailors from a naval contingent on the ship of General Roca during the former Argentine President's recent visit to Rio. *Correio da Manhã*, May 8, 1907.

76. Theodore Roosevelt, "Brazil and the Negro," *Outlook*, vol. 106 (Feb. 21, 1914), 410. The translation appeared in *Correio da Manhã* Apr. 7, 1914.

77. Sílvio Romero, "Prefácio" to Tito Lívio de Castro, *Questões e problemas* (São Paulo, 1913), xxiii–xxvii.

78. *Ibid.*

79. E. Franklin Frazier, *The Negro in the United States*, rev. ed. (New York, 1957), 186.

80. Batista de Lacerda, *O Congresso*, 98–100. Brazilian intellectuals' view of the U.S. was indicated by the passing reference of the poet Olavo Bilac to "everyday lynchings in North America." Olavo Bilac, *Crítica e fantasia* (Lisbon, 1904), 145.

81. Manuel de Oliveira Lima, *Nos Estados Unidos: Impressões políticas e sociais* (Leipzig, 1899), 21–22. Joaquim Nabuco argued in 1895 that race prejudice was less prevalent in Brazil because the monarchy had worked to combat it, whereas Republican regimes, such as in the U.S., tended to reinforce it. Joaquim Nabuco, *O Dever dos monarchistas: Carta ao almirante Jacequay* (Rio de Janeiro, 1895), 7–9.

82. Oliveira Lima, *Nos Estados Unidos*, 52–53.

83. *Ibid.*, 52.

84. José Veríssimo, article in *Jornal do Comércio*, Dec. 4, 1899.

85. Medeiros e Albuquerque, *A Tribuna do Rio*, Dec. 11, 1899.

86. Afrânio Peixoto, *Romances Completos* (Rio de Janeiro, 1962), 209–10. Peixoto was also a well-known medical doctor and popularizer of public health doctrines—discussed in chapter 4.

87. Clayton Sedgwick Cooper, *The Brazilians and Their Country* (New York, 1917), 23–25.

88. Roosevelt, "Brazil and the Negro," 410–11.

89. One chronicler of Rio de Janeiro, for example, recounted how inexorably the population of that city had grown whiter between 1880 and 1900, Luiz Edmundo, *O Rio de Janeiro do meu Tempo*, 5 vols. (Rio de Janeiro, 1957), vol. I, 45–46. The process of "whitening" of Rio de Janeiro had begun in the mid-nineteenth century as slaves were shifted out of the city to the rapidly expanding coffee plantations. Mary Catherine Karasch, "Slave Life in Rio de Janeiro, 1808–1850" (Ph.D. diss., University of Wisconsin, 1972), 555.

CHAPTER 3

1. The most satisfactory political history of the Old Republic (1889–1930) is the excellent study by Edgard Carone, *A República velha: Evoluçao política* (São Paulo, 1971). The Brazilian historian-diplomat Oliveira Lima was a good example of the intellectuals' concern over the effect of political stability on their country's future. See, for example, Manoel de Oliveira Lima, *Sept ans de République au Brésil: 1889–1896* (Paris, 1896), 38.

2. The case of Rio Grande do Sul has been carefully studied in

Joseph L. Love, *Rio Grande do Sul and Brazilian Regionalism, 1882–1930* (Stanford, Calif., 1971).

3. The pioneer work on the realities of the electoral system in the provinces in Victor Nunes Leal, *Coronelismo, enxada e voto* (Rio de Janeiro, 1948). Much insight on the system in Ceará may be found in Ralph della Cava, *Miracle at Joaseiro* (New York, 1970). A case study on Bahia for a later period shows how the system continued: Eul-soo Pang, "The Revolt of the Bahian *Coronéis* and the Federal Intervention of 1920," *Luso-Brazilian Review*, vol. VIII (No. 2, Dec. 1971), 3–35.

4. The manner in which the Paulista oligarchy took over direction of the Republic from the military is well told in June E. Hahner, *Civilian-Military Relations in Brazil, 1889–1898* (Columbia, S.C., 1969).

5. Much contemporary reporting on the event is included in Honorato Caldas, *O Marechal de ouro* (Rio de Janeiro, 1898).

6. The manipulation of the coffee market which began in 1906 has been given its first careful analysis in Thomas Halsey Holloway, "The Brazilian Coffee Industry and the First Valorization Scheme of 1906–07" (M.A. thesis, University of Wisconsin, 1971). An extremely valuable collection of data and analysis on the economic history of the Old Republic can be found in Annibal Villanova Villela and Wilson Suzigan, *Política do governo e crescimento da economia brasileira, 1889–1945* (Rio de Janeiro, 1973).

7. Paulo Cavalcanti, *Eça de Queiroz, agitador no Brasil,* 2nd ed. (São Paulo, 1966).

8. The Jacobins have been little studied. I am grateful to Professor June E. Hahner for allowing me to consult her unpublished paper "Portuguese and Radicals in Rio de Janeiro."

9. Cited in João [Pinheiro] Chagas, *De Bond: Alguns aspectos da civilização brasileira* (Lisbon, 1897), 149–51. Unfortunately I was not able to consult a collection of *O Jacobino*.

10. Cited in Barbosa Lima Sobrinho, *Desde quando somos nacionalistas?* (Rio de Janeiro, 1963), 43.

11. Luiz Edmundo, *O Rio de Janeiro do meu tempo* (Rio de Janeiro, 1957), vol. V, 1000.

12. Barbosa Lima Sobrinho, *Desde quando,* 44.

13. Everardo Backheuser, *O Professor* (Rio de Janeiro, 1947), 185–86.

14. Raul Pompéia, Introduction to Rodrigo Octávio, *Festas nacionais* (Rio de Janerio, 1893), i–xxiii.

15. Edmundo, *O Rio de Janeiro do meu tempo,* vol. V, 1002–4; Delgado de Carvalho, *História diplomática do Brasil* (São Paulo, 1959), 178–79.

16. Nationalist consciousness in literary criticism is traced in Afrânio Coutinho, *A Tradição afortunada* (Rio de Janeiro, 1968), and

Ronald Dennis, "Brazilian Literary Nationalism Among the Critics, 1870–1900" (Ph.D. diss., University of Wisconsin, 1972). Dennis argues convincingly, and in refutation of Coutinho, that the interest of the leading critics in literary nationalism per se declined steadily from the mid-1870's to 1900. For a stimulating analysis of the tensions between local and cosmopolitan tendencies in Brazilian literature, see Antônio Cândido, *Literatura e sociedade* (São Paulo, 1965).

17. Machado de Assis, "Notícia da Atual Literatura Brasileira: Instinto de Nacionalidade," in Machado de Assis, *Obra completa*, 3 vols. (Rio de Janeiro, 1962), vol. III, 801–9.

18. The manifesto was published over the signature of Sílvio Romero and is reprinted in Sílvio Romero, *Novos Estudos de literatura contemporânea* (Paris, n.d. [1898]), 259–66. The style, as well as the fact that it was reprinted in this collection, strongly suggest that it was written by Romero. Mendonça, *Sílvio Romero, de corpo inteiro*, 142.

19. Academia Brasileira de Letras, *Discursos acadêmicos: 1897–1906* (Rio de Janeiro, 1934), 20–21.

20. Joaquim Nabuco, *Minha formação* (Rio de Janeiro, 1957), 46–47. Even the two literary critics, José Veríssimo and Araripe Júnior, who had campaigned for a more "national" literature in the 1870's, had lost their enthusiasm by the 1890's. Araripe Júnior simply did not discuss the issue any more and Veríssimo in 1908 confessed that he had abandoned his earlier "nationalistic" position. Dennis, "Brazilian Literary Nationalism," 213.

21. Graça Aranha, "A Literatura Atual no Brasil," *Revista Brazileira*, XIII (Jan.–Mar. 1898), 198.

22. *Gazeta de Notícias*, September 8, 1907. The imitative quality of Brazilian culture in this era is stressed in João Cruz Costa, *Panorama da história da filosofia no Brasil* (São Paulo, 1960), 67–68. One young journalist reacted strongly to the atmosphere and wrote in 1910: "On one hand, there is the supercivilized Brazil that thinks and dresses along with Paris, that has intellectual ambitions and literary neuroses, that reads Anatole [France], and that discusses the most refined ideas while detesting the tropics. On the other hand, there is the crude Brazil of the forest, the victim of invasions and upheavals, fetishistic and naked, separated by four hundred years from the other Brazil." Gilberto Amado, *O Paiz*, Sept. 11, 1910.

23. *O Paiz*, Dec. 26, 1910.

24. Monteiro Lobato, *A Barca de Gleyre: Quarenta anos de correspondência literária entre Monteiro Lobato e Godofredo Rangel* (São Paulo, 1944), 268.

25. Brito Broca, *A Vida literária no Brasil: 1900*, 2nd ed. (Rio de Janeiro, 1960), 143–49. The Brazilian obsession with European fashions was described by the literary critic Sousa Bandeira as an example of what the French (!) critic Jules Gaultier called "Bovaryism"—living in

the illusion of a romanticized self-image, à la Flaubert's *Madame Bovary*. João Carneiro de Sousa Bandeira, *Páginas literárias* (Rio de Janeiro, 1917), 63.

26. The lack of literary originality in this period (and up to 1920) is stressed in the authoritative study by Lúcia Miguel-Pereira, *Prosa de ficção de 1870 a 1920* [Álvaro Lins, ed., *História da literatura Brasileira*, vol. XII] (Rio de Janeiro, 1957); see also Alfredo Bosi, *O Pré-Modernismo* [*A Literatura brasileira*, vol. V] (São Paulo, 1966). A leading contemporary critic bemoaned the lack of originality in his survey of the Brazilian literary scene written in 1913. José Veríssimo [de Mattos], *Letras e literatos* (Rio de Janeiro, 1936), 7–17. But Veríssimo thought the difficulty stemmed from Brazil's failure to pick up the latest and most stimulating currents from Europe!

27. See, for example, the collection of pieces in Coelho Neto, *Scenas e Perfis* (Rio de Janeiro, 1910).

28. Edmundo, *O Rio de Janeiro do meu tempo*, vol. V, 924–25.

29. Peixoto later explained the context in which he had made the often-quoted statement: Homero Senna, *República das letras: 20 Entrevistas com Escritores* (Rio de Janeiro, 1957), 83–102.

30. Cited in José Lopes Pereira de Carvalho, *Os membros da Academia Brasileira em 1915* (Rio de Janeiro, n.d.), 386.

31. Medeiros e Albuquerque, *Em voz alta: Conferências literárias* (Rio de Janeiro, 1909), 131.

32. Edmundo, *O Rio de Janeiro do meu tempo*, vol. IV, 761.

33. Elysio de Carvalho, *Five O'Clock* (Rio de Janeiro, 1909), 28–31.

34. *Ibid.*, dedication page.

35. Elysio de Carvalho, *As modernas correntes estéticas na literatura brasileira* (Rio de Janeiro, 1907), 123.

36. Edmundo, *O Rio de Janeiro do meu tempo*, vol. III, 584–85.

37. João do Rio, *Cinematógrafo* (Pôrto, 1909), 215, 312, 278.

38. João do Rio, ed., *O Momento literário* (Rio de Janeiro n.d. [1908?]), 7, 69, 204, 225, 319.

39. Coelho Neto, *Scenas e perfis*, 215.

40. João do Rio, *O Momento literário*, 3, 9, 71, 79, 285.

41. *Ibid.*, 75.

42. *Ibid.*, 264–65; Carvalho, *As Modernas correntes estéticas*, 206–7. Carvalho's arrogance infuriated Sousa Bandeira, who classified him among the "Philistines, hams, and inane mediocrities who also inspire nausea and pain, above all, pain," Sousa Bandeira, *Páginas literárias*, 44.

43. In 1903, on the fourteenth anniversary of the Republic, the famous poet Olavo Bilac wrote that "the Republic has had a sad and dim puberty. . . . The only certainty is that no one is satisfied." Olavo Bilac, *Crítica e fantasia* (Lisbon, 1904), 248. I gained many ideas for

this chapter from the sensitive analysis in Gilberto Freyre, *Ordem e progresso*. Reactions to the sense of inadequacy are discussed especially on page clxii.

44. João Carneiro de Sousa Bandeira, *Estudos e ensaios* (Rio de Janeiro, 1904), 2, 3, 7.

45. *Ibid.*, 7.

46. Sousa Bandeira, *Páginas literárias* (Rio de Janeiro, 1917), 146–47.

47. Afonso Celso, *Porque me ufano do meu país* (Rio de Janeiro, 1901).

48. *Ibid.*, 3.

49. *Ibid.*, 199.

50. Magalhães de Azeredo, *Homens e livros* (Rio de Janeiro, 1902), 279. For another patriotic schoolbook (printed in Europe!) with a similarly breathless approach to Brazil's "fabulous" natural resources, see Virgílio Cardoso de Oliveira, *A Patria brazileira* (Brussels, 1930). Two examples of schoolbooks published in 1861 and 1873 which were enthusiastic about Brazil's natural resources, climate, and immense territory are cited in Erasmo d'Almeida Magalhães, "Notas aos Estudos sôbre o Português Falado no Brasil," *Revista do Instituto de Estudos Brasileiros* No. 4 (1968), 53. Afonso Celso was in part drawing on this Romantic tradition in Brazilian thought.

51. *Commercio de São Paulo*, Nov. 2, 1901. Gilberto Freyre described Afonso Celso as belonging to the school of "apologetic literature" which had arisen "as a kind of corrective to the despair which for some time had overtaken Brazilians when thinking about the circumstances and the origins—whether ethnic, historical or social—of the Luso-American people." Freyre, *Ordem e progresso*, vol. I, clxvii.

52. Luiz Edmundo, *O Rio de Janeiro do meu tempo*, vol. II, 279; João do Rio, *A Alma encantadora das ruas* (Rio de Janeiro, 1908), 277–78. The translation of the poem is mine.

53. *O Estado de São Paulo*, Sept. 11, 1903.

54. The articles appeared in *O Estado de São Paulo*, Sept. 12, 1903, and succeeding issues.

55. Olavo Bilac, *Crítica e fantasia* (Lisbon, 1904), 195.

56. Nilo Peçanha, *Impressões da Europa* (Nice, n.d. [1912?], 277–88.

57. Rodrigo Octávio, *Le Brésil: sa culture, son liberalisme* (n.p., n.d. [1912?]), 23.

58. *Ibid.*, 8.

59. João Capistrano de Abreu, *Caminhos antigos e povoamento do Brasil* (Rio de Janeiro, 1889). For detail on this important historian, see Hélio Vianna, *Capistrano de Abreu: Ensaio bibliográfico* (Rio de Janeiro, 1955), and José Honório Rodrigues, "Capistrano de Abreu and Brazilian Historiography," in E. Bradford Burns, ed., *Perspectives on Brazilian History* (New York, 1967), 156–80.

60. João Capistrano de Abreu, *Capítulos de história colonial* (Rio de Janeiro, 1907); Rodrigues, "Capistrano de Abreu," 175.

61. *Correspondéncia de Capistrano de Abreu*, ed. by José Honório Rodrigues, 3 vols. (Rio de Janeiro, 1954–56), vol. I, 226; vol. II, 21. My translation of the latter letter is taken from Burns, ed., *Perspectives on Brazilian History*, 80.

62. The most satisfactory biography is Sylvio Rabello, *Euclides da Cunha*, 2nd ed. (Rio de Janeiro, 1966). Another well-known biography is Eloy Pontes, *A Vida dramática de Euclides da Cunha* (Rio de Janeiro, 1938). Unless otherwise indicated all citations of Euclides' writings are from the *Obra completa*, edited by Afrânio Coutinho (Rio de Janeiro: Ed. José Aguilar, 1966), 2 vols., which includes the extensive bibliography on Euclides (with some additions) published in *Revista do Livro* (Rio de Janeiro), No. 15 (Sept. 1959). The most systematic analyses of Euclides' thought have been written by Marxists: Nelson Werneck Sodré, "Euclides da Cunha: A Intuição e a Superstição," a chapter in Sodré's *A Ideologia do colonialismo: Seus reflexos no pensamento brasileiro* (Rio de Janeiro, 1961), 103–66; Clóvis Moura, *Introdução ao pensamento de Euclides da Cunha* (Rio de Janeiro, 1964).

63. Da Cunha, *Obra completa*, vol. I, 543–66. During the Empire the paper carried the title of *A Província do São Paulo*. After the proclamation of the Republic in 1889, it became *O Estado de São Paulo*, thereby reflecting the change in constitutional language.

64. Cruz Costa, "Euclides da Cunha e os Filósofos," *Revista Brasiliense*, No. 25 (Sept.–Oct. 1959), 110–20.

65. Da Cunha, *Obra completa*, vol. I, 580–81.

66. *Ibid.*, 625.

67. Reprinted in da Cunha, *Obra completa*, vol. I, 575–82.

68. *Os Sertões* has become one of the most thoroughly studied works in Brazilian literature. A careful analysis of its origins may be found in Olímpio de Sousa Andrade, *História e interpretação de "Os Sertões"* (Rio de Janeiro: Edart, 1960), which is based on extensive study of available sources. *Os Sertões* was given a superb English translation by Samuel Putnam: *Rebellion in the Backlands* (Chicago, 1944).

69. The change in Euclides' attitude can be seen in the diary he kept while covering the revolt. It was published posthumously and is reprinted in da Cunha, *Obra completa*, vol. II, 491–572.

70. One of the few contemporaries who immediately saw the larger implications of Canudos was Afonso Arinos, the sensitive monarchist writer who had an uncommonly deep understanding of the *sertão*. Just after the defeat of the rebels in 1897, he wrote: "this struggle deserves to be studied . . . in its basic origins as a social phenomenon highly important for psychological investigation and for an understanding of the Brazilian character," Afonso Arinos, *Notas do dia* (São Paulo: Andrade Melo, 1900), 133. An important new interpreta-

tion of Canudos is offered in Ralph della Cava, "Brazilian Messianism and National Institutions: A Reappraisal of Canudos and Joaseiro," *Hispanic American Historical Review*, XLVIII (No. 3, Aug. 1968), 402–20.

71. Viriato Correia, "Euclides da Cunha" in *A Illustração brasileira*, Aug. 15, 1909, reprinted in da Cunha, *Obra completa*, vol. I, 474. Details of the printing history are given in Francisco Venancio Filho, *A Glória de Euclides da Cunha* (São Paulo, 1940), 60–68.

72. A very useful collection of the initial reviews was printed by Euclides' publishers: *Os Sertões: Juizos críticos* (Rio de Janeiro: Laemmert, 1904).

73. One contemporary critic described it as an "unrestrained, cataclysmic style perhaps most appropriate for describing abnormal events, social revolutions, and personal disasters." Araripe Júnior, "Dois Grandes Estilos," reprinted in Da Cunha, *Obra completa*, vol. I, 98. Sixty years later Manuel Bandeira, the great Modernist poet, referred to Euclides' "virile, somewhat barbarous prose," *ibid.*, 629.

74. Euclides' views on race are spelled out in greatest detail in the section of *Os Sertões* on "man": *Obra completa*, vol. II, 137–236. Nelson Werneck Sodré argues that only after careful consultation of "the best sources of colonialist ideology" did Euclides propound ideas of racial inferiority. As evidence Sodré points out the racist interpretation apparent in *Os Sertões* was not evident in Euclides' earlier account, *Diário de uma expedição*. Sodré, *A Ideologia do colonialismo*, 137–39. Euclides' ideas on race and ethnography are examined in Clóvis Moura, *Introdução ao pensamento de Euclides da Cunha*, 74–101. Gilberto Freyre was one of the first to acknowledge how greatly Euclides had been influenced by the racist assumptions of his era: Gilberto Freyre, *Atualidade de Euclides da Cunha* (Rio de Janeiro, 1943), 13–19. One critic has argued that Euclides' views were not of the rigid mechanistic variety of Buckle or Ratzel, since a total application of their ideas would have ruled out the tragic quality so evident in *Os Sertões*. Antônio Cândido, "Euclides da Cunha, sociólogo," *Estado de São Paulo*, Dec. 13, 1952, quoted in Sousa Andrade, *História e interpretação*, 208.

75. Euclides da Cunha, *Rebellion in the Backlands*, 84–85.

76. Da Cunha, *Obra completa*, vol. II, 193–214. Euclides may have been influenced in this interpretation by Nina Rodrigues, "A Loucura epidémica de Canudos," *Revista Brazileira*, III, tomo XII (Nov. 1, 1897), 129–44.

77. *Os Sertões: Juizos críticos*. While discussing different "races," for example, Euclides often referred to "our race." A later book by Euclides da Cunha, *Contrastes e confrontos* (Pôrto, 1907) provoked one reviewer to express great skepticism about the racist sociological theories still being imported from Europe. Sousa Bandeira, *Páginas*

literárias, 22–28. Yet Euclides' "irritating parenthesis," which repeated the theory of the degeneracy of mixed bloods, continued to be cited as authoritative by other Brazilian writers. See, for example, Alcides Bezerra, *Ensaios de crítica e philosofia* (Parahyba, 1919), 251–53.

78. The most balanced and detailed analysis of *Canaã* is the long introduction which Antonio Alatorre wrote for Spanish translation published in Mexico: Graça Aranha, *Canaán* (México, 1954), vii–lii. Alatorre's essay includes extensive references to earlier criticism of the novel both in Brazil and abroad. Augusto Emílio Estellita Lins, *Graça Aranha e o "Canaã"* (Rio de Janeiro, 1967), is a lengthy and disorganized attempt to relate *Canaã* to the rest of Aranha's work and to furnish details on the locale in Espírito Santo where real-life incidents evidently inspired Aranha's story.

79. There is no scholarly biography of Aranha. Citations of his works are from José Pereira da Graça Aranha, *Obra completa* (Rio de Janeiro, 1969), which includes an essay on Aranha by Gilberto Freyre, as well as a detailed bibliography of works on Aranha. The controversy over Aranha's role in the origins of the Brazilian Modernist Movement has undoubtedly tended to overshadow interest in his earlier career.

80. The translations are from the English edition published in the U.S.: Graça Aranha, *Canaan*, trans. by Mariano Joaquin Lorente (Boston, 1920), 56–57.

81. *Ibid.*, 57.

82. Typical was the long review by Félix Pacheco which appeared in the *Jornal do Comércio* in 1902. Pacheco praised Aranha as a "first-class stylist" and a "profound thinker" and compared *Canaã* to Zola's *Travail*. The review included long excerpts from the dialogue between Milkau and Lentz, with the reviewer implying that Milkau held the clear advantage. The review was later reprinted in book form: Félix Pacheco, *A Chanaan de Graça Aranha* (Rio de Janeiro, 1931). The novel was praised by José Veríssimo (a leading literary critic and fellow member of the Brazilian Academy of Letters), José Veríssimo, *Estudos de literatura brasileira*, Fifth Series (Rio de Janeiro, 1905), 15–35. Another critic, Nestor Vítor, praised the novel but expressed many more doubts about its merit as an original literary work: *Obra crítica de Nestor Vítor* (Rio de Janeiro, 1969), 293–302. The influence of Aranha's work on the younger generation is described in Orris Soares, "Graça Aranha: O Romance–Tese e Canaan," in Aurélio Buarque de Hollanda, ed., *O Romance brasileiro* (Rio de Janeiro, 1952), 203–21. Aranha's novel attracted praise abroad, which undoubtedly increased his prestige at home. See, for example, Guglielmo Ferrero's favorable review of the French translation in *Le Figaro*, Oct. 31, 1910. Ferrero, whom Baron Rio Branco, the Brazilian Foreign Minister, had carefully cultivated, referred to *Canaã* as "the novel of contemporary America."

83. One contemporary critic wrote a review article specifically

comparing Euclides de Cunha and Graça Aranha and their approach to the question of the Brazilian's adaptation. Sousa Bandeira, *Páginas literárias*, 5–12.

84. Among other anti-racist statements the most uncompromising was Álvaro Bomilcar, *O Preconceito de raça no Brasil* (Rio de Janeiro, 1916). In a postscript Bomilcar explained that the book was written in 1911, but delayed in publication. Another writer who had condemned the "perfidious theory" of racial inferiority was the literary critic Alencar Araripe Júnior in his Introduction to Clóvis Beviláqua, *Esboços e fragmentos* (Rio de Janeiro, 1899), L.

85. This point is brought out clearly in Dante Moreira Leita, *O Caráter nacional brasileiro: História de uma ideologia*, 2nd ed. (São Paulo, 1969), 258–59.

86. Bomfim, *A América latina: Males de origem* (Rio de Janeiro, n.d. [1903?]).

87. *Ibid.*, 3.

88. *Ibid.*, 278.

89. *Ibid.*, 306.

90. *Ibid.*, 284.

91. *Ibid.*, 287–88.

92. *Ibid.*, 299–300.

93. *Ibid.*, 280–81. Sílvio Romero devoted an entire book to a refutation of Bomfim's *A América latina* which he labeled "a mass of errors, sophisms, and blundering contradictions." He called Bomfim's views on ethnography "a veritable comedy." Romero dismissed Bomfim's belief in racial equality as a "cock-and-bull story" and an "illusion." Prevailing theories of racial differences, Romero argued, had been established by "sincere, objective, strictly scientific investigation." Sílvio Romero, *A América latina* (Pôrto, 1906), 11, 203–4, 212.

94. Bomfim, *A América latina*, 398.

95. *Ibid.*, 180–81.

96. *Ibid.*, 342.

97. *Ibid.*, 189.

98. *Ibid.*, 378.

99. *Ibid.*, 263, 399. Later Bomfim published a series of volumes giving his revisionist version of Brazil's history, applying the interpretation he had spelled out in *A América latina*. He continued to attack the racist views still current in Brazil, which were often based on a "poorly assimilated Mendelianism." His aggressive tone was even more evident: "without fear of denial it can be stated that racial mixture, in the case of the Brazilian population, has been an advantage and not an evil," Bomfim, *O Brasil na América: Caracterização da formação brasileira* (Rio de Janeiro, 1929), 176–77. He attacked the "ruling classes" for having "inhumanely, unpatriotically and assininely" regarded the *caboclo* and Negro as "inferiors." Bomfim, *O Brasil nação: Realidade da*

soberania brasileira (Rio de Janeiro, 1931), vol. II, 243. Another volume in his revisionist history was *O Brasil na História: Deturpação das tradições: Degradação política* (Rio de Janeiro, 1931). He was honored by having his writing published in an anthologized volume of the famous "Brasiliana" series begun in the 1930's: Manoel Bomfim, *O Brasil* (São Paulo, 1935), with a short "explanatory note" by Carlos Maul.

100. The most complete study of Alberto Tôrres is Barbosa Lima Sobrinho, *Presença de Alberto Tôrres: Sua vida e pensamento* (Rio de Janeiro, 1968). Earlier studies by Tôrres enthusiasts such as A. Saboia Lima, *Alberto Tôrres e a sua obra* (Rio de Janeiro, 1918), and Candido Moto Filho, *Alberto Tôrres e o tema da nossa geração* (São Paulo, 1931), although valuable as evidence of Tôrres' influence, consist largely of uncritical summaries of his writings. For a skeptical view of the coherence of Torres' thought, see W. Douglas McLain, Jr., "Alberto Tôrres, Ad Hoc Nationalist," *Luso-Brazilian Review*, IV (No. 2, Dec. 1967), 17–34. An index to the principal themes in Torres' works (including newspaper articles) is given in the form of a concordance in Alcides Gentil, *As Idéias de Alberto Tôrres* (São Paulo, 1932). Tôrres published a number of newspaper articles, only some of which were incorporated into his two major books: *O Problema nacional* (Rio de Janeiro, 1914) and *A Organização nacional* (Rio de Janeiro, 1914). Subsequent citations will be to the books. My careful reading of these newspaper articles revealed no basic divergences from, nor additions to, the ideas developed in book form.

101. Alberto Tôrres, *O Problema nacional*, 45–49; Tôrres, *Le Problème mondial* (Rio de Janeiro, 1913), 138.

102. Tôrres, *Problema nacional*, 12, 137; Alberto Tôrres, *Organização Nacional*, 11, 84, 196.

103. Tôrres, *Problema nacional*, XX–XXI, 65, 76–82.

104. Tôrres, *Organização nacional*, 155, 182, 208; Tôrres, *Problema nacional*, XVII, 133.

105. Tôrres, *Organização nacional*, 194; Tôrres, *Problema nacional*, 121; Alberto Tôrres, *As Fontes da vida no Brasil* (Rio de Janeiro, 1915), 44.

106. Tôrres, *Organização nacional*, XXXIX, 155; Tôrres, *Problema nacional*, 122, 150.

107. Tôrres, *Organização nacional*, XL, 44: Tôrres, *Problema nacional*, 14, 32–34, 39, 55, 84, 109; Tôrres, *As Fontes da vida*, 30, 41.

108. Tôrres, *Problema nacional*, 24–25.

109. Tôrres, *Organização nacional*, 197; Tôrres, *Problema nacional*, 41, 116.

110. Tôrres, *As Fontes da vida*, 19; Tôrres, *Problema nacional*, XXI–XXIII.

111. Tôrres, *Organização nacional*, XXVI, 125, 212, 241, 248; Tôrres *Problema nacional*, XXIII, 5.

112. Tôrres, *Problema nacional*, XV, 13, 38, 43, 106; Tôrres, *Organização nacional*, XXVI, 167, 185, 189. Barbosa Lima Sobrinho unconvincingly attempted to downplay Tôrres' agrarianism, perhaps because it was such an anachronism alongside his economic nationalism: Lima Sobrinho, *Presença de Alberto Tôrres*, 347–48.

113. Tôrres, *Organização nacional*, 145, 158–59, 173, 204. The detailed constitutional revisions are spelled out on pages 219–311.

114. A very complete discussion of Tôrres' influence on later Brazilian thought is given in Lima Sobrinho, *Presença de Alberto Tôrres*, 457–520.

CHAPTER 4

1. Afonso de'Escragnolle Taunay, *A Missão artística francesa* (Rio de Janeiro, 1956); the best general source on these institutions is Azevedo, *Brazilian Culture*.

2. When pushed by his ministers, however, he fully supported the use of foreign personnel to assist in the building of institutions essential to Brazil's material development—such as the invitation to the French mission led by Henri Gorceix in 1874, to help found the School of Mines in Ouro Prêto. Azevedo, *Brazilian Culture*, 175, 182–83, 250–52, 398–405.

3. The British contribution is clearly analyzed in Graham, *Britain and the Onset of Modernization*, especially Chapters 2 and 5. For an earlier, more impressionistic account, see Gilberto Freyre, *Inglêses no Brasil* (Rio de Janeiro, 1948).

4. Rio-Branco wrote and had published in Paris a laudatory biography of Emperor Pedro II under the pseudonym B. Mossé: *Dom Pedro II, Empereur du Brésil* (Paris, 1889). He describes his propaganda efforts in his letters to the Emperor: Miguel do Rio Branco, ed., *Correspondência entre D. Pedro II e o Barão Rio-Branco* (São Paulo, 1957), 25, 51, 62–63.

5. Caio Prado Júnior, "A Imigração brasileira no passado e no futuro," in Prado, *Evolução política do Brasil e outros estudos*, 2nd ed. (São Paulo, 1957), 243–61.

6. For an example, see José Ricardo Pires de Almeida, *L'Agriculture et les industries au Brésil* (Rio de Janeiro, 1889). For earlier examples of such literature, see S. Dutot, *France et Brésil* (Paris, 1857); Hippolyte Carvallo, *Études sur le Brésil: Au Point de Vue de L'Emigration et du Commerce Français* (Paris, 1858); and V. L. Baril [Comte de la Hure], *L'Empire du Brésil: Monographie complète de l'Empire sud-Américain* (Paris, 1862). The latter was subsidized by subscriptions, undoubtedly from Brazilians.

7. Luiz Viana Filho, *A Vida do Barão do Rio Branco* (Rio de Janeiro, 1959), 146.

8. Afrânio Peixoto, *Ramo de louro: Novos ensaios de crítica e de história*, 2nd ed. (São Paulo, 1942), 241–44.

9. Heitor Lyra, *História de Dom Pedro II*, 3 vols. (São Paulo, 1938–40), vol. II, 312; Georges Raeders, *D. Pedro II e o Conde de Gobineau* (São Paulo, 1938), 52.

10. Papers of Salvador de Mendonça, Biblioteca Nacional, Manuscript Section, I, 4, 22, 13.

11. Fernando Bastos de Avila, *L'immigration au Brésil* (Rio de Janeiro, 1956); T. Lynn Smith, *Brazil: People and Institutions*, rev. ed. (Baton Rouge, La., 1963), chapter VIII. For examples of Brazilian liberal thinking on the need to attract white immigrants in the 1860's, see David Gueiros Vieira, "Protestantism and the Religious Question in Brazil, 1850–1875" (Ph.D. diss., American University, 1972), 599–611.

12. Efforts to promote immigration in the late Empire are documented and analyzed in Michael M. Hall, "The Origins of Mass Immigration in Brazil, 1871–1914" (Ph.D. diss., Columbia University, 1969).

13. *O Império do Brasil na exposição universal de 1867 em Paris* (Rio de Janeiro, 1867), 3.

14. Júlio Constancio de Villeneuve, ed., *Relatório sôbre a exposição universal de 1867* (Paris, 1868), vol. I, cxxiii.

15. *L'Empire du Brésil à l'exposition de Vienne en 1873* (Rio de Janeiro, 1873), 19–20; 165.

16. *O Império do Brasil na exposição universal de 1876 em Philadelphia* (Rio de Janeiro, 1875), [unnumbered page at front of book].

17. M. F.-J. Santa-Anna Nery, ed., *Le Brésil en 1889* (Paris, 1889), i–iii. Perhaps the Brazilians felt easier in participating in an exposition now that they no longer had to explain the continued existence of slavery in their country.

18. *Ibid.*, x–xi.

19. Luiz Joaquim de Oliveira Castro, *Le Brésil vivant*, 3rd ed. (Paris, 1891), vol. IX, 3, 5.

20. Domingos Jaguaribe, *Influence de l'esclavage et de la liberté* (Brussels, 1893), 113, 117, 145.

21. Afrânio Peixoto, *Clima e doenças do Brasil* (Rio de Janeiro, 1907). For similar attempts by Brazilian scholars and publicists to defend their country from the charge of being dangerously unhealthful, see Eurico Gonçalves Bastos, *Contribución para a climatologia brasileira* [Tese apresentada a Faculdade de Medicina do Rio de Janeiro em 26 de março de 1897] (Rio de Janeiro, 1897); Joaquim A. de Oliveira Botelho, *Apuntes sobre el clima del Brasil* (Santiago de Chile, 1901); and Arthur Orlando, *Clima brasileiro* [3° Congresso de Geografia] (Rio de Janeiro, 1911). Additional detail on other writings in this line may be found in an unpublished paper by Professor Donald B. Cooper (of Ohio State University): "Brazil's Long Fight Against Epidemic Disease: 1849–1917 (with Special Emphasis on Yellow Fever)." Interestingly enough, Brazil was apparently free of epidemic disease

until about 1850 and up to then was considered one of the safest countries for white immigrants. I am grateful to Professor Cooper for allowing me to consult his paper. Actually, yellow fever was never totally eliminated from Rio de Janeiro. In 1907 there were still thirty-nine deaths from yellow fever in Rio, and a moderate epidemic recurred in 1928 (seventy-three deaths). Yellow fever was virtually eliminated in its epidemic form, but jungle yellow fever has persisted until the present day, although claiming relatively few deaths.

22. *Correio da Manhã*, Nov. 4, Dec. 27, 29, 1904. Vidal devoted many columns to urging a more aggressive policy of promoting immigration. *Correio da Manhã*, Mar. 12, June 18, Aug. 11, Oct. 15, Nov. 9, 1903; Mar. 1, June 18, 1904; Jan. 1, Nov. 30, 1905; May 9, 1911; June 5, 1912; Apr. 7, 1914. Concern over the image projected abroad was expressed in editorials in the *Correio da Manhã* on Oct. 17, Dec. 12, 1908; May 23, 1913.

23. J. Fernando Carneiro, *Imigração e colonização no Brasil* (Rio de Janeiro, 1950), 32.

24. *Correio da Manhã*, Dec. 18, 1910. *Correio da Manhã*, Jan. 21, 1911.

25. Caio de Menezes, *A Raça Allemã* (Pôrto Alegre, 1914), 61.

26. *Ibid.*, 57.

27. Comisão: Louisiana Purchase Exposição, 1904., *Relatório apresentado ao Exm. Sr. Lauro Severiano Müller . . . pelo General F. M. de Souza Aguiar* (Rio de Janeiro, 1905). Evidence of the miserable living conditions for the poor in Rio de Janeiro could be found, for example, in the two articles by Everardo Backheuser, "Onde Moram os Pobres," *Renascença*, No. 13 (Mar. 1905) and No. 15 (May 1905).

28. *Gazeta de Notícias*, July 29, 1907; Typical of the efforts to promote Brazil's image in Europe was the trip of the literary critic Medeiros e Albuquerque in 1910. See the column by "Joe" (João do Rio) in *Gazeta*, Sept. 11, 1910.

29. Artur Orlando, *O Panamericanismo* (Rio de Janeiro, 1906), 44. The prevailing view was summarized by the journalist (later to become a national newspaper mogul) A. Chateaubriand, who wrote in 1918: "Up to now we have lived in the faith that we would be regenerated by a transfusion of new European blood in the process of national race mixture." "A Superstição Colonizadora," *Correio da Manhã*, Feb. 1, 1918.

30. João de Barro [pseud. of Rodrigo Octávio], "Chronica," *Renascença*, No. 3 (May 1904).

31. Luiz Edmundo, *O Rio do Janeiro*, vol. III, 613; IV, 773–74. The same author notes: "The odor of animal droppings figured so prominently among Rio's traditions that a leading dandy, the symbolist poet Guerra Duval, decided to join the foreign service. By poetic justice his first post was Paraguay. . . ." *Ibid.*, 512–13.

32. Afrânio Peixoto, *Poeira da estrada*, 2nd ed. (São Paulo, 1921), 86.

33. Directoria Geral de Estatística, *Boletim commemorativo da exposição nacional de 1908* (Rio de Janeiro, 1908), V–VII.

34. João do Rio, *Cinematographo*, 277, 281.

35. *Ibid.*, 286, 289.

36. In *Ordem e progresso*, Gilberto Freyre devoted much attention to Rio Branco's image-guilding efforts, as does Brito Broca, *Vida literária*, chapter XVI. Some contemporaries were skeptical of Rio-Branco's efforts. João do Rio thought the Foreign Minister was being taken in by visiting European journalists who could do little in return for the fees they collected from the Brazilian government. João do Rio, *Cinematografo*, 223–30.

37. Luiz Edmundo, *O Rio Janeiro do meu tempo*, vol. IV, 896–900; Otto Prazeres, "Aspectos do Rio Branco,"˙ *Revista do Instituto Histórico e Geográfico Brasileiro*, vol. 244 (July–Sept. 1959), 343–45.

38. Broca, *Vida literária*, 155. There is much witty gossip about "image" promotion by the Brazilian Foreign Office in Manoel de Oliveira Lima, *Memórias* (Rio de Janeiro, 1937). I learned a great deal about the era between the late Empire (late 1880's) and the early 1920's from the detailed scrapbooks of newspaper and magazine clippings which Oliveira Lima and his wife assembled over the years—until his death in 1928. The scrapbooks are housed, along with Lima's correspondence and personal library, at the Oliveira Lima Library at the Catholic University of America in Washington, D.C. For detail on this interesting figure's career, see Manuel de Oliveira Lima, *Obra seleta* (Rio de Janeiro, 1971), which was edited and given a long biographical introduction by Barbosa Lima Sobrinho.

39. Joaquim Nabuco had been Rio-Branco's first choice to head the Brazilian delegation. For background on the conference, see E. Bradford Burns, *The Unwritten Alliance: Rio-Branco and Brazilian-American Relations* (New York, 1966), 116–26. Typical of the Brazilian press reaction was this account: "The role which Rui Barbosa has played at the Conference has contributed more to the prestige and good reputation of Brazil than all the propaganda we promoted and paid for during these last twenty years." *Gazeta de Notícias*, Aug. 7, 1907. Much was made of how Rui was said to have impressed European statesmen. See, for example, the remarks attributed to the French parliamentarian, Leon Bourgeois: "I had never imagined . . . that outside of a few European centers there was any ambiance capable of producing a man of Sr. Barbosa's culture. He would do honor to the intellectual elite of *any* nationality." *Renasçenca*, No. 47 (Jan. 1908), 6. Rui has since been considered a national hero for his role at the Hague conference, as in the standard biography, Luiz Viana Filho, *A Vida de Rui Barbosa* (São Paulo, 1949), 331–53. This interpretation was rudely

challenged in a revisionist biography: R. Magalhães Júnior, *Rui, o homem e o mito* 2nd ed. (Rio de Janeiro, 1965), 281–305. Magalhães' charge that some of Rui's ecstatic press coverage had been bought at Brazilian government expense brought indignant replies, such as Salomão Jorge, *Um Piolho na asa da Águia* (São Paulo, 1965), 263–76.

40. Thomas E. Skidmore and Thomas Holloway, "New Light on Euclides da Cunha: Letters to Oliveira Lima, 1903–1909," *Luso-Brazilian Review*, VIII (No. 1, Summer 1971), 30–55; Viana Filho, *Vida do Barão do Rio Branco*, 335. Details of Euclides' work in the Foreign Ministry may be found in Francisco Venâncio Filho, *Rio-Branco e Euclides da Cunha* (Rio de Janeiro, 1946). Euclides' official report of the trip to the Purús is included in *Obra completa*, vol. I, 681–734. He had planned to write a book about Amazonia, but had completed only a few chapters when he died. They were included in the posthumously published volume *À Margem da história* (Porto, 1909) and are reprinted in *Obra completa*, vol. I, 223–77. For a detailed study of this phase of Euclides' career, see Leandro Tocantins, *Euclides da Cunha e o paraíso perdido* (Rio de Janeiro, 1968).

41. A detailed account of Rio-Branco's policy toward the United States is given in Burns, *The Unwritten Alliance*. Rio-Branco's speech welcoming the delegates included a proud recital of Brazil's recent accomplishments, such as the rebuilding of Rio de Janeiro. Barão do Rio-Branco, *Obras*, vol. IX: *Discursos* (Rio de Janeiro, 1948), 95–98.

42. Rodrigo Octávio in *Renasçenca*, No. 31 (Sept. 1906). The entire issue was devoted to the conference. For an example of the favorable publicity Rio-Branco's policy received in Brazil, see Alcides Gentil, *O Brasil e o internacionalismo: À Margem das idéias e dos atos do Barão do Rio-Branco* (Rio de Janeiro, 1913). The praise was so fulsome that one is led to wonder who financed the book.

43. After a dinner at Itamaratí in honor of Ferrero, Graça Aranha sent Rio Branco his congratulations: "I had the delicious illusion that Cicero was being received by Pericles. We are dining in Athens." On Rio Branco's role: "As Athenians we would be able to say to the Historian of Antiquity that Rio Branco's youthful oath was the same as the young Greek on the altar of the Goddess: 'I will not leave my country diminished, rather I will make it greater.'" Viana Filho, *A Vida do Rio Branco*, 379. Unfortunately for Rio-Branco, Ferrero's wife, shortly after the visit on which she accompanied her husband to Brazil, published a travel book describing the indolence and unreliable character of the Brazilians. It was a disconcerting example of how the selling efforts could backfire. Gina Lombroso Ferrero, *Nell 'America Meridionale (Brasile–Uruguay–Argentina)* (Milan, Italy, 1908), cited in Broca, *Vida literária*, 162–63.

44. Francisco de Assis Barbosa, "Flutuações do Pan-Americanismo," *Revista do Instituto Histórico e Geográfico Brasileiro*, CCLXIII (Apr.–June 1964), 112.

45. Lucy Maffei Hutter, *Imigração italiana em São Paulo, 1880–1889: Os primeiros contactos do imigrante com o Brasil* (Tese de Doutoramento, Departamento de História da Faculdade de Filosofia, Letras e Ciências Humanas da Universidade de São Paulo, 1971), 127–48.

46. There is no comprehensive, detailed study of immigration policy in Brazil for the period between 1870 and 1930. The dissertations by Michael Hall and Lucy Maffei Hutter offer valuable information on the late Empire. A starting point for the entire span of the Empire and the Republic is Fernando Carneiro, *Imigração e colonização no Brasil*. Even reliable statistical series are not easy to establish. Figures published by the state government of São Paulo (which kept the best records) often vary from those published by the federal government. The legal history is traced in Péricles de Mello Carvalho, "A Legislação imigratória do Brasil e sua evolução," *Revista de Imigração e Colonização*, I (No. 4, Oct. 1940), 719–36.

47. Decreto N. 528 of June 28, 1890.

48. J. Fernando Carneiro, *Imigração e Colonização no Brasil*, 31.

49. Paula Beiguelman, *A Formação do povo no complexo cafeeiro: Aspectos políticos* (São Paulo, 1968), 128–29.

50. A well-documented study of this program may be found in Lucy Maffei Hutter, *Imigração italiana em São Paulo, 1880–1889*.

51. "Relatório apresentado por Martinho Prado Jr. à Directoria da Sociedade Promotora de Imigração em 18 de Novembro de 1887" reprinted in *In Memoriam: Martinho Prado Junior* (São Paulo, 1944), 351–58.

52. Data on expenditures and the number of immigrants admitted may be found in publications of the São Paulo state government: *Boletim do Departamento do Trabalho Agricola*, Nos. 73–74 (1932), 67–68; *Boletim da Directoria de Terras, Colonização e Imigração*, No. 1 (Oct. 1937).

53. The *Sociedade Central* had, after initial enthusiasm, opposed the Paulista program of subsidized immigration. The Society was dissolved in 1891. Hall, "The Origins of Mass Immigration in Brazil," 80.

54. There were persistent worries about the sharp regional imbalance in the distribution of the immigrants. One of the first to urge an effort to attract immigrants to the neglected areas, especially the North and Northeast, was Sílvio Romero, *A Imigração e o futuro da raçã portuguesa no Brasil* (Rio de Janeiro, 1891), which was reprinted in Romero, *Discursos* (Pôrto, 1904), 309–16. Romero subsequently became alarmed at the concentration of German-speaking immigrants in the southern provinces of Rio Grande do Sul, Santa Catarina, and Paraná, where he thought the German government had sinister designs. Romero, *O Allemanismo no sul do Brasil* (Rio de Janeiro, 1906), reprinted in Romero, *Provocações e debates* (Pôrto, 1910), 115–69. For a vigorous reply in defense of the German immigrants in Paraná, see

Alcides Munhoz, *O Sr. Sílvio Romero e o allemanismo no sul do Brasil* (Curitíba, 1907).

55. In 1904, for example, after the Italian Foreign Ministry's directive of 1902 had prohibited subsidized immigration, two Brazilian writers expressed alarm over the much greater flow of Italian immigrants to the United States which "for some years has been trying to slow down the immigrant wave, rejecting the poor and sick and only permitting the disembarcation of those who have at least five hundred francs savings. Nevertheless, the Italians rush there in masses, full of enthusiasm and confidence in the future. What a contrast with the Brazilian Republic! We offer racial affinities, the advantages of language, customs and climate, even free passage, but all in vain. They turn their backs on us and go to blend into the Anglo-Saxon race." L. P. Barretto and Santos Werneck proposal (of 1904) to the Sociedade Paulista de Agricultura, quoted in Beiguelman, *A Formação do povo no complexo cafeeiro*, 112–13. A similar concern over Brazil's competitive position vis-à-vis Argentina and the United States may be found in Alcides Bezerra, *Ensaios de crítica*, 258; and the editorial "O Brasil na Europa," *Correio da Manhã*, May 9, 1907. It must have given Brazilians great pleasure to read the headline "Clemenceau affirma a superioridade do Brasil sôbre a Argentina" on a story commenting on interviews with Clemenceau after his tour of South America in 1910. *Correio da Manhã*, Oct. 27, 1910.

CHAPTER 5

1. Precise income estimates are impossible, but rough comparisons in the mid-1890's showed Argentina to have a per capita income approximately equal to that of Germany and Holland and higher than those of Austria, Spain, and Italy. Michael G. Mulhall, *Industries and Wealth of Nations* (London, 1896), 391. Brazil, along with the rest of Latin America, was not even included in the Mulhall survey—an indication of Brazil's relatively disorganized state of data-gathering facilities. Celso Furtado estimated Brazil's annual per capita income at $106 in 1900 but unfortunately did not explain how his estimate was reached. Celso Furtado, *The Economic Growth of Brazil* (Berkeley, Calif., 1963), 164.

2. In his typically hyperbolic style, Romero had used Euclides' theme of the struggle to achieve an authentic nationality in order to launch his own denunciation of Brazil's leaders whom he accused of being "thrilled to enjoy fat positions" while being "bemuddled by the twin mirages of foreign capital and foreign labor, as if these had been created just for our use and offered to us for nothing. . . ." He gave an exaggerated description of foreign economic control and warned that

Brazil had "arrived at the twentieth century—the century which will decide our destiny—completely unequipped for the struggle." The speech is reprinted in Romero, *Provocações e debates*, 335–400. Sitting in the audience was the President of Brazil, Afonso Pena, which so embarrassed Romero's fellow Academy members that they decided to screen all future Academy addresses, Broca, *Vida literária*, 66–67. Romero was referring to Euclides' phrase in an article published in 1900: "We have condemned ourselves to civilization: Either we progress or we disappear." da Cunha, *Obra completa*, vol. I, 342.

3. For a discussion of this crisis, see the excellent survey of Brazilian political history between 1889 and 1930 in Edgar Carone, *A República velha: Evolução política*. An important new analysis of the "kindergarten" political group is offered in Alberto Venâncio Filho, "Carlos Peixoto e o 'Jardim da Infância,' " *Digesto Econômico*, No. 226 (July–Aug. 1972), 109–29.

4. Rui's speeches and campaign documents may be found in Rui Barbosa, *Contra o militarismo: Campanha eleitoral de 1909 a 1910*, First Series (Rio de Janeiro, n.d.); *Contra o militarismo: Discursos em S. Paulo, Santos e Campinas, campanha eleitoral de 1909 a 1910*, Second Series (Rio de Janeiro, n.d.); *Contra o militarismo* (Discurso Financeiro): *campanha eleitoral de 1909 a 1910*, Second Series (Rio de Janeiro, n.d.); *Excursão eleitoral aos estados da Bahia e Minas Gerais, manifestos á nação* (São Paulo, 1910).

5. Barbosa, *Excursão eleitoral*, 233–339.

6. A graphic description of the revolt's effect on elite opinion is given by Gilberto Amado in *O Paiz*, Nov. 27, 1910, which is reprinted in the only secondary work on the revolt: Edmar Morel, *A Revolta da chibata*, 2nd ed. (Rio de Janeiro, 1963), 17–21.

7. James Bryce, *South America: Observations and Impressions* (New York, 1912), 419–21. Bryce's doubts and questions were given further publicity—with virtually no critical commentary—in Oliveira Lima's review in *O Estado de São Paulo*, Dec. 29, 1912. Bryce's disturbing reflections on Brazil's future were often cited by subsequent Brazilian writers, much as Agassiz and Buckle had been earlier. Forty years later in an article written in 1952, Gilberto Amado was still indignant about Bryce's book: "Bryce was a liberal English jurist full of Victorian prejudices and incapable in his mediocrity of seeing and feeling Brazil's greatness or of doing justice to the Brazilian people, who are not inferior to any other people—quite the contrary." Gilberto Amado, *Sabor do Brasil* (Rio de Janeiro, 1953), 46.

8. For details on how the Brazilian sympathizers of the Allies and the Central Powers lined up, see Broca, *A Vida literária*, 265–71. Broca notes that the literary mentality in Brazil experienced little change during the first two years of the European war.

9. Article by Joaquim Eulalio, *O Estado de São Paulo*, Oct. 23,

1914, reprinted from *O Jornal do Comércio*, Oct. 22, 1914. For a typical statement from a pro-Allied propagandist see the Chapter on "le Brésil et la guerre européenne" by Medeiros e Albuquerque in Santiago Argüello et al., *L'Amérique Latine et la Guerre Européenne:* Part I (Paris, 1916), 35–48.

10. The play is reprinted in Afrânio Peixoto, *Parábolas* (Rio de Janeiro, 1920), 140–80.

11. Article by Joaquim de Sampaio Ferraz, *Jornal do Comércio,* Oct. 17, 1915.

12. Estevão Leitão de Carvalho, *Memórias de um soldado legalista* (Rio de Janeiro, 1961), vol. I, 208.

13. The speech was given on September 26, 1914. *Anais da Câmara dos Deputados,* 1914, vol. VI, 575–602. Dunshee de Abranches was the most prolific anti-interventionist writer. His major effort was *A Ilusão brasileira* (Rio de Janeiro, 1917).

14. By 1917 Capistrano de Abreu thought the war had become "completely commercial," since the "French and English peddlers no longer disguise their purpose—to monopolize South America." Capistrano Abreu, *Correspondência* (ed. by José Honório Rodrigues), 3 vols. (Rio de Janeiro, 1954–56), vol. III, 39–40.

15. Article by Oliveira Lima, *O Estado de São Paulo,* Sept. 28, 1914.

16. Arbivohn [pseudo. of Raymundo Bandeira], *O Perigo prussiano no Brasil* (Rio de Janeiro, 1914).

17. Menezes, *A Raça alemã.*

18. *Diário Alemão: Supplemento Português do "Deutsche Zeitung de São Paulo,"* May 9, 1915.

19. *O Paiz,* Nov. 12, 1914.

20. *O Paiz,* June 28, 1915.

21. José Maria Bello, *Ensaios políticos e literários* (Rio de Janeiro, 1918), 222.

22. Capistrano de Abreu, *Correspondência,* vol. I, 41.

23. Miguel Calmon [du Pin e Almeida], *Tendências nacionais e influências estrangeiras* (Bahia, 1922), 60.

24. *In Memoriam: Miguel Calmon, sua vida e sua obra* (Rio de Janeiro, 1936), 54–56.

25. The speech was delivered on October 9, 1915, and is reprinted in Olavo Bilac, *A Defesa nacional: Discursos* (Rio de Janeiro, 1965), 23–28. There were many earlier editions, the first of which was published by the Liga de Defesa Nacional in 1917.

26. The law (N. 1860) was dated January 4, 1908. It was passed by the Congress on December 11, 1907. The debates on the bill are in *Anais da Câmara dos Deputados,* 1907, VI, Part I, 213 ff.

27. Some of his speeches are collected in Olavo Bilac, *Últimas conferências e discuros* (Rio de Janeiro, 1924). Bilac enjoyed lavish

press coverage. For an example of a Rio daily reporting an enthusiastic reception for his speaking appearance in Belo Horizonte, see *A Tribuna*, Aug. 26, 1916.

28. Coelho Neto, *Falando* (Rio de Janeiro, 1919), 115–28.

29. Luiz Vianna Filho, *A Vida de Rui Barbosa* (São Paulo, 1949), 390–92. For a bibliography of sources on this famous incident, see Regina Monteiro Real, *Rui Barbosa em Buenos Aires* (Rio de Janeiro, 1969).

30. Abrahão Ribeiro article in *O Estado de São Paulo*, Aug. 4, 1916; Oliveira Lima article in *Diário de São Paulo*, July 27, 1916; articles in *Jornal do Comércio*, July 29, 1916, and *A Noite*, July 28, 1916.

31. Afonso Arinos, "A Unidade da Patria" which is reprinted in Arinos, *Obra completa* (Rio de Janeiro, 1969) 885–95, where the date of the lecture is incorrectly given as 1917, the date of its publication in pamphlet form. Olavo Bilac said in 1917 that Arinos' lecture in 1915 had been "the first cry of alarm and the first creative act in the campaign of regeneration we are conducting . . . ," Bilac preface to Afonso Arinos, *Lendas e tradições brasileiras* (São Paulo, 1917), iii. The latter volume was a collection of lectures given by Arinos in São Paulo in 1915 on Brazilian popular culture, part of an exhibition on Brazilian folkoric art and music. Arinos made the purpose of this exhibition clear: "For a century we have been looking to the outside, to the foreigner; now let us look at ourselves," *ibid.*, 30. The leading critical study of Arinos remains Tristão de Athayde [Alceu Amoroso Lima], *Affonso Arinos* (Rio de Janeiro, 1922), reprinted in Lima, *Estudos literários*, vol. I, 533–621. Much valuable information is to be found in the three-part series "Affonso Arinos: Centenário" published in *Minas Gerais: Suplemento Literário*, No. 87 (Apr. 27, 1968), No. 88 (May 4, 1968), and No. 89 (May 11, 1968).

32. João do Rio, *Adiante!* (Lisbon, 1919), 79. Similar sentiments were evident in a Rio de Janeiro lecture: "Patriotismo," in João do Rio, *Sésamo* (Rio de Janeiro, 1917), 173–96.

33. João do Rio, *Adiante!*, 85.

34. *Ibid.*, 74, 85.

35. For another example of a belle époque literary critic who became more nationalistic during the war, see the contrast between the earlier and later articles in Matheus de Albuquerque, *Da Arte e do patriotismo* (Rio de Janeiro, 1919). The contrast was clearly noted by Alceu Amoroso Lima in his 1919 review of Albuquerque's book, reprinted in Lima, *Estudos literários* (Rio de Janeiro, 1966), vol. I, 160–64.

36. An appeal to use the Army as a vehicle for education and mobilization was made soon after passage of the law: Capitão Liberato Bittencourt, *Pelo exército* (Rio de Janeiro, 1907), which was a speech

delivered to the Associação dos Empregados no Comércio do Rio de Janeiro.

37. The critical Congressman was Maurício de Lacerda, who dismissed Bilac's appearances at rallies as "buffoonery," *Anais da Câmara dos Deputados,* 1916, XII, 288–89; 357–63.

38. The officers are listed in *Discursos proferidos na sessão solemne de posse do Conselho Deliberativo de Liga Nacionalista de São Paulo, no Instituto Histórico no dia 26 de Julho de 1917* (São Paulo, 1917). There is information on the later activities of the Liga Nacionalista in José Carlos de Macedo Soares, *Justiça* (Paris, 1925), 58–71.

39. *Ibid.,* 7–12.

40. For an example of this literature, see A. de Sampaio Doria, *O Que o cidadão deve saber: Manual de instrução cívica* (São Paulo, 1919).

41. Alvaro Octavio de Alencastre, *O Problema nacional* (Rio de Janeiro, 1917), 13, 18, 8, 25, 23.

42. Oliveira Lima article in *Diário de Pernambuco,* Apr. 22, 1917. The strongly interventionist *O Estado de São Paulo* found Lima's change in position still too equivocal: *O Estado de São Paulo,* Apr. 24, 1917.

43. Brazilian Ministry for Foreign Affairs, *The Brazilian Green Books: Consisting of Diplomatic Documents Relating to Brazil's Attitude with Regard to the European War, 1914–1917* (ed. by Andrew Boyle) (London, 1918), 87.

44. J. Lloyd Mecham, *A Survey of United States-Latin American Relations* (Boston, 1965), 100–102.

45. President Wenceslau Braz described the U.S. as a belligerent to whom "we are bound by a traditional friendship and by similarity of political opinion in the defense of the vital interests of America and the principles accepted by International Law." *Brazilian Green Book,* 40; Mecham, *Survey of U.S.-Latin American Relations,* 447. For a careful analysis of Brazil's policy toward the U.S. from 1902 to 1912, see E. Bradford Burns, *The Unwritten Alliance: Rio-Branco and Brazilian-American Relations* (New York, 1966).

46. Valente de Andrade, *A Aliança necessária entre o Brasil e a América do Norte: O Brasil e o Pan-Americanismo* (São Paulo, 1917). This pamphlet is an article that was published in the *Jornal do Commercio* (São Paulo edition), Apr. 8, 1917.

47. J. F. de Assis Brasil, *Idéia de patria* (São Paulo, 1918), 54–55.

48. Coelho Neto, *Falando,* 138, 255–57.

49. *Anais da Câmara dos Deputados,* 1917, I, 659–62.

50. Delgado de Carvalho, *História diplomática,* 378.

51. *A Razão,* Jan. 1, 1917; *Diário de Notícias da Bahia,* Feb. 9, 1917.

52. *A Noite*, Mar. 10, 1917.

53. *Anais da Câmara dos Deputados*, 1917, I, 686–87.

54. Front-page reports, accompanied by photographs of the sacked shops, appeared in *Jornal do Recife*, Nov. 8 and 9, 1917. The relative mildness of the Brazilian harassment of Germans and Germano-Brazilians is stressed in Gerhard Bruun, *Deutschland und Brasilien, 1889–1914* (Köln, 1971), 274–82.

55. Percy Alvin Martin, *Latin America and the War* (Baltimore, 1925), 30–106.

56. Although there was a minor propaganda campaign in Brazil to whip up fear of the threat of an Argentine invasion of Brazil (with the Argentines perhaps getting German support). See, for example, Sargento Albuquerque [pseud.?], *Em Caminho da guerra: A Cilada argentina contra o Brasil* (Rio de Janeiro, 1917); and *Revista da Semana*, XVIII, No. 27 (Aug. 11, 1917), where notice was given of a pamphlet, *Nuestra guerra*, purportedly an Argentine plan for invading and conquering Brazil.

57. Olavo Bilac, *Últimas conferencias e discursos*, 44; *O Governo Wencelsáo: 1914–1918* (n.p., 1918), 109–10; Augusto de Bulhões, *Leopoldo de Bulhões: Um Financista de princípios, 1856–1928* (Rio de Janeiro, n.d.), 511–30.

58. Azevedo, *Brazilian Culture*, 421, 443.

59. Basílio de Magalhães, *O Grande doente de América do Sul* (Rio de Janeiro, 1916), 42.

60. Tobias Monteiro, *Funcionários e doutores* (Rio de Janeiro, 1917), 5, 10, 13, 15. A very similar indictment of the ornamental culture still plaguing Brazil was given in "Dos Homens Chamados 'Prácticos' e a sua Influência no Brasil," an essay by Gilberto Amado first published in 1918 and reprinted in Amado, *Grão de areia e outros estudos* (Rio de Janeiro, 1948), 126–50.

61. Monteiro, *Funcionários e doutores*, 21–22.

62. *Ibid.*, 25–26.

63. *Ibid.*, 26.

64. *Ibid.*, 22, 38–39.

65. Assis Brasil, *Idéia da pátria*, 26–28.

66. One of the leaders in the movement was A. Carneiro Leão, whose *O Brasil e a educação popular* (Rio de Janeiro, 1917) includes a number of his lectures in 1915 and 1916. For other evidence of this reform movement, see Antônio Leão Velloso, "Educação Brasileira," *Correio da Manhã*, June 18, 1917.

67. Calmon, *Tendências*, 59; Evidence of the continuing discrimination against Brazilian mulattoes may be found in the works of the contemporary mulatto novelist Lima Barreto, especially his novels *Recordações do escrivão Isaís Caminha* (Lisbon, 1909) and *Clara dos Anjos* (Rio de Janeiro, 1922–23), which are reprinted in Afonso Hen-

riques de Lima Barreto, *Obras completas* (São Paulo, 1956), vols. I and V. For an excellent critical biography of this author, see Francisco de Assis Barbosa, *A Vida de Lima Barreto*, 3rd ed. (Rio de Janeiro, 1964).

68. Calmon, *Tendências*, 10-11.

69. The date of Amado's speech was December 11, 1916. *Anais da Câmara dos Deputados*, 1916, XIV, 707-33. Essentially the same text was later published under the title "As Instituições Políticas e o Meio Social no Brasil" in Gilberto Amado, *Grão de areia* (Rio de Janeiro, 1919). For further detail on the interesting career of Amado, see Homero Senna, *Gilberto Amado e o Brasil* (Rio de Janeiro, 1968).

70. The statement is in a letter dated 1917 and first printed in *Grão de areia*. I used a later edition: Gilberto Amado, *Grão de areia e outros estudos* (Rio de Janeiro, 1948). The quotation is on 53. It is interesting that the two terms used by Amado (*cafuso and curiboca*) both involved an Indian mixture—he did not mention mulatto, the unambiguous term for a mixture of white and black. On the other hand, *cafuso* was an extremely unflattering term. Amado later became very proud of this early statement acknowledging Brazil to be a "República mestiça," as in Amado, *Sabor do Brasil* (Rio de Janeiro, 1953), 45-46. In a newspaper article in early 1914 Amado had already argued that "None of the three races which contributed to the make-up of our nationality has predominated to the point of imposing its physiognomy on our race." *O Paiz*, Jan. 24, 1914.

71. Basilio de Magalhães, *O Grande doente da America do Sul* (Rio de Janeiro, 1916), 14-15.

72. *Ibid.*, 17.

73. *Ibid.*, 6-7, 56.

74. *Ibid.*, 56.

75. *Ibid.*, 54, 42.

76. *Ibid.*, 40, 17.

77. Faith in "whitening" continued to be a common assumption of the elite, as could be seen in the introductory statement (by Bulhões Carvalho) to the official *Anuário estatística do Brasil: 1º Ano: 1908-1912* (Rio de Janeiro, 1916), published by the Ministério da Agricultura, Indústria e Comércio. Bulhões Carvalho noted that Brazil was headed for "a great future when its national type is definitively fixed by the complete assimilation of varying ethnic groups and the subsequent purification of the races by crossing with foreign elements of differing origins."

78. *Revista do Brasil*, I (No. 1, Jan. 1916), 1-5.

79. See Edgard Cavalheiro, "Monteiro Lobato e a *Revista do Brasil*," *Revista Brasiliense*, No. 1 (Sept.-Oct. 1955), 5-14; Cavalheiro, *Monteiro Lobato: Vida e obra*, 3rd ed., 2 vols. (São Paulo, 1962), I, 149-92; and Lannoy Dorin, "A 'Revista do Brasil,'" *Revista Brasiliense*, No. 45 (Jan.-Feb. 1963), 52-67.

80. Afrânio Peixoto, *Minha terra e minha gente* (Rio de Janeiro, 1916), 5. Ironically enough, the book was printed in Lisbon. Peixoto's contrast between shallow optimism and debilitating pessimism was given an interesting analysis in José Antonio Nogueira, "Narcisos e Jeremias," *Revista do Brasil*, II (No. 6, Junho 1916), 111–21.

81. *Ibid.*, 206, 222. Peixoto was fully conscious of Bryce's doubts about the capacity of the Brazilian elite. He quoted from Bryce in a footnote on page 225.

82. *Ibid.*, 228–29.

83. João do Rio, *No Tempo de Wenceslau* (Rio de Janeiro, 1917), 60–61.

84. José Maria Bello, *Ensaios políticos*, 176–77. This chapter is undated but was probably written late in the war.

85. This was noted by Alceu Amoroso Lima in his literary commentaries soon after the war. See, for example, his reviews in June 1919 reprinted in Lima, *Estudos literários*, I, 84–90. One of the writers most explicit about the war's stimulus to nationalism was José Maria Bello, *Ensaios políticos*, 136–43.

86. Bilac, *Últimas conferências*, 46. Similar statements are scattered through the wartime speeches of Bilac in this volume. What most worried Bilac was the possibility that Brazil might break up into smaller territorial units, *ibid.*, 133–34.

87. For an example of a literary intellectual who had been an outspoken apologist for the imitative culture of pre-war Rio de Janeiro but who now became a propagandist for economic nationalism, see Elysio de Carvalho, *Brasil, potencia mundial: Inquérito sôbre a indústria siderúgica no Brasil* (Rio de Janeiro, 1919). Carvalho urged the creation of a national steel industry, noting that "the European war revealed to us the profoundly dangerous situation which results from our country's strict dependence on foreign goods for the functioning of its industries," *ibid.*, 9. For an analysis of the debates over industrialization, see Nícia Vilela Luz, *A Luta pela industrialização do Brasil* (São Paulo, 1961).

88. The effect of World War I on Brazilian industrialization has been significantly reinterpreted by recent research in economic history. Earlier it had been argued that the war accelerated industrialization, as in Roberto Simonsen, *Brazil's Industrial Evolution* (São Paulo, 1939). Evidence disproving any acceleration is given in Nathaniel Leff, "Long-Term Brazilian Economic Development," *Journal of Economic History*, XXIX (No. 3, Sept. 1969), 473–93; Warren Dean, *The Industrialization of São Paulo, 1880–1945* (Austin, Tex., 1969), chapter VI; and Werner Baer and Annibal V. Villela, "Industrial Growth and Industrialization: Revisions in the Stages of Brazil's Economic Development," *The Journal of Developing Areas*, VII (No. 2, Jan. 1973), 217–34.

89. Delgado de Carvalho, *História diplomática*, 385–89. The mood of self-confidence is very evident in the newspaper articles sent to *O*

Paiz by João do Rio, the correspondent at Versailles, which are reprinted in João do Rio, *Na Conferência de Paz, I: Do Armisticio de Foch á paz de guerra* (Rio de Janeiro, 1919); and in Alcides Bezerra's "A Paz e seus Problemas," in Bezerra, *Ensaios de crítica*, 261–63. Brazil's stormy membership in the League culminated in formal withdrawal in 1926 when her aspirations to a permanent seat were frustrated, in part by lack of support from the other Latin American delegations. For a defense of the Brazilian position, see João Pandiá Calogeras, *O Brasil e a Sociedade de Nações* (São Paulo, 1926), which is a reprint of an article in *O Commentario*, No. 6, June 30, 1926.

CHAPTER 6

1. Documents of the campaign may be found in Rui Barbosa, *Campanha presidencial: 1919* (Bahia, 1919).

2. A clear description of these revolts and the evolving political crisis is given in Edgard Carone, *A República velha*, 319–92. Carone's companion volume, *A República velha: Instituições e classes sociais* (São Paulo, 1970), gives socio-economic and institutional information which is very useful for understanding the context of the younger generation's discontent.

3. One angry author gave his polemic a title that reversed the chauvinist rhetoric common before 1914: Francisco Lagreca, *Porque não me ufano de meu paiz* [*Why I am not proud of my country*] (São Paulo, 1919).

4. A. Carneiro Leão et al., *Á Margem da historia da república* (Rio de Janeiro, 1924).

5. Another of the contributors was J. A. Nogueira, whose chapter was taken from his earlier book-length version offering the same kind of nationalist message: J. A. Nogueira, *Sonho de gigante* (São Paulo, 1922).

6. Hermes Lima, a prominent jurist born in 1902, remarked: "My generation, which began to think about politics after the Great War of 1914, was greatly influenced by the tendency to judge the constitutional structure of monarchical Brazil and the Constitutional regime of 1891 as servile imitations of foreign models, lacking any correspondence to Brazilian reality." Hermes Lima, *Notas à vida brasileira* (São Paulo, 1945), 5. The changing mood could be seen in the speech of the class orator at the Faculdade de Ciências Jurídicas e Sociaes in Rio de Janeiro in December 1919. In attempting to answer why Brazil had progressed so much more slowly than the United States, he specifically rejected the racist determinism of Lapouge and Le Bon, citing Alberto Tôrres as having "forever demonstrated the falsity of these pretentiously arrogant doctrines." Generoso Ponce Filho, *Porque estamos*

atrazados? (Rio de Janeiro, 1920). One of the most articulate nationalist intellectuals was Vicente Licínio Cardoso, who relentlessly attacked those Brazilian writers who continued contributing to "this bizarre and strange situation of being intellectual bastards of the Europeans. . . ." Vicente Licínio Cardoso, *Vultos e idéias* (Rio de Janeiro, 1924), 257. For a sympathetic study of Cardoso's thought, see Lourenço Filho, "Vicente Licínio Cardoso e os Estudos Sociais," *Educação e Ciências Sociais,* vol. VIII (No. 15, Sept. 1960), 9–32. The best secondary source on nationalist thought in the 1920's is the excellent survey in the first volume of Jorge Nagle, *Educação e Sociedade no Brasil, 1920–1929: Tese de concurso de Docência Geral da Faculdade de Filosofia, Ciências e Letras de Araraquara* (Araraquara, 1966), 2 vols. For a study which extends into the 1930's, see Ludwig Lauerhass, Jr., "Getúlio Vargas and the Triumph of Brazilian Nationalism: A Study of the Rise of the Nationalist Generation of 1930" (Ph.D. diss., University of California, Los Angeles, 1972).

7. My brief analysis of Brazilian Modernism draws upon Wilson Martins, *The Modernist Idea,* trans. by Jack E. Tomlins (New York, 1970), which is a translation of the third edition of the Brazilian original; John Nist, *The Modernist Movement in Brazil* (Austin, 1967); Mário da Silva Brito, *História do modernismo brasileiro,* vol. I: *Antecedentes da semana de arte moderna,* 2nd ed. (Rio de Janeiro, 1964); and Afrânio Coutinho, *An Introduction to Literature in Brazil* (New York, 1969), 210–54.

8. Di Cavalcanti, the famous Modernist painter, described the cultural atmosphere he and his fellow rebels faced in São Paulo as having been dominated by "the idiotic academicism of the literary and artistic critics at the leading newspapers, the conceit of the vain and verbose literary hangers-on, well set up in the business and political world, and the deadening presence of Brazilian and foreign stuffed shirts. . . ." Emiliano Di Cavalcanti, *Viagem da minha vida* (Rio de Janeiro, 1955), 108.

9. São Paulo had also produced a cadre of articulate reformers who saw São Paulo as the model for national development. As one wrote: "The state of São Paulo is the guarantee of our national future . . . and the brilliant lighthouse showing all Brazil the course to follow . . . in implementing the new ideas. Its present vigor is a result of the educational organization given it by the founders of the Republic. . . ." Mário Pinto Serva, *Patria nova* (São Paulo, 1922). This brand of strong Paulista regionalism could be traced back to the late Empire, when the rapidly expanding coffee economy gave Paulistas confidence. Pinto Serva wrote extensively on the need for educational reform, much in the vein of the reformers such as Carneiro Leão who had begun their campaign during the war. Although he was a Northeasterner by background (Pernambuco), Carneiro Leão enthusiastically

joined the promoters of São Paulo as a national model: A. Carneiro Leão, *São Paulo em 1920* (Rio de Janeiro, 1920). Their emphasis on education was obviously based on environmentalist assumptions. For background on São Paulo in this era, see Richard M. Morse, *From Community to Metropolis: A Biography of São Paulo, Brazil* (Gainesville, Fla., 1958), 200–290.

10. The conflicting interpretations of Graça Aranha's role are discussed in Coutinho, *Introduction to Literature in Brazil*, 221–22. The autobiographical comments in [João] Peregrino Júnior, *O Movimento modernista* (Rio de Janeiro, 1954), and in Peregrino Júnior's interview with Brito Broca in *Letras e Artes*, February 3, 1952, picture Aranha as a lonely and largely forgotten man who found in the Modernist movement an opportunity to indulge his "combative nature and exuberant temperment."

11. The most penetrating study of this fascinating and complex figure is Telê Porto Ancona Lopez, *Mário de Andrade: Ramais e caminho* (São Paulo, 1972).

12. *Macunaíma* is reprinted in Mário de Andrade, *Obras completas*, IV (São Paulo, 1944). Andrade's difficult work was given a sympathetic and lucid explication in M. Cavalcanti Proença, *Roteiro de Macunaíma* (São Paulo, 1955).

13. The movements in the other states are summarized in Coutinho, *Introduction to Brazilian Literature*, 225–27. Detail on the Northeastern movement, with emphasis on Gilberto Freyre's role, is given in José Aderaldo Castello, *José Lins do Rego: Modernismo e regionalismo* (São Paulo, 1961), 27–67; and Freyre, *Região e Tradição* (Rio de Janeiro, 1941). Freyre's alleged distortions of the history of Regionalism in Recife have been angrily attacked in Joaquim Inojosa, *O Movimento modernista em Pernambuco* (Rio de Janeiro, 1968–69), 3 vols., especially vol. I. For Minas, see Fernando Correia Dias, *O Movimento modernista em Minas* (Belo Horizonte, 1971).

14. The antecedents of Modernism are well summarized in Coutinho, *An Introduction to Literature in Brazil*, 211–19. Modernism's links with the past are stressed also in Brito Broca, "À Margem do Modernismo," *Letras e Artes*, Feb. 17, 1952, and "Quando Teria Começado Modernismo?" *Letras e Artes*, July 20, 1952.

15. For a stimulating essay on the development of nativist themes in Brazilian literature, with special emphasis on Modernism, see José Guilherme Merquior, "Poesia y Sociedad en la Literatura Brasileña," *Aportes*, No. 8 (Apr. 1968), 20–38. Looking back on the Modernist Movement in 1940, Mário de Andrade concluded that it had "formulated a descriptivist nationalism which, if it produced poor poetry, systematized the scientific study of the nation's people" in sociology, folklore, and geography. Mário de Andrade, "Modernismo," reprinted in *Obras completas, XX: O Empalhador de passarinho* (São Paulo, 1955), 185–89.

16. The increased confidence produced by the literary revolution of Modernism can be seen clearly in the autobiographical statements of Brazilian writers in such collections of the early 1940's as Mário Neme, *Plataforma da nova geração* (Pôrto Alegre, 1945); Silveira Peixoto, *Falam os escritores:* Segunda Série (Curitiba, 1941); and Edgard Cavalheiro, ed., *Testamento de uma geração* (Pôrto Alegre, 1944). Despite their frequent criticisms of the "superficiality" of the Modernists, almost all agreed, implicitly or explicitly, that Modernism had created the condition for a new sense of cultural identity.

17. Quoted in Lycurgo Santos Filho, *Pequena história da medicina brasileira* (São Paulo, 1966), 118. I have not been able to locate the original source of this often-repeated quotation. The phrase was being cited in newspaper stories by Antonio Leão Velloso on the need for public health measures: *Correio da Manhã,* Oct. 1, 1916 and Dec. 9, 1917.

18. The standard biography is Edgard Cavalheiro, *Monteiro Lobato: Vida e obra,* 3rd ed. (São Paulo, 1962), 2 vols.

19. The quotation is from a two-part book review, published in the student literary journal, *O Minarete,* July 30 and Aug. 6, 1903, and reprinted in [José Bento] Monteiro Lobato, *Obras completas* (São Paulo, 1961) vol. XIV, 109–13.

20. Monteiro Lobato, *A Barca de Gleyre* (São Paulo, 1944), 133. These strongly racist passages of Lobato's letter of February 3, 1908, were suppressed in the version of Lobato's correspondence published in the *Obra completa* (São Paulo, 1961), vol. XI, 207.

21. The original article entitled "Urupês" was published in *O Estado de São Paulo,* Dec. 23, 1914, and is reprinted in Monteiro Lobato, *Obras completas,* vol. I, 277–92.

22. For a discussion of the popular concept of the *caboclo,* see Antônio Cândido [Mello e Souza], *Os Parceiros do Rio Bonito* (Rio de Janeiro, 1964), 60. The definitions of caboclo in Ramos, *Le Métissage au Brésil,* 55, stress the Indian or white-Indian connotations.

23. Idelfonso Albano, *Jéca Tatú e Mané Chique-Chique* (Rio de Janeiro, n.d.). One reviewer suggested that instead of choosing between the two portraits of Lobato and Albano, "the top leaders in the country" ought to "accept the reality of 'Jéca Tatú' in order to convert him afterwards . . . into a dauntless and invincible 'Mané Chique-Chique.'" José Maria Bello, *A Margem dos livros* (Rio de Janeiro, 1923), 169.

24. The speech was given March 20, 1919, and reprinted in Rui Barbosa, *Campanha presidencial: 1919* (Bahia, 1919), 107–69. Rui's speech opened with the citation of Lobato's portrait of Jéca Tatú, which was excellent advertising since Rui's speeches were elaborately covered by the press. As one of Lobato's friends noted: "This is the ultimate praise, Rui never cites a living author but he's made an exception for you." Cavalheiro, *Monteiro Lobato,* I, 183. Lobato had sent a

copy of *Urupês* to Rui Barbosa with the dedication: "To Rui Barbosa, the first, with respects from Monteiro Lobato, the last," Brito Broca, "A Literatura na Biblioteca de Rui Barbosa," *Jornal de Letras* (Nov. 1949).

25. The phrase occurred in a letter to Alberto Rangel dated April 20, 1919. Lobato, *A Barca de Gleyre*, 391.

26. The point is stressed by one of Lobato's publishing colleagues: Leo Vaz, *Páginas vadias* (Rio de Janeiro, 1957), 71–72. Jéca Tatú also became a symbol of the regionalist literature which the Modernists wanted to reject. Brito, *História do modernismo brasileiro*, I, 201–2.

27. Racist assumptions still appeared in the rhetoric of some public health advocates. Gouvêa de Barros, for example, who had directed the Sanitary Service in Pernambuco, attributed the miserable state of the population to two factors: "the anthropological and ethnological factors contributing to the make-up of the Brazilian man" and the "complete abandonment in which this weak man confronts a hostile environment." *Anais da Câmara dos Deputados: Sessões de 18 a 31 de outubro de 1916*, vol. XI (1921), 478.

28. Belisário Pena and Artur Neiva, *Viagem científica pelo norte da Bahia, sudoeste de Pernambuco, sul do Piauí e de norte de Goiás* (Rio de Janeiro, 1918). It had originally been printed in *Memorias do Instituto Oswaldo Cruz*, VIII, No. 3 (1916).

29. An editorial of August 25, 1918 (newspaper unnamed), cited by Azevedo Sodré in a Congressional speech, *Anais da Câmara dos Deputados: Sessões de 20 a 31 de agôsto de 1918*, vol. VII (1919), 606.

30. Belisário Pena, *Saneamento do Brasil*, 2nd ed. (Rio de Janeiro, 1923), 34. A useful study of Pena is Alberto Dinís, *O Dinamismo patrioticamente construtivo de Belisário Pena* (Rio de Janeiro, 1948). Azevedo, *Brazilian Culture*, 184.

31. See chapter 4, above. Excerpts from Peixoto's lecture upon assuming the professorship in 1916 are reprinted in Leonidio Ribeiro, *Afrânio Peixoto* (Rio de Janeiro, 1950), 62–64. Peixoto's message in defense of the Brazilian climate was delivered to generations of medical students in Rio. It is summarized in Peixoto, *Clima e saúde* (São Paulo, 1938).

32. Antonio Leão Velloso, "Ministério de Saúde Publica," *Correio da Manhã*, Aug. 26, 1918. F. Saturnino Rodrigues de Brito, *Saneamento do Rio Grande* (Pôrto Alegre, 1918); and Brito, *Saneamento de Recife* (Recife, 1917) For examples of newspaper support for the campaign, see *O Correio da Manhã*, Oct. 23, 1916, Feb. 2, June 4, Dec. 28, 1917, Jan. 23, Feb. 4, May 10, 13, 28, 1918.

33. In the fourth edition of *Urupês* he issued a formal *mea culpa*: "I must implore the pardon of poor Jéca. I didn't know, my dear Jéca, that you were that way because of terrible diseases. Now it's proven that in your blood and intestines you have a zoo of the worst kind. It's

all those merciless bugs that have made you swollen, ugly, lazy, motionless. Is it your fault? Obviously not." Monteiro Lobato, *Urupês*, 4th ed. (São Paulo, 1919), "Explicação desnecessária." The shift in Lobato's position was duly noted by the contemporary literary critic Agrippino Grieco in a review of *Urupês* written in 1925–26 and reprinted in Grieco, *Gente nova do Brasil: Veteranos-alguns Mortos* (Rio de Janeiro, 1935), 358–60.

34. The articles are included in *Problema vital* (the title of the book in which they were later published), which is reprinted in Monteiro Lobato, *Obras completas*, First Series (São Paulo, 1961), vol. VIII, 220–340. The quotations in the text are from the latter edition.

35. One of Lobato's friends later denied that the creator of Jéca had reversed his position, recalling that Lobato had refused in conversation to accept the argument that Jéca was the result, not the cause. Leo Vaz, *Páginas vadias* (Rio de Janeiro, 1957), 89–90. Vaz was not the only friend to hear Lobato's continuing doubts about Brazil's racial health. On April 9, 1919, Lobato wrote Alberto Rangel a despairing letter about Brazil's plight: "The world is for those who *can*, and the Brazilian—coming from the Portuguese, the Negro and I don't know what else—*can't*. . . ." Alberto Rangel papers, Arquivo Nacional, Rio de Janeiro. I am indebted to Professor Stanley Hilton for this reference. While visiting the United States in 1928 Lobato wrote Oliveira Vianna: "You know what I came to find in this country? An infinite despair— the certainty of what I had suspected, that race is everything and that we have no race . . . Gobineau, Gobineau. . . ." Letter dated Dec. 22, 1928, Oliveira Vianna Archive, Niteroi. I am indebted to James Lauer for this reference. Whatever doubts Lobato continued to express privately, the reversal in his public stance was unmistakable.

36. For my brief survey of studies of the African and Afro-Brazilian I have used as a starting point Artur Ramos, *O Negro na Civilização brasileira* (Rio de Janeiro, 1956), chapter XIV ("Os Estudos científicos sôbre o Negro no Brasil"); and José Honório Rodrigues, *Brazil and Africa* (Berkeley, Calif., 1965), especially 36–52. An invaluable bibliographical guide is provided in the relevant sections of Donald Pierson, *Survey of the Literature on Brazil of Sociological Significance Published up to 1940* (Cambridge, Mass., 1945), which was also published in Rubens Borba de Moraes and William Berrien, eds., *Manual bibliográfico de estudos brasileiros* (Rio de Janeiro, 1949), 789–857. The latter manual's section on "Folklore" is also an important bibliographical survey, *ibid.*, 285–317.

37. Sílvio Romero, *História da literatura brasileira* (Rio de Janeiro, 1888), 2 vols.

38. The most inclusive work by Raimundo Nina Rodrigues was *Os Africanos no Brasil* (São Paulo, 1932), a posthumous edition of papers edited by Homero Pires.

39. João do Rio [João Paulo Coelho Barreto], *As Religiões no Rio* (Rio de Janeiro, 1906).

40. A collection of papers was published in Manoel Querino, *Costumes africanos no Brasil* (Rio de Janeiro, 1938). Information on this relatively little-known writer on the African in Brazil may be found in Gonçalo de Athayde Pereira, *Prof. Manuel Querino: Sua Vida e suas Obras* (Bahia, 1932). Querino furnished the model for the character of Pedro Archanjo, the hero of Jorge Amado's novel, *Tent of Miracles*. Professor Bradford Burns' article, "Black on Black: Manuel Querino's Interpretation of the African Contribution to Brazil," will appear in a forthcoming issue of the *Journal of Negro History*.

41. There is no full-length study of Roquette-Pinto. I have relied on Álvaro Lins, *Ensaio sôbre Roquette-Pinto e a ciência como Literatura* (Rio de Janeiro, 1967); and Pedro Gouvêa Filho, *E. Roquette-Pinto: O Antropólogo e Educador* (Rio de Janeiro: Ministerio da Educação e Cultura: Instituto Nacional de Cinema Educativo, 1955); and the obituary by Fernando de Azevedo in *Revista de Antropologia*, vol. 2 (No. 2, Dec. 1954), 97–101.

42. The shift in scientific thought about race among Anthropologists is traced in George Stocking, *Race, Culture and Evolution;* detail on American thinking may be found also in I. A. Newby, *Jim Crow's Defense: Anti-Negro Thought in America, 1900–1930* (Baton Rouge, La., 1965).

43. E. Roquette-Pinto, *Rondonia: Antropologia; Etnografia* (Rio de Janeiro, 1917). This first edition was published as part of *Archivos do Museu Nacional* (Rio de Janeiro), vol. XX (1917). The text was expanded in later editions, of which the fourth was published in the Brasiliana Series (São Paulo, 1938).

44. See, for example, his praise for Euclides in Roquette-Pinto, *Ensaios brasileiros* (São Paulo, 1941), 132–38.

45. The following citations are taken from his essay "O Brasil e a Antropogeografia," reprinted in Edgar Roquette-Pinto, *Seixos rolados* (Rio de Janeiro, 1927), 45–79, which is identified there as a lecture delivered in 1912, although one biographer dates it as September 1914: Gouvêa Filho, *Roquette-Pinto*, 14.

46. Roquette-Pinto showed an unusual appreciation of the importance of mass media and their possibilities for accelerating national integration. He founded the Radio Society of Rio de Janeiro in 1923 and the Instituto Nacional do Cinema Educativo in 1936.

47. Roquette-Pinto, *Seixos rolados*, 59–62. Nonetheless, Roquette-Pinto was capable of stressing whitening for foreign audiences. In a lavishly produced volume aimed at investors abroad, he noted that "In this country no prejudice against color exists, and the negro, in place of preserving his entity by selection and segregation, becomes absorbed in the white masses, whose numbers increase year by year. Before long he

will thus disappear altogether. . . ." Roquette-Pinto, "Archeology and Ethnography" in *Twentieth Century Impressions of Brazil* (London, 1913), 55.

48. Roquette-Pinto, *Rondonia*, 1st ed., 201.

49. The quotations from this paragraph and the following one are taken from "Eçulides da Cunha, Naturalista," reprinted in Roquette-Pinto, *Seixos rolados*, 263–301. Álvaro Lins gives this essay two different dates: 1917 and 1920, Lins, *Ensaio sôbre Roquette-Pinto*, 31–63.

50. He lauded both Bomfim and Tôrres for their pioneering attacks on racist thought: Roquette-Pinto, *Ensaios brasileiros*, 63–65; 91–94.

51. Cited in Lins, *Ensaio sôbre Roquette-Pinto*, 94.

52. Roquette-Pinto, "Discurso de Posse," Academia Brasileira de Letras, *Discursos acadêmicos*, vol. VII (1927–32) (Rio de Janeiro, 1937), 85–86.

53. Among Ramos' many publications are *As Culturas negras no mundo novo* (Rio de Janeiro, 1937) and *O Folk-lore negro do Brasil* (Rio de Janeiro, 1935).

54. Papers from the first (1934) Congress have been published in two volumes: *Estudos Afro-brasileiros* (Rio de Janeiro, 1935) and Gilberto Freyre et al., *Novos estudos afro-brasileiros* (Rio de Janeiro, 1937). Papers from the second (1937) Congress are included in Edison Carneiro and Aydano do Couto Ferraz, eds., *O Negro no Brasil* (Rio de Janeiro, 1940).

55. Gilberto Freyre, *The Masters and the Slaves*, trans. by Samuel Putnam (2nd English-language edition, New York, 1956). The first American edition was published in 1946. The first Brazilian edition of *Casa-Grande e senzala* was published in Rio de Janeiro in 1933.

56. *Sobrados e mucambos* was first published in São Paulo in 1936. An extensively revised second edition was published in 1951 and a third edition appeared in 1961. The first edition was subtitled "Decadência do Patriarchado Rural no Brasil," to which was added in the subtitle of the second edition "e Desenvolvimento do Urbano." The American edition, *The Mansions and the Shanties*, was translated and edited by Harriet de Onís (New York, 1963). There is evidence that Freyre originally planned only one volume on the "formação da familia brasileira sob o regimen de economia patriarchal," as it was expressed in the subtitle of the first edition of *Casa-Grande e Senzala*. Freyre's study has now grown to a projected seven volumes, under the general title *Introdução à história de sociedade patriarchal no Brasil*. See the Preface to the Second English-language edition, *The Masters and the Slaves*, liv. The evolution in the subtitles might lead one to speculate that Freyre began by attempting to interpret the history of the family in terms of the social system and ended by interpreting Brazilian social history in terms of the family.

57. Freyre has explained how he himself had to be liberated from

an ethnic inferiority complex about Brazil. Describing his graduate studies in anthropology at Columbia University in the early 1920's Freyre wrote: "Once upon a time, after three straight years of absence from my country, I caught sight of a group of Brazilian seamen—mulattoes and *cafusos* [mixture of Indian and black]—crossing Brooklyn Bridge. I no longer remember whether they were from [the] São Paulo or from [the] Minas Gerais [referring to the names of the Brazilian ships in harbor], but I know that they impressed me as being the caricatures of men, and there came to mind a phrase from a book on Brazil written by an American traveler: 'the fearfully mongrel aspect of the population.' That was the sort of thing to which miscegenation led. I ought to have had some one to tell me then what Roquette Pinto had told the Aryanizers of the Brazilian Eugenics Congress in 1929: that these individuals whom I looked upon as representative of Brazil were not simply mulattoes or *caufsos* but *sickly* ones. It was my studies in anthroplogy under the direction of Professor Boas that first revealed to me the Negro and the mulatto for what they are—with the effects of environment or cultural experience separated from racial characteristics." *The Masters and the Slaves*, xxvi–xxvii.

58. João Cruz Costa, *Contribuição à história das idéias no Brasil* (Rio de Janeiro, 1956), 440. The extraordinary influence of *Casa-Grande e senzala* would have been impossible if Freyre had not been able to cite this scientific evidence. His book therefore had to be based in part on the writings of other Brazilian investigators who had anticipated many of his questions. His accomplishment was to have transformed this evidence into a new approach to Brazilian history. Some recent evaluations of Freyre's influence have tended to neglect the importance of the intellectual movement on whose work he was able to draw. See, for example, Frank Tannenbaum's introduction to *The Mansions and the Shanties* and his *Ten Keys to Latin America* (New York, 1962), 123–25.

59. The twenty-fifth anniversary of the publication of *Casa Grande e senzala* furnished the occasion for a commemorative volume containing sixty-four essays written in tribute to the book's "influence on the modern culture of Brazil." *Gilberto Freyre: Sua ciência, sua filosofia, sua arte: Ensaios sôbre o autor de "Casa-Grande e senzala" e sua influência na moderna cultura do Brasil, commemorativos do 25º aniversário da publicação desse seu livro* (Rio de Janeiro, 1962). Even if one discounts the efforts of some of his more pious admirers to canonize Freyre, these essays offer impressive evidence of the enormous influence which *Casa-Grande e senzala* has had on the cultural elite of Brazil. In the words of Emílio Willems, "Freyre's success has been that of a genuine culture hero." Review of the eighth edition of *Casa-Grande e senzala*, *Hispanic American Historical Review*, XXV (Aug. 1955), 411. For earlier evaluations, see Diogo de Melo Meneses, *Gil-*

Ferdinand ?

berto Freyre (Rio de Janeiro, 1944); Fernand Braudel, "A Travers un Continent d'Histoire," *Annales d'Histoire Sociale* (1943), 3–20; and Lewis Hanke, "Gilberto Freyre: Brazilian Social Historian," *Quarterly Journal of Inter-American Relations*, I (July 1939), 24–44.

60. Freyre also provoked some intemperate dissent in Brazil. In 1939 the right-wing Catholic press labeled him "the Pornographer of Recife." See Samuel Putnam's article on "Brazilian Literature" in the *Handbook of Latin American Studies*, 5 (1939), 357.

61. Freyre went on to develop his interpretation of Brazil's multi-racial heritage in more controversial form. The third volume in his history of patriarchical society in Brazil (published in Brazil in 1959) covered the years between the founding of the Republic in 1889 and the end of World War I and analyzed the agony of the Brazilian elite as they faced up to the reality of a society which did not fit the soon-to-be archaic categories of scientific racist thought. Freyre, *Ordem e progresso*. For a critical review, see Thomas E. Skidmore, "Gilberto Freyre and the Early Brazilian Republic: Some Notes on Methodology," *Comparative Studies in Society and History*, VI (No. 4, July 1964), 490–505. Even before World War II Freyre had developed his theory of "Luso-tropicalism," which assumed a unique Portuguese gift for achieving supposedly harmonious multi-racial societies, as in Freyre, *O Mundo que o Português criou* (Rio de Janeiro, 1940). For the very negative reaction of a contemporary Paulista intellectual to Freyre's extreme admiration for the Portuguese, see Paulo Duarte's letter of August 17, 1941, in Paulo Duarte, ed., *Mário de Andrade por êle mesmo* (São Paulo, 1971), 203–13. Freyre's exaggerated conception of the Portuguese lack of racial prejudice later produced much wider criticism, especially in the context of his defense of Portuguese policy in her African provinces in the 1960's.

62. Mário de Andrade, "O Samba Rural Paulista," *Revista do Arquivo Municipal*, vol. 41 (Nov. 1937), 37–116; and Andrade's chapter in *Estudos afro-brasileiros* (Rio de Janeiro, 1935).

63. Edison Carneiro, *Religiões negras* (Rio de Janeiro, 1936).

64. It is important to understand that black nationalism has not been an important social or intellectual force in Brazil since 1870 (the influence earlier of runaway slave communities is a separate question). In the 1920's and 1930's there was a short-lived movement to unite blacks, but it had relatively little effect, either on behavior or the prevailing racial ideology. When Getúlio Vargas suppressed the "Brazilian Negro Front" (founded 1931), along with all other independent political groups, shortly after the advent of the authoritarian Estado Nôvo (1937–45), the black solidarity movement suffered a mortal blow. Florestan Fernandes, *A Integração do negro à sociedade de classes* (Rio de Janeiro, 1964), chapter 4. Researchers should note that the valuable bibliographical references on this topic in the Brazilian edition of Fer-

nandes' book have been largely eliminated in the American edition: *The Negro in Brazilian Society*, 187–233.

65. Neiva cited Batista de Lacerda as the authority for his prediction of a century, after which "the entire world will consider us white, except for the United States which . . . today still considers the Portuguese people less than perfectly white because of the transfusion of Moorish blood." Neiva's article appeared in 1921 and is reprinted in Arthur Neiva, *Daqui e de longe: Chronicas nacionais e de viagem* (São Paulo, n.d. [1927?]), 111–18.

66. The debate may be found in the *Anais da Câmara dos Deputados*, 1921, vol. VI (Rio de Janeiro, 1923), 623–37. The debate was held on July 29, 1921.

67. *Anais de Câmara dos Deputados*, 1923, vol. X (Rio de Janeiro, 1928), 140–49. The debate took place on October 22, 1923.

68. Clóvis Beviláqua's response is printed in Bruno Lobo, *Japonezes no Japão; no Brasil* (Rio de Janeiro, 1926), 140–42.

69. Peixoto's letter to Fidelis Reis is in Lobo, *Japonezes no Japão; no Brasil*, 143–44.

70. Robert M. Levine, "Some Views on Race and Immigration during the Old Republic," *The Americas*, XXVII (Apr. 1971), 373–80. Subsequent quotations are taken from this article.

71. Hiroshi Saito, *O Japonês no Brasil* (São Paulo, 1961), 47.

72. E. Roquette-Pinto, *Ensaios de antropologia brasileira* (São Paulo, 1933), 69–75; Azevedo Amaral, *O Comentário*, July 4, 1929; and *Iº Congresso Brasileiro de Eugenia* (Rio de Janeiro, 1929). I am indebted to James Lauer for these references.

73. As a Paulista educational reformer expressed it: "a century from now the United States will have between twenty and thirty million strong and vigorous blacks in a system of complete social segregation and will therefore face the gravest ethnic problem within the country. Not so in Brazil. A century from now we shall have one hundred and fifty million inhabitants, almost all white, but having peacefully accomplished the absorption of the other elements." Mário Pinto Serva, *O Enigma brasileiro* (São Paulo, n.d.), 21. Serva's book was published in the late 1920's.

74. Fernando H. Mendes de Almeida, *Constituições do Brasil* (São Paulo, 1963), 301–2.

75. The debate is reprinted in a collection of the speeches involving the São Paulo delegation: *A Ação da bancada paulista "Por São Paulo unido" na Assembléa Constituinte* (São Paulo, 1935), 364–413.

76. *Ibid.*, 367–85. Similar sentiments could be found in an officially endorsed (by the Departamento Nacional de Publicidade e Estatística) textbook of anthropo-geography published in 1935: "Gobineau's doctrine of exaggerated racism is undoubtedly erroneous. But an awareness of the role which ethnic groups play vis-à-vis nationalities and a zeal for the preservation of racial unity ought to be essential con-

cerns in South American countries." Ovidio da Cunha, *Directrizes da anthropo-geographia brasiliense* (Rio de Janeiro, 1935), 215.

77. The constitutional provisions are in Mendes de Almeida, *Constituições*, 470, 664. For a discussion of the background of this legislation, see Manuel Diégues Júnior, *Imigração, urbanização e industrialização* (Rio de Janeiro, 1964), 334–55.

78. A critical analysis of Oliveira Vianna's racial theories may be found in Nelson Werneck Sodré, *A Ideologia do colonialismo: Seus reflexos no pensamento brasileiro* (Rio de Janeiro, 1961), 169–267. I benefitted greatly from reading the preliminary draft of a doctoral dissertation on Oliveira Vianna (as one among three case studies in the intellectual history of Brazil in the 1920's and 1930's) by James Lauer.

79. Oliveira Vianna, *Populações meridionais do Brasil*, vol. I, 5th ed. (São Paulo, 1952), 13. Since Vianna did not make revisions in subsequent editions of his major books, I have cited the later, more readily accessible editions.

80. F. J. Oliveira Vianna, "O Povo brazileiro e sua evolução," in Ministerio da Agricultura, Industria e Commercio: Directoria Geral de Estatística, *Recenseamento do Brasil realizado em 1 de Setembro de 1920*, vol. I: *Introducção* (Rio de Janeiro, 1922), 279–400. It was later published separately as *Evolução do povo brasileiro*. I have used the fourth printing (which the Brazilians often call "editions") (Rio de Janeiro, 1956), which was unchanged from the original.

81. *Ibid.*, 178–82, 188–90.

82. The official explanation for the dropping of race was given in "Historico e Instrucções para a Execução do Recenseamento de 1920," *Recenseamento do Brazil realizado em 1 de Setembro 1920*, 488–89. The question is discussed also in Arthur Ramos *O Negro brasileiro*, 2nd ed. (São Paulo, 1940), 17–18. Roquette-Pinto gave the following estimate of the racial composition of the Brazilian population in 1922:

Brancos (whites)	51 per cent
Mulatos (mulattoes)	22
Caboclos (primarily white-Indian mixture)	11
Negros (blacks)	14
Indios (indians)	2

E. Roquette-Pinto, "Nota sôbre os Tipos Antropológicos do Brasil," *Archivos do Museu Nacional*, XXX (1928), 309. Interestingly, these figures showed whites to be 1 per cent higher than the 50 per cent that Roquette-Pinto had estimated in his calculation for Batista Lacerda in 1912 (discussed above in Chapter 2).

83. Vianna, *Evolução do povo*, 182–85, 175. Vianna made his most comprehensive argument that only by assimilation could non-whites make any contribution to modern civilization in his *Raça e assimilação* (Rio de Janeiro, 1932).

84. Very favorable reviews of the first volume of *Populações*

Meridionais do Brasil came from influential younger literary critics who were generally identified with the reaction against the intellectual assumptions of the older generation. Alceu Amoroso Lima praised the book on December 27, 1920, hardly mentioning Vianna's Aryanism: Lima, *Estudos literários,* vol. I, 292–96. Aggripino Grieco called it "the vertical column of Brazilian Sociology," although he thought necessary (and not contradictory) to add: "It is only regrettable that Sr. Oliveira Vianna gives great importance . . . to certain Anthropo-Sociological factors. He's among those who still believe in craneometry, in cephalic indices and other complications from the books of Vacher de Lapouge. Nowadays that has all been relegated to the realm of fiction." Grieco, *O Jornal,* July 8, 1923, reprinted in *Revista do Brasil,* vol. XXV (No. 93, Sept. 1923), 77–81. Even Nelson Werneck Sodré, who was later to publish such an uncompromising attack on Vianna's racism (1961: cited above), found nothing fundamental to criticize when he wrote a long review article on Vianna published in 1942. Nelson Werneck Sodré, *Orientações do pensamento brasileiro* (Rio de Janeiro, 1942), 59–75.

85. Even when some critics thought they had refuted Vianna's racist assumptions, they proved very close to his concept of "Aryanization." Almachio Diniz, for example, quoted at length from Bomfim to disprove Vianna, and yet had trouble proving the differences between Vianna's conclusion and his own belief that miscegenation was producing a progressively whiter mixed blood. He thought racial mixture was producing "a new type, varying according to the climatic conditions. . . . This is occurring slowly, not because the Brazilian is Aryanizing himself . . . , but because the white is more numerous, and has defeated the other groups in adapting to the environment, which in turn does not favor the perpetuation of the native types . . . nor of the Negro types. . . ." Almachio Diniz, *História racial do Brasil* (São Paulo, 1934), 336, 371–73. An officially published information pamphlet of the 1920's referred to the "process of intense aryanization" then under way: Costa Miranda, *Synopse da actualidade brasileira* (Rio de Janeiro: Ministério da Agricultura, Indústria e Comércio: Serviço de Informações, 1928), 5.

86. Vianna, *Evolução do povo,* 158.

87. Freyre described Vianna as "the greatest exponent of a mystic Aryanism who has as yet arisen among us," Freyre, *Masters and the Slaves,* 306. One contemporary critic thought Freyre's masterpiece ("this superb volume") could be traced directly back to the influence of Vianna and Alberto Tôrres: Grieco, *Gente nova,* 217–18.

88. In fact, Vianna may have sensed the trend. After 1938 (the year of third edition of *Raça e assimilação*) he published no book-length study treating race per se. In 1932 he had announced that two volumes on that subject were in preparation: *O Ariano no Brasil* and

Antropologia social (prospective titles later changed to *Raça e Seleções etnicas* and *Raça e Seleções Telúricas*), but they remained unpublished when he died in 1951.

89. Paulo Prado, *Retrato do Brasil: Ensaio sôbre a tristeza brasileira*, 6th ed. (Rio de Janeiro, 1962). The original text remained unchanged through many reprintings. The leading student of the literature on Brazilian national character described Prado's book as the "first rigorously psychological interpretation of our history and our national character." Moreira Leite, *O Caráter nacional brasileiro*, 262.

90. Prado, *Retrato do Brasil*, 155.

91. *Ibid.*, 158–59.

92. *Ibid.*, 158–60.

93. *Ibid.*, 174, 182.

94. *Ibid.*, 179.

95. For an example of contemporary attacks on Prado's determinism, see Grieco, *Gente nova*, 267–70. Prado's portrait provoked a debate over Brazilian national character which continued for the next decade and a half. Among the earliest replies was Eduardo Friero, *O Brasileiro não é triste* (Belo Horizonte, 1931).

96. João Pandiá Calogeras, *A History of Brazil* (New York, 1963), 30. This is a reprint of the English translation first published in 1939. The original Brazilian edition bore the title *Formação histórica do Brasil* and was published in 1930, by which time Calogeras had been Minister of War, Minister of Finance, and Minister of Agriculture. A confident description of the whitening process had been given earlier in the decade by Elysio de Carvalho, *Os Bastiões da nacionalidade* (Rio de Janeiro, 1922), 190: and in Ronald Carvalho and Elysio de Carvalho, *Affirmações, um agapé de intelectuaes* (Rio de Janeiro, 1921), 40. As we have seen earlier, Elysio de Carvalho's lack of originality and enthusiasm made him a reliable bellweather of the predominant cultural mood. For another enthusiastic foreign endorsement of the whitening process in Brazil, see Rüdiger Bilden, "Brazil, Laboratory of Civilization," *The Nation*, CXXVIII, No. 3315 (Jan. 16, 1929), 71–74.

97. For a study which puts the Integralist movement into the context of the radicalization of politics in the 1930's, see Robert M. Levine, *The Vargas Regime: The Critical Years, 1934–1938* (New York, 1970). A wealth of new information is provided in Hélgio Henrique Casses Trindade, "L'Action intégraliste brésilienne: Un mouvement de type fasciste des années 30." (Thesis: Fondation Nationale des Sciences Politiques, Paris, 1971).

98. As, for example, in Gustavo Barroso, *O Que O Integralista Deve Saber* (Rio de Janeiro, 1935), 119–33.

99. There is a succinct discussion of these measures in Karl Loewenstein, *Brazil Under Vargas* (New York, 1942), 205–11.

100. Detail on Nazi designs on southern Brazil may be found in

Jürgen Hell, "Das 'südbrasilianische Neudeutschland': Der annexion-
istische Grundzug der wilhelminischen und nazistischen Brasilien-
politik, 1895–1938," in *Der Deutsche Faschismus in Lateinamerika,
1933–1943* (Berlin, 1966), 103–24. The diplomatic implications of the
Brazilian campaign to speed up the assimilation of the German-speakers
is analyzed in Käte Harms-Baltzer, *Die Nationalisierung der deutschen
Einwanderer und ihrer Nachkommen in Brasilien als Problem der
deutschbrasilianischen Beziehungen, 1930–1938* (Berlin, 1970). There
is much information on the attitudes of Germano-Brazilians in Loewenstein, *Brazil Under Vargas*, 155–204.

101. The manifesto is reprinted in Arthur Ramos, *Guerra e
relações de raça* (Rio de Janeiro, 1943), 171–74. For another Sociologist's attempt to refute racist theories both on the grounds of their lack
of scientific respectability and on the grounds that they were the stalk-
ing horse of "mystic Pan-Germanism," see [João] Rodrigues de Meréje,
O Problema da Raça (São Paulo, n.d. [1934]).

102. Reprinted in Ramos, *Guerra e relações de raça*, 177–80.

103. Basic behavioral attitudes in Brazilian race relations have
probably remained largely constant since 1870, independent of the
theoretical justifications given them (documentation on this question is
admittedly very sketchy). There would appear to be a parallel to the
relationship between race theories and racial behavior in the United
States. One scholar who studied the scientific attitudes of racial inferiority in the U.S. between 1859 and 1900 concluded that "The subject of race inferiority was beyond critical reach in the late nineteenth
century. Having accepted science and its exalted doctrinaires, American society betrayed no sentiment, popular or otherwise, that looked to
a remodeling of its social or political habits of race. . . . Dissent about
the character of evolution had little bearing on the concept of race inferiority and much less upon the derivation of its racist ideas." Haller,
Outcasts from Evolution, 210. In Brazil, on the other hand, a de facto
faith in miscegenation (i.e., whitening) was beyond the critical reach
even of scientific racist theory.

104. Fernando de Azevedo, *Brazilian Culture: An Introduction to
the Study of Culture in Brazil*, trans. by William Rex Crawford (New
York, 1950), 40–41. The first Brazilian edition was issued as an official
government publication: Instituto Brasileiro de Geografía e Estatística,
Commisão Censitária Nacional: *Recenseamento geral do Brasil:* National Series, vol. I: Introdução, Tomo I: Fernando de Azevedo, *A Cultura brasileira* (Rio de Janeiro, 1943). Azevedo had been invited by
President Vargas to head the Commisão Censitária Nacional, but declined. Fernando de Azevedo, *História de minha vida* (Rio de Janeiro,
1971), 191. Azevedo explains the background of his involvement in
writing the introduction to the census in the Preface to the third Brazilian edition of *A Cultura Brasileria* (São Paulo, 1958).

105. Confidence in the continuing whitening process was often expressed after the census of 1940, as in Pierre Deffontaines, "A População branca no Brasil," *Boletim Geográfico*, III, No. 32 (Nov. 1945), and Angelo Bittencourt, "A Nossa gente de côr," *Boletim Geográfico*, ano IV, No. 45 (Dec. 1946).

106. Eugene Gordon, *An Essay in Race Amalgamation* (Rio de Janeiro, 1951) [Ministry of Foreign Relations, Cultural Division]. The author was a student at the University of California. In his Foreword Gilberto Freyre suggested that Brazil's racial solution "becomes of greater importance day by day as an experiment and perhaps as an example to be followed."

107. In his comparative analysis of Brazilian and U.S. race relations, Carl Degler has persuasively argued that the "mulatto escape hatch" is the key to understanding how Brazil developed a multi-racial society instead of the bi-racial system which prevailed in the United States. Degler, *Neither Black Nor White.*

108. For an excellent analysis of the historiography of national character studies in Brazil, see Dante Moreira Leite, *O Caráter nacional brasileiro* (São Paulo, 1969).

109. Vianna Moog, *Bandeirantes e pioneiros* (Rio de Janeiro, 1955), later translated and published in the United States under the title *Bandeirantes and Pioneers* (New York, 1964).

110. The UNESCO-sponsored research in Brazil grew out of the effort of a UNESCO Committee to establish a scientifically acceptable definition of "race." Professor Métraux, a well-known French Anthropologist and Director of UNESCO studies on race relations, enthusiastically supported the Brazilian project. For an explanation of the research plan and a synthesis of the conclusions drawn from the studies, see Roger Bastide, "Race Relations in Brazil," *UNESCO International Social Science Bulletin*, IX, No. 4 (1957), 495–512. An earlier report, written in popular form, was given by the major researchers in *Courier* (UNESCO), V, Nos. 8–9 (Aug.-Sept. 1952), 6–15. For a skeptical view of the UNESCO-sponsored research, see an article published by Edison Carneiro in 1953 and reprinted in his *Ladinos e crioulos* (Rio de Janeiro, 1964), 102–18. Carneiro was one of the pioneer researchers on Afro-Brazilian religion and other aspects of African influence in Brazil.

111. The two most important works produced under UNESCO sponsorship were Charles Wagley, ed., *Race and Class in Rural Brazil* (Paris, 1952), and Roger Bastide and Florestan Fernandes, *Relações raciais entre negroes e brancos em São Paulo* (São Paulo, 1955). Details on the background of the research may be found in the prefaces to both books. For a collection of Fernandes' later articles, see his *O Negro no mundo dos brancos* (São Paulo, 1972).

112. Looking back on the research he had helped direct, Charles

Wagley observed: "It is curious that although these UNESCO studies were motivated by showing a positive view of race relations in one part of the world (i.e., Brazil) from which it was thought that the rest of the world might learn something, they actually modified the world's view of race relations in Brazil." Personal communication from Charles Wagley, September 21, 1973. The present-day picture is well summarized in Degler, *Neither Black Nor White*, Chapter III, and is cast in the form of six propositions about Brazilian race relations in John Saunders, "Class, Color, and Prejudice: A Brazilian Counterpoint," in Ernest Q. Campbell, ed., *Racial Tensions and National Identity* (Nashville, Tenn., 1972), 141–65. Both Degler and Saunders give detailed citations of the relevant research works. A description of the background of this new research is given by one of Fernandes' students in Octavio Ianni, *Raças e classes sociais no Brasil* (Rio de Janeiro, 1966), 3–40.

113. Typical was the article "Existe Preconceito de Côr no Brasil," *Realidade*, Oct. 1967. Citations of other press stories may be found in Abdias do Nascimento, *O Negro revoltado* (Rio de Janeiro, 1968), 23–30. For citations of press stories appearing during 1946, see Rodrigues Alves, *A Ecologia do grupo afro-brasileiro* (Rio de Janeiro, 1966), 30–36. See also *Ebony* for July and Sept. 1965.

114. Florestan Fernandes, *The Negro in Brazilian Society* (New York, 1969), xv, 137–39. This is a translation and condensation of the longer original work: *A Integração do negro à sociedade de classes* (Rio de Janeiro, 1964), 2 vols. One of the most thorough-going critics of previous elite opinion on race and race relations was Guerreiro Ramos, whose writings of the early 1950's are collected in Ramos, *Introdução crítica à sociologia brasileira* (Rio de Janeiro, 1957).

115. One of the earliest examples was Mary W. Williams, "The Treatment of Negro Slaves in the Brazilian Empire," *Journal of Negro History*, XV (No. 3, July 1930). The most important work in this vein was Frank Tannenbaum, *Slave and Citizen* (New York, 1946), which greatly influenced the widely read work of Stanley Elkins *Slavery: A Problem in American Institutional and Intellectual Life* (Chicago, 1959). I gained a number of ideas from the general analysis of U.S. and Brazilian interpretations of slavery and race relations in Brazil given in Leslie B. Rout, Jr., "Sleight of Hand: Brazilian and American Authors Manipulate the Brazilian Racial Situation, 1910–1951," *The Americas*, XXIX (No. 4, Apr. 1973), 471–88.

116. Marvin Harris, *Patterns of Race in the Americas* (New York, 1964). The important revisionist trend since the early 1950's in Brazilian scholarly work on slavery has been analyzed in an excellent historiographical survey by Richard Graham, "Brazilian Slavery Reexamined: A Review Article," *Journal of Social History*, III (No. 1, Fall 1969), 30–52.

117. The issue was fully debated in a public session of the Comissão Censitária Nacional on September 9, 1969, where several leading sociologists presented their views. At the conclusion of the meeting the Commission decided by a split vote to exclude both color and religion from the 1970 census questionnaire. Instituto Brasileiro de Geografia e Estatística: Comissão Censitária Nacional, "Ata Dos Trabalhos: 6a Sessão Ordinária, September 9, 1969" (typescript). The decision drew angry criticism from Edison Carneiro and Afonso Arinos, who both argued that despite the admitted variability of the application of color categories an attempt should be made to continue gathering data. *Correio da Manhã*, Jan. 30, 1970. An editorial praising the decision and stressing the extreme unreliability of responses to questions about color was published in *Diário de Notícias*, Feb. 15, 1970.

118. Edison Carneiro et al., *80 anos de abolição: O Negro brasileiro* (Rio de Janeiro, 1968), 63, 67. Sources on the still-born attempt at a black nationalist revival since 1945 are given in Abdias do Nascimento, *O Negro revoltado* (Rio de Janeiro, 1968). Further information on the literary attempts in Brazil to emphasize blackness may be found in Preto-Rodas, *Negritude as a Theme in the Poetry of the Portuguese-Speaking World*, chapter 2. The failure of black nationalism in Brazil was a logical result of the predominance of the "whitening ideal" *throughout* Brazilian society. The relative lack of interest in the Brazilian black, per se, among "colored intellectuals" in Bahia in the 1930's was noted by the American sociologist Donald Pierson, *Negroes in Brazil*, 2nd ed., 220.

119. Edison Carneiro, for example, accused the organizers (which included Nascimento) of the First Congress of the Brazilian Negro (1950) of trying to "enunciate racist statements." Carneiro, *Ladinos e Crioulos*, 116.

NOTES ON SOURCES AND METHODOLOGY

1. In 1872 the illiteracy rate was 66.4 per cent, in 1890 67.2 per cent, in 1900 58.8 per cent, and in 1920 60.1 per cent. Azevedo, *Brazilian Culture*, 428. As late as 1940 the official figures showed that fewer than half of the children in the 7–11 age bracket were enrolled in primary school. Robert J. Havighurst and J. Roberto Moreira, *Society and Education in Brazil* (Pittsburgh, 1965), 85.

2. There were some notable exceptions to the rule that all intellectuals held higher degrees. Machado de Assis, Brazil's most famous novelist and the President of the Brazilian Academy of Letters, lacked even a secondary education, while Capistrano de Abreu, the most original historian of the era, had no higher degree. Nonetheless, such exceptions were rare among the intellectual spokesmen for the elite analyzed in this study.

3. For an analysis of the most cited authors in twelve secondary works on socio-political thought, see Wanderley Guilherme dos Santos, "A Imaginação político-social brasileira," *Dados*, Nos. 2/3 (1967), 182–93. For an example of the kind of secondary source that can be very helpful to intellectual historians, see Fernando Sales, "Livros novos de 1920," *Revista do Livro*, No. 44 (1970), 37–53, which is a brief survey of the fifty-eight principal authors whose works were published in 1920.

4. References to the large literature on the role of intellectuals in widely varying societies may be found in two issues of *Daedalus* devoted to "Intellectuals and Tradition," *Daedalus* (Spring 1972), and "Intellectuals and Change," *Daedalus* (Summer 1972).

5. For discussions of the role of intellectuals in developing societies, see Edward Shils, "The Intellectuals in the Political Development of the New States," *World Politics*, XII (No. 3, Apr. 1960), 329–68; and John Friedmann, "Intellectuals in Developing Societies," *Kyklos*, XIII (1960), 514–43.

6. The most perceptive discussion of this cultural ethos is Brito Broca, *A Vida literária no Brasil: 1900*, 2nd ed. (Rio de Janeiro, 1960). Clear evidence of the dominance of literary prestige in the intellectual world can be seen in the role played by the Brazilian Academy of Letters. From its founding in 1897 it included prominent figures who had no claim to significant literary accomplishments, if defined to mean poetry, drama, fiction, or literary criticism. Scientists such as Oswaldo Cruz and Roquette-Pinto, jurists such as Pedro Lessa and Clóvis Beviláqua, and politicians such as Lauro Müller and Rui Barbosa were all Academy members. Competition to win election to a chair after the death of one of the forty members often provoked bitter rivalries among the intellectuals. It was customary for aspirants to declare their candidacy and solicit votes among the incumbent members. The style of such self-promotion can be seen in the case of Euclides da Cunha who successfully campaigned for election. Thomas E. Skidmore and Thomas H. Holloway, "New Light on Euclides da Cunha: Letters to Oliveira Lima, 1903–1909," *Luso-Brazilian Review*, VIII (No. 1, June 1971), 30–55. Much information on the Academy for this period may be found in José Lopes Pereira de Carvalho, *Os Membros da Academia Brasileira em 1915* (Rio de Janeiro, n.d.), which is an anthology of excerpts from members' works along with bio-bibliographical sketches.

7. For a contemporary estimate of the market for books, see *Revista do Brasil*, No. 63 (Mar. 1921), 278–80. Data on the circulation of periodicals at the end of the decade of the 1920's is given in Departamento Nacional de Estatística, *Estatística da imprensa periódica no Brasil: 1929–1930* (Rio de Janeiro, 1931). For details on Monteiro Lobato's efforts to expand book publishing and distribution, see Edgard Cavalheiro, *Monteiro Lobato: Vida e obra*, 2 vols., 3rd ed. (São Paulo, 1962), I, 193–212.

8. As Capistrano de Abreu said of Coelho Neto, "he had the disadvantage of writing for a living. . . ." Capistrano de Abreu, *Correspondência*, II, 98. For a wealth of detail (if rather disorganized) on the role of the press, see Nelson Werneck Sodré, *História da imprensa no Brasil* (Rio de Janeiro, 1966).

9. João do Rio, *O Momento literário* (Rio de Janeiro, n.d. [1908?]).

10. The distinguished literary critic Antônio Cândido has argued that the essay of ideas has been "the most characteristic and original feature of our thought." Cândido, *Literatura e sociedade*, 157. The essay has been seen by scholars of Spanish American literature as an important form of literary expression. For an example of how this approach can produce a stimulating contribution to intellectual history, see Martin S. Stabb, *In Quest of Identity: Patterns in the Spanish American Essay of Ideas, 1890–1960* (Chapel Hill, N.C., 1967).

11. Among these works are Antonio Paim, *História das idéias filosóficas no Brasil* (São Paulo, 1967); João Camilo de Oliveira Tôrres, *História das idéias religiosas no Brasil* (São Paulo, 1968); Nelson Saldanha, *História das idéias políticas no Brasil* (Recife, 1968); Vamireh Chacon, *História das idéias socialistas no Brasil* (Rio de Janeiro, 1965); and José Antônio Tobias, *História das idéias estéticas no Brasil* (São Paulo, 1967).

12. Studies of schoolbooks and educational methods can tell us much about how the elite hoped to socialize future generations of Brazilians. For works in this area, see Leonardo Arroyo, *Literatura infantil brasileira* (São Paulo, 1968); and Miriam Moreira Leite, *O Ensino da história no primário e no ginásio* (São Paulo, 1969).

13. For an effort to do this elsewhere in Latin America, see Juan F. Marsal, *El Intelectual latinoamericano: Un simposio sobre sociología de los intelectuales* (Buenos Aires, 1970).

Selected Bibliographical Index

This is an index of short titles used for works cited more than once. References are to the location of the full citation (for example, 260, n. 14, is page 260, note 14), where the author's full name and publishing information may be found. Because of possible confusion due to multiple names in Portuguese, the reader may need to look in more than one place. Newspapers and magazines are excluded from this index.

Bibliography to the 1993 Edition

Adorno, Sergio. 1988. *Os Aprendizes do Poder: O Bacharelismo Liberal na Política Brasileira*. Rio de Janeiro: Paz e Terra.

Alves Filho, Aluizio. 1979. *Pensamento Político no Brasil: Manoel Bomfim, um Ensaísta Esquecido*. Rio de Janeiro: Achiame.

Andrews, George Reid. 1991. *Blacks and Whites in São Paulo, Brazil: 1888–1988*. Madison: University of Wisconsin Press.

Arquivo Nacional. 1988. *Guia Brasileiro de Fontes para a História da África, da Escravidão Negra e do Negro na Sociedade Atual*. 2 vols. Rio de Janeiro: Departamento de Imprensa Nacional.

Azevedo, Celia Maria Marinho de. 1987. *Onda Negra, Medo Branco: O Negro no Imaginário das Elites Século XIX*. Rio de Janeiro: Paz e Terra.

Azevedo, Thales de. 1975. *Democracia Racial: Ideologia e Realidade*. Petrópolis: Vozes.

Barcelos, Luiz Claudio, et. al. 1991. *Escravidão e Relações Raciais no Brasil: Cadastro da Produção Intelectual (1970–1990)*. Rio de Janeiro: Centro de Estudos Afro-Asiáticos.

Bastos, Elide Rugai. 1986. "Gilberto [Freyre] e a Questão Nacional." In *Inteligência Brasileira*, ed. Reginaldo Moraes et al. São Paulo: Brasiliense.

Brookshaw, David. 1983. *Raça e Cor na Literatura Brasileira*. Porto Alegre: Mercado Aberto.

Cadernos Negros 14. 1991. São Paulo: Quilombhoje.

Camargo, Oswaldo de. 1986. *A Razão da Chama: Antologia de Poetas Negros Brasileiros*. São Paulo: GRD.

Carvalho, José Murilo de. 1991. "A Utopia de Oliveira Viana." *Estudos Históricos* 7:82–99.

Chaloub, Sidney. 1986. *Trabalho, Lar e Botequim*. São Paulo: Brasiliense.

———. 1990. *Visões da Liberdade*. São Paulo: Companhia das Letras.

CNBB (Conferencia Nacional dos Bispos do Brasil). 1988. *Ouvi o Clamor deste Povo: Manual*. Brasília: Centro de Pastoral Popular.

Colina, Paulo. 1982. *Axé: Antologia Contemporanea da Poesia Negra Brasileira*. São Paulo: Global.

Corrêa, Mariza. 1987. *História da Antropologia no Brasil (1930–1960)*. São Paulo: Vértice.

Costa, Haroldo. 1982. *Fala, Crioulo*. Rio de Janeiro: Record.

Da Matta, Roberto. 1987. "A Originalidade de Gilberto Freyre." *Boletim Informativo e Bibliográfico de Ciências Sociais* 24:3–10.

Diacon, Todd A. 1991. *Millenarian Vision, Capitalist Reality: Brazil's Contestado Rebellion, 1912-1916*. Durham: Duke University Press.

Dimas, Antonio. 1983. *Tempos Eufóricos: Analise da Revista Kosmos, 1904–1909*. São Paulo: Ática.

Faoro, Raymundo. 1974. *Machado de Assis: A Piramide e o Trapézio*. São Paulo: Nacional.

Fernandes, Florestan. 1989. *Significado do Protesto Negro*. São Paulo: Cortez.

Fonseca, Edson Nery da. 1983. *Um Livro Completa Meio Seculo*. Recife: Massangana.

Fontaine, Pierre-Michel, ed. 1985. *Race, Class and Power in Brazil*. Los Angeles: Center for Afro-American Studies, University of California, Los Angeles.

Galvão, Walnice Nogueira. 1976. *Saco de Gatos*. São Paulo: Duas Cidades.

———. 1974. *No Calor da Hora*. São Paulo: Ática.

———, ed. 1985. *Os Sertões: Edição Crítica*. São Paulo: Brasiliense.

Gledson, John. 1984. *The Deceptive Realism of Machado de Assis*. Liverpool: Francis Cairns.

———. 1986. Machado de Assis: *Ficção e História*. Rio de Janeiro: Paz e Terra.

Gomes, Angela de Castro, and Marieta de Moraes Ferreira. 1989. "Primeira República: Um Balanço Historiográfico." *Estudos Históricos* 4:244–80.

Gomes, Heloisa Toller. 1988. *O Negro e o Romantismo Brasileiro*. São Paulo: Atual.

Haberly, David T. 1983. *Three Sad Races: Racial Identity and National Consciousness in Brazilian Literature*. Cambridge: Cambridge University Press.

Hall, Michael, et al. 1989. "Imigrantes." *Trabalhadores: Publicação Mensal do Fundo de Assistência a Cultura* 3. Campinas: Prefeitura Municipal de Campinas, Secretaria de Cultura, Esportes e Turismo.

Hallewell, Laurence. 1982. *Books in Brazil: A History of the Publishing Trade*. Metuchen, N.J.: Scarecrow.

Hasenbalg, Carlos Alfredo. 1979. *Discriminação e Desigualdades Raciais no Brasil*. Rio de Janeiro: Graal.

Hasenbalg, Carlos, and Nelson do Valle Silva. 1988. *Estrutura Social, Mobilidade e Raça*. São Paulo: Vértice.

———. 1990. "Raça e Oportunidades Educacionais no Brasil." *Estudos Afro-Asiáticos* 18:73–91.

Hellwig, David J. 1992. *African-American Reflections on Brazil's Racial Paradise*. Philadelphia: Temple University Press.

Holloway, Thomas H. 1980. *Immigrants on the Land: Coffee and Society in São Paulo, 1886–1934*. Chapel Hill: University of North Carolina Press.

———. 1989. "'A Healthy Terror': Police Repression of *Capoeiras* in Nineteenth-Century Brazil." *Hispanic American Historical Review* 69 (4): 637–76.

Ianni, Octavio. 1978. *Escravidão e Racismo*. São Paulo: Hucitec.

———. 1987. *Raças e Classes Sociais no Brasil*. 3rd ed. São Paulo: Brasiliense.

Instituto Panamericano de Geografia e Historia. 1987. *Legislación y Política Inmigratoria en el Cono Sur de America: Argentina, Brasil, Uruguay*. Mexico: Organización de los Estados Americanos.

Janotti, Maria de Lourdes Monaco. 1986. *Os Subversivos da República*. São Paulo: Brasiliense.

Landers, Vasda Bonafini. 1988. *De Jeca a Macunaíma: Monteiro Lobato e o Modernismo*. Rio de Janeiro: Civilização Brasileira.

Levi, Darrell E. 1987. *The Prados of São Paulo, Brazil*. Athens: University of Georgia Press.

Lovell, Peggy A., ed. 1991. *Desigualdade Racial no Brasil Contemporaneo*. Belo Horizonte: CEDEPLAR, Universidade Federal de Minas Gerais.

Luebke, Frederick C. 1987. *Germans in Brazil: A Comparative History of Cultural Conflict During World War I*. Baton Rouge: Louisiana State University Press.

Maciel, Cleber da Silva. 1987. *Discriminações Raciais: Negros em Campinas (1888–1921)*. Campinas: UNICAMP.

Maggie, Yvonne. 1989. *Catálogo: Centenario da Abolição*. Rio de Janeiro: CIEC, Nucleo da Cor, Universidade Federal do Rio de Janeiro.

Marotti, Giorgio. 1987. *Black Characters in the Brazilian Novel*. Los Angeles: Center for Afro-American Studies, University of California,

Los Angeles.

Marson, Adalberto. 1979. *A Ideologia Nacionalista em Alberto Torres*. São Paulo: Duas Cidades.

Martins, Wilson. 1976-78. *História da Inteligência Brasileira*. 7 vols. São Paulo. Cultrix.

Massi, Fernanda. 1989. "Franceses e Norte-Americanos nas Ciências Sociais Brasileiras (1930–1960)." In *História das Ciências Sociais no Brasil*, ed. Sérgio Miceli, vol. 1, pp. 410–59. São Paulo: Vértice.

Meade, Teresa, and Gregory Alonso Pirio. 1988. "In Search of the Afro-American 'Eldorado': Attempts by North American Blacks to Enter Brazil in the 1920s." *Luso-Brazilian Review* 25 (1): 85–110.

Medeiros, Jarbas. 1978. *Ideologia Autoritária no Brasil, 1930–1945*. Rio de Janeiro: Fundação Getúlio Vargas.

Miceli, Sérgio. 1979. *Intelectuais e Classe Dirigente no Brasil (1920–1945)*. São Paulo: DIFEL.

——. 1989. *História das Ciências Sociais no Brasil*. Vol. 1. São Paulo: Vértice.

Miranda, Maria do Carmo Tavares de. 1988. *Á Memória de Gilberto Freyre*. Recife: Massangana.

Mota, Carlos Guilherme. 1978. *Ideologia da Cultura Brasileira, 1933–1974*. São Paulo: Ática.

Moura, Clovis. 1976. *O Preconceito de Cor na Literatura de Cordel*. São Paulo: Resenha Universitária.

——. 1983. *Brasil: Raízes do Protesto Negro*. São Paulo: Global.

——. 1988. *Sociologia do Negro Brasileiro*. São Paulo: Ática.

——. 1990. *As Injustiças de Clio: O Negro na Historiografia Brasileira*. Belo Horizonte: Oficina de Livros.

Nachman, Robert G. 1977. "Positivism, Modernization and the Middle Class in Brazil." *Hispanic American Historical Review* 57 (1):1–23.

Nascimento, Abdias do. 1982. *O Negro Revoltado*. Rio de Janeiro: Nova Fronteira.

——. 1978. *O Genocídio do Negro Brasileiro*. Rio de Janeiro: Paz e Terra.

Needell, Jeffrey D. 1987. *A Tropical Belle Epoque: Elite Culture and Society in Turn-of-the-Century Rio de Janeiro*. Cambridge: Cambridge University Press.

Novaes, Regina Reyes, and Maria da Graça Floriano. 1985. *O Negro Evangélico*. Rio de Janeiro: Instituto de Estudos da Religiâo.

Oliveira, Lucia E. Garcia de, Rosa Maria Porcaro, and Tereza C. N. Araujo. 1985. *O Lugar do Negro na Força de Trabalho*. Rio de Janeiro: Departamento de Estudos e Indicadores Sociais (DEISO), Instituto Brasileiro de Geografia e Estatística.

Oliveira, Lucia Lippi. 1990. *A Questão Nacional na Primeira República*. São Paulo: Brasiliense.

Queiroz, Paulo Edmur de Souza. 1975. *A Sociologia Política de Oliveira Vianna*. São Paulo: Convívio.

Queiroz, Suely Robles Reis de. 1986. *Os Radicais da República: Jacobinismo: Ideologia e Ação 1893–1897*. São Paulo: Brasiliense.

Queiroz Júnior, Teófilo de. 1975. *Preconceito de Cor e a Mulata na Literature Brasileira*. São Paulo: Ática.

Ricci, Maria Lucia de Souza Rangel. 1990. *Guarda-Negra: Perfil de uma Sociedade em Crise*. Campinas: Ricci.

Rodrigues, José Honório.. 1988a. *História da História do Brasil*. Vol. 2, tom. 1 [*A Historiografia Conservadora*]. São Paulo: Nacional.

———. 1988b. *História da História do Brasil*. Vol. 2, tom. 2 [*A Metafísica do Latifúndio: O Ultrareacionário Oliveira Vianna*]. São Paulo: Nacional.

Rosemberg, Fulvia, and Regina Pahim Pinto. 1987. "Raça Negra e Educação." *Cadernos de Pesquisa* 63.

Schwartz, Stuart B. 1992a. *Slaves, Peasants, and Rebels: Reconsidering Brazilian Slavery*. Urbana: University of Illinois Press.

———. 1992b. "Brazilian Ethnogenesis: Mamelucos, Mestiços, and Pardos." Paper delivered at the Conference on Le Nouveau Monde-Mondes Nouveaux: L'Expérience Américaine, June 2–4, Ecole des Hautes Etudes en Sciences Sociales, Paris.

Schwarz, Roberto. 1977. *Ao Vencedor as Batatas*. São Paulo: Duas Cidades.

———. 1990. *Um Mestre na Periferia do Capitalismo: Machado de Assis*. São Paulo: Duas Cidades.

Sevcenko, Nicolau. 1983. *Literatura Como Missão: Tensões Sociais e Criação Cultural na Primeira República*. São Paulo: Brasiliense.

Silva, Nelson do Valle. 1981. "Cor e o Processo de Realização Sócio-Econômica." *DADOS* 24 (3):391–409.

———. 1985. "Updating the Cost of Not Being White in Brazil." In *Race, Class and Power in Brazil*, ed. Pierre-Michel Fontaine, pp. 42–55. Los Angeles: Center for Afro-American Studies, University of California, Los Angeles.

Skidmore, Thomas E. 1985. "Race and Class in Brazil: Historical Perspectives." In *Race, Class and Power in Brazil*, ed. Pierre-Michel Fontaine, pp. 11–24. Los Angeles: Center for Afro-American Studies, University of California, Los Angeles.

———. 1991. "Fato e Mito: Descobrindo um Problema Racial no Brasil." *Cadernos de Pesquisa* (S.P.) 79 (November):5–16.

———. 1992. "Bi-Racial U.S. vs. Multi-Racial Brazil: Is the Contrast Still Valid?" Paper delivered at the Conference on Racism and Race Relations in the Countries of the African Diaspora, April 6–9, Rio de Janeiro.

———. 1993. "The Myth-Makers: Architects of Brazilian National Identity." In *Cambridge History of Latin American Literature*, ed. Roberto Gonzalez-Echevarria and Enrique Pupo-Walker. Cambridge: Cambridge University Press. Forthcoming.

Souza, Neusa Santos. 1983. *Tornar-se Negro: As Vicissitudes da Identidade do Negro Brasileiro em Ascenção Social*. Rio de Janeiro: Graal.

Spitzer, Leo. 1989. *Lives in Between: Assimilation and Marginality in Austria, Brazil, West Africa, 1780–1945*. Cambridge: Cambridge University Press.

Stepan, Nancy Leys. 1991. *"The Hour of Eugenics": Race, Gender, and Nation in Latin America*. Ithaca: Cornell University Press.

Vainfas, Ronaldo. 1986. *Ideologia e Escravidão: Os Letrados e a Sociedade Escravista no Brasil Colonial*. Petrópolis: Vozes.

———. 1986. *Trópico dos Pecados*. Rio de Janeiro: Campus.

Veja. 1985. August 28.

Venancio Filho, Alberto. 1977. *Das Arcadas ao Bacharelismo: 150 Anos de Ensino Jurídico no Brasil*. São Paulo: Perspectiva.

Ventura, Roberto. 1991. *Estilo Tropical: História Cultural e Polêmicas Literárias no Brasil, 1870–1914*. São Paulo: Companhia das Letras.

Vieira, Evaldo Amaro. 1976. *Oliveira Vianna e o Estado Corporativo*. São Paulo: Grijalbo.

Viotti da Costa, Emília. 1982. *A Abolição*. São Paulo: Global.

———. 1985. *The Brazilian Empire: Myths and Histories*. Chicago: University of Chicago Press.

Winant, Howard. 1992. "Rethinking Race in Brazil." *Journal of Latin American Studies* 24 (1):173–92.

Wood, Charles H., and José Alberto Magno de Carvalho. 1988. *The Demography of Inequality in Brazil*. Cambridge: Cambridge University Press.

Index

Peixoto, Afrânio, 73–74, 94–95,
129, 132, 149, 169–70, 183,
196
Peixoto, Floriano, 81–82, 86–87
Pena, Afonso, 79, 83, 102, 174
Pena, Belisario, 182–83
Pereira, Miguel, 180
Pernambuco, 85
Pessoa, Epitácio, 174
Pestana, Nestor Rangel, 158
Picchia, Menotti del, 178
Pimentel, Figueiredo, 95
Pinheiro, João, 147
Pinto, Edgar Roquette, see
Roquette-Pinto, Edgar
political system: of the Empire,
3–6, 9, 15; of the republic,
79–84, 145–49, 174–75
"polygenist hypothesis," 49–52,
54–55, 115, 188
Pompéia, Raul, 86–87, 145
Pontes, Carlos, 114n.
Portugal, 7; see also Lusophobia
positivism, 10, 11–14
Prado, Antônio da Silva, 38,
127–28
Prado, Eduardo, 125, 145
Prado, Paulo, 203–5
prejudice in Brazilian race relations, 22–23, 24, 47, 129–30,
155, 165, 180, 198, 272
Public Food Commission, 162
public health: problems, 34, 169,
180, 182–84, 191; programs,
129–30, 132, 183; see also
malaria; yellow fever
Puerto Rico, 8

Quatrefages de Breu, Jean Louis
Armand de, 115n.
Queiroz, Eça de, 85, 93
Querino, Manoel, 185

race mixture, 23, 29–30, 31, 35–
37, 39–43, 46, 54–55, 60–61,
65–67, 73–77, 106–8, 111,
165–67, 169, 173, 187–88,
191–92, 195–96, 202, 204,
207, 209, 238; see also black
race; Indians; mulatto; white
race; "whitening"
"racial democracy" myth, 216–
17
racism: among abolitionists, 21–
22, 26; and immigration policy, 25, 198–200; as basis for
race relations, 44, 64, 214;
Brazilian theories of, 34–37,
58–64, 77, 111–12, 164–67,
169, 185, 187–92, 197, 200–
204; "scientific" theories of,
29–31, 34–37, 49–53, 77, 116,
200–203, 206–7; see also
"whitening"
Ramos, Artur, 190, 206, 240
Rangel, Alberto, 271
Rangel, Godofredo, 93
Ratzel, Friedrich, 118, 186, 200
Rebellion in the Backlands, see
Os Sertões
Rebouças, André, 17, 18, 48
"Recife School," 10, 11, 131,
195
Regionalism, 179
Reis, Fidelis, 194–95, 197
Reis, Joaquim Silveira dos, 101
Renan, Ernest, 10, 17
Republican party, 8, 9, 15, 19,
79–80
Revista Brasileira, 90, 110
Revista do Brasil, 167–68
Ribeiro, René, 216
Ribeiro, Tomás, 87
Rio, João do, 94, 96–97, 133,
149, 155–56, 170, 185, 222

About the Author
Thomas Skidmore is Céspedes Professor of History and
Director of the Center for Latin American Studies at Brown
University. He is the author of *Politics in Brazil, 1930–1964:
An Experiment in Democracy, The Politics of Military Rule in
Brazil, 1964–1985*, and, with Peter Smith, *Modern Latin
America*, third edition.

Library of Congress Cataloging-in-Publication Data
Skidmore, Thomas E.
Black into white : race and nationality in Brazilian thought /
with a preface to the 1993 edition and bibliography [by]
Thomas E. Skidmore.
Originally published: New York : Oxford University Press,
1974. With a new pref. and bibliography.
Includes index.
ISBN 0-8223-1320-0 (pbk.)
1. Brazil—Race relations. I. Title.
F2659.A1s55 1993
305.8'00981—dc20   92-28497   CIP